Studies in Immigration and Culture
Royden Loewen, Series editor

Families, Lovers, and their Letters
Italian Postwar Migration to Canada

Sonia Cancian

University of Manitoba Press

University of Manitoba Press
Winnipeg, Manitoba
Canada R3T 2M5
www.umanitoba.ca/uofmpress

Printed in Canada on chlorine-free, 100% post-consumer recycled paper.

Cover design: Doowah Design
Interior design: Karen Armstrong Graphic Design

Library and Archives Canada Cataloguing in Publication

Cancian, Sonia, 1965–
        Families, lovers, and their letters : Italian postwar migration to Canada / Sonia Cancian.

(Studies in immigration and culture series, ISSN 1914-1459 ; 4)
Includes bibliographical references.
ISBN 978-0-88755-715-6 (pbk.).—ISBN 978-0-88755-187-1 (bound)

        1. Italians—Canada—Correspondence. 2. Italian Canadians—Correspondence. 3. Italians—Correspondence. 4. Canada—Emigration and immigration—Social aspects. 5. Italy—Emigration and immigration—Social aspects. 6. Canada—Emigration and immigration—History—20th century. 7. Italy—Emigration and immigration—History—20th century. I. Title. II. Series: Studies in immigration and culture ; 4

FC106.I8C35 2010   305.85'1071   C2009-906724-2

The University of Manitoba Press gratefully acknowledges the financial support for its publication program provided by the Government of Canada through the Book Publishing Industry Development Program (BPIDP) and the Canada Council for the Arts, and the support of the Province of Manitoba through the Book Publishing Tax Credit, the Book Publisher Marketing Assistance Program, and the Manitoba Arts Council.

ENVIRONMENTAL BENEFITS STATEMENT

University of Manitoba Press saved the following resources by printing the pages of this book on chlorine free paper made with 100% post-consumer waste.

TREES	WATER	SOLID WASTE	GREENHOUSE GASES
5	2,310	140	480
FULLY GROWN	GALLONS	POUNDS	POUNDS

Calculations based on research by Environmental Defense and the Paper Task Force.
Manufactured at Friesens Corporation

FSC
Mixed Sources
Cert no. SW-COC-001271
© 1996 FSC

TABLE OF CONTENTS

For my children, Lorenzo and Arianna

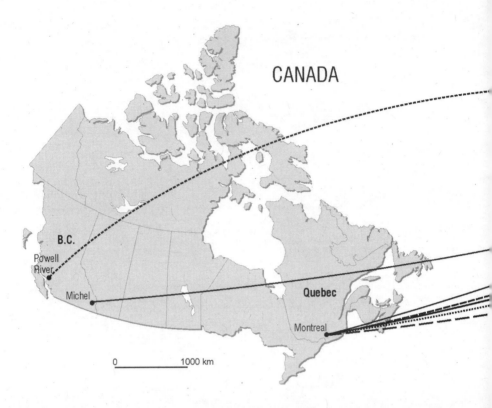

CANADA

B.C.

Powell
River

Michel

Quebec

Montreal

0 ———— 1000 km

THE LETTER WRITERS

Dante del Moro in Powell River, BC—Sara Franceschetti in
Arcugnano, Vicenza

∞

Gianlorenzo Colonello in Michel, BC, and Montreal—Luciano Colonello
and Marianna Domenica in Spilimbergo, Pordenone

∞

Clara Renzi in Montreal—Maurizio Trevisan in Venice

∞

Clara Renzi and Maurizio Trevisan in Montreal—
Laura Adaggi in Venice

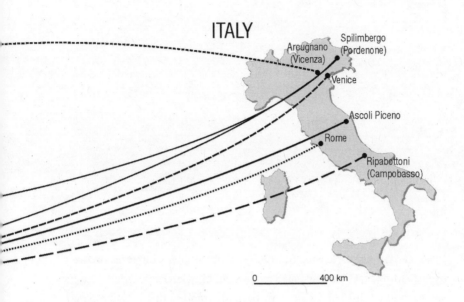

ITALY

Arcugnano (Vicenza)

Spilimbergo (Pordenone)

Venice

Ascoli Piceno

Rome

Ripabottoni (Campobasso)

0 ———— 400 km

Maddalena Franchi in Montreal—Daniela Perini in Ascoli Piceno

❧

Lucia Valessi and Domenico Losanto in Montreal—
Carmela Losanto in Ripabottoni, Campobasso

❧

Ester di Leonardi in Montreal—Giordano Rossini
in Rome

❧

ACKNOWLEDGEMENTS

IN REFLECTING BACK to early beginnings of my scholarly interests, two axes come to mind that have fascinated me as a child and later as an adult—letters and migration. In 1986, I visited my paternal grandmother in Spilimbergo, Pordenone, for a few days—a comforting respite from my stay in Siena where I was attending an intensive course on Italian language and culture at a school for foreigners. As a daughter of Italian immigrants in Canada who had learned early on about the graceful offerings of Italian culture, on this personal adventure, I sought to capture my parents' dream of a return to their homeland. Just as they had desired to return—but never did indefinitely—I too dreamed of living in Italy. This trip to Siena was an attempt to make it more plausible for me. In those rare moments of quiet solidarity at her home, I inquired with my grandmother about her life story. As she began to recount her youthful years, suddenly, she was on her way to her bedroom. Within a few minutes she returned with an ordinary-looking white shoebox. Standing above me, she opened the box, and there they were—the love letters she and my grandfather had written to each other when they were in their late twenties. I was mesmerized. As she opened one of the envelopes, there on the thin, nearly transparent paper with ink bleeding through was my grandfather's calligraphy crystallizing words of affection for my grandmother while he had been away in Amiens, France. The words, *tuo per sempre* (yours forever), immediately struck me. In that moment, I realized that my grandparents too had been in love, and that they too had been separated by migration and, like millions of others, had turned to letter writing to remain emotionally connected despite the physical distance that separated them. Shortly after their wedding in 1929, Giovanni Cancian emigrated to Amiens to work in a cinder-brick factory. A work life that was too arduous for him to endure, he returned home to his wife a short time later and concentrated his efforts on supporting his family as *bracciante* (day labourer) in his hometown while working the rented land as *contadino* and growing magnificent crops to sustain his family. Until his eyesight receded, Giovanni had been the letter writer of the family. As his niece recalled recently, he was the first to respond to letters and the first to send news to kin about family and friends.

For decades, my grandmother had archived these wafer-thin, neatly folded love letters, packed upright in that old white shoebox that she stored in her room among her precious things. I have only faint memories of our conversation on that day in November 1986, nonetheless, the excitement I felt when she showed me her letters remains with me. As I held in my hands these precious words, I remember wanting to ask her if I could borrow them and have them photocopied. But I did not have the courage, and the letters were soon returned to their original box, never to be seen again.

Families, Lovers, and their Letters is a revised version of my doctoral dissertation prepared for the PhD in Humanities program at the Centre for Interdisciplinary Studies in Society and Culture at Concordia University, Montreal.

This book on the letters of families and lovers in the context of Italian postwar migration to Canada would not have been possible without the generous support and encouragement of family, friends, and colleagues.

My first and most profound debt is extended to the individuals and families in Canada and Italy who have so generously shared with me their personal letters and their life stories. Without their trust, care, and friendship, this book would not have come into existence. I am extremely grateful to each of them and their families for welcoming me into their homes, for sharing their hearts and their memories, and for entrusting me with their epistolary treasures.

I would also like to thank the families and individuals who graciously gave permission for the letters and photos to be reprinted in this book. Readers should note that all names have been changed to pseudonyms.

I owe an enormous debt of gratitude to my thesis supervisors, Graham Carr and Sally Cole at Concordia University in Montreal and Bruno Ramirez at the Université de Montréal. As the project evolved over the years, they have provided crucial advice and much-needed encouragement and inspiration. I owe heartfelt gratitude to each of them for the intellectual guidance and critical support they provided at all stages of the project. In particular, I thank Bruno Ramirez for his extraordinary support and intellectual generosity at the final stages of the project.

I thank Franca Iacovetta for her highly constructive comments and insightful suggestions at the dissertation defence, and for her continued encouragement for the project. I am also grateful to Steven High for his perceptive comments and suggestions, and for his support.

For her intellectual generosity and enthusiastic response to my project, I thank my postdoctoral supervisor, Donna R. Gabaccia. Her extraordinary inspiration, encouragement, and support came at a crucial point of the project. I am deeply grateful to her.

At the Immigration History Research Center of the University of Minnesota, I thank the friendly and helpful staff and colleagues who welcomed me as postdoctoral visiting scholar while I was there.

For stimulating classroom discussions, I thank the graduate students that Donna Gabaccia and I team-taught in the interdisciplinary history seminar "Studies of Migration across Nations and Disciplines," in the winter of 2008 at the University of Minnesota.

In Montreal, at the Centre d'Études Éthniques des Universités Montréalaises and the Groupe de Recherche Diversité Urbaine at the Université de Montréal, I thank Deirdre Meintel for her kind welcome to the Centre, and her encouragement and support.

A special thank-you is extended to colleagues and friends who have generously shared suggestions and comments on parts of my manuscript and related papers that I presented in recent years at international scholarly conferences. I especially thank Laura Ahearn, Loretta Baldassar, Bina Freiwald, David Gerber, Dirk Hoerder, Haven Hawley, Thora Martina Herrmann, Royden Loewen, Leo Lucassen, Jeffrey Pilcher, Mary Anne Poutanen, Linda Reeder, Matteo Sanfilippo, Gabriele Scardellato, Suzanne Sinke, Jana Vizmuller-Zocco, and Joel Wurl.

This project was supported by a doctoral and postdoctoral fellowship received through the generosity of the Social Sciences and Humanities Research Council of Canada and the Fonds Québécois de la Recherche sur la Société et la Culture. I gratefully acknowledge the financial support received at Concordia University during the research and writing of my dissertation.

At the University of Manitoba Press, I thank Royden Loewen for his initial interest in my manuscript. For their scrupulous editing, I thank Glenn Bergen and Heidi Harms. I also thank Cheryl Miki, and I am grateful to David Carr for guiding me through the steps of turning the manuscript into a book. The humanity and kindness of everyone at the University of Manitoba Press has made the publishing experience an extremely positive one. I also thank the two anonymous readers selected by the University of Manitoba Press for their critical reading and helpful suggestions in improving the manuscript. All faults in the book are mine.

For their perennial cheerfulness and sustenance throughout the highs and lows of the project, I thank my friends, Maddalena Marinari, Serena Pani, and Elizabeth Zanoni.

For their support and encouragement at various stages of the project, I thank especially Shawna Atkins, Ester Cancian, Lina D'Eramo, Michael Kavoliunas, Wanda Palma, and Assunta Sauro.

For their continued encouragement and loving support, I thank my sister Nadia, my brothers Johnny and Robert, and especially my mother, Maria Lemmo Cancian, and my father, Luciano Cancian. I thank my late grandmother, Maria Domenica (Rosina) Moscato. While she had never been taught to read and write, she, along with my parents, valiantly encouraged me and provided much-needed help with my domestic responsibilities.

Finally, I thank my children, Lorenzo and Arianna who have accompanied me on this journey since its beginnings. The determination, relentlessness and conviction with which I carried to completion this book would not have been possible without them. With much love and appreciation, this book is for them.

Ascoli Piceno, Italy, 1960

Families, Lovers, and their Letters

A family reunion after years of separation. San Giovanni in
Galdo, Campobasso, Italy, 1961

INTRODUCTION

"It was like seeing you here..."

Dearest son I am writing this letter to you letting you know that a few days ago we received your letter, we are happy to hear that you are well, the same is for us, even your grandmother is in good health again. So you advised us that a young man from Casarsa has arrived in Italy and that you gave him ten dollars, so he brought us the money a few days ago with his cousin they came by motorcycle, however he said he will come back to visit us on the day of San Rocco. We thank you very much for the dollars... your father Luciano

Dear son Gianlorenzo... thank you for the ten dollars that you sent us through the hands of your friend. It was like seeing you here.

—Luciano Colonello and Marianna Domenica to
Gianlorenzo Colonello, 8 August 1956

BORN IN 1932 in the rural outskirts of Spilimbergo situated *al di quà* (on this side) of the Tagliamento River in the Friuli-Venezia Giulia region, Gianlorenzo Colonello had heard numerous stories throughout his childhood and youth about kin migrating to distant corners of the world. A few years before the start of the First World War, his maternal grandfather left Spilimbergo to work for a brief period in the forest and logging industry in Arizona, and at about the same time, his grandfather's brother left to work in California, and was later joined by his son in the late 1940s. Before and after the Second World War, other family members would direct their compass southward, northward and westward to work and settle in countries such as the United States, Argentina, Colombia, Belgium, France, and Canada. By the time Gianlorenzo came of age, his mother spoke with him about seeking economic opportunities through migration—pointing to family members abroad who could serve as networks of support for him. In this family, migration has been a long-standing alternative to the grim realities of low employment and dearth of economic opportunities that younger and older men and women experienced in their hometown throughout the twentieth century.[1]

The epistolary reflections written by the parents of Gianlorenzo, and included in the above epigraph, induce us to imagine the parents of this young migrant rushing to respond to their son's letter received through the hands of a fellow migrant. The desire to transcend physical barriers and respond quickly, so that their son could also receive word from them as expediently as possible, is juxtaposed by the ardent wish for an imminent reunion. We also imagine his mother, a middle-aged woman, turning to her kitchen table and immersing herself in the writing of *una bella lettera*, communicating to him her *pensieri*, her thoughts or concerns, in the best way she could, despite her limited years of schooling.

In migration movements occurring in the post-Second World War era, correspondence remained one of the key media of communication bridging the distances, near or far, between loved ones.[2] While scholars throughout the twentieth century have explored a number of facets related to correspondence exchanged in a process of migration, recent years have seen the publication of several exciting new collections of scholarly works on the immigrant letter. New conceptual frameworks, new analytical approaches, and ever-widening opportunities for working with letters shared between migrants and their significant others have been the hallmark of this scholarship. Within a few short months of each other, three important historical and interdisciplinary studies appeared and demonstrated the range of research and methodologies being applied to the study of personal correspondence resulting from migration.[3]

Families, Lovers, and their Letters engages with a multidisciplinary historiography grounded in social history, migration history, feminist ethnography, and literary studies. It draws its findings predominantly from one primary source, letters of people who lived in primarily oral cultures and did not normally employ literary expression in their everyday lives. These letters were written "in the moment" on both sides of the ocean as migration was bringing changes to the daily lives, life dreams, and opportunities of migrants and their loved ones. This study addresses two main research questions: First, what do the personal letters of ordinary individuals reveal about the impact of migration experienced by Italian migrants in Canada and their kin and lovers who remained in Italy during the postwar years? Second, what strategies and social, cultural, and emotional responses to migration do the letters reveal from the viewpoint of these actors? Drawing on an analysis of over 400 private letters belonging to six different families, I explore the multiple layers of significance that these letters hold both historically and anthropologically in conversation with the rapidly growing scholarly interest in immigrants' letters. The letters I analyze have been drawn from an original archive of 800 letters that I located and collected. These letters are unique in scope and original in the sense that they have never previously been archived or analyzed. Both individually and collectively, they offer a new source on the history of postwar Italian migration to Canada. Largely of a private and semi-private nature,[4] these letters take us inside the minds and hearts of ordinary people whose personal and family identities and circumstances were most affected by the realities of international migration.[5]

My interest in the topic stems from an earlier project in which I examined nineteen immigrants' letters belonging to four families in Canada.[6] In that study, I offered a detailed analysis of the letters by exploring their linguistic particularities. I argued that the linguistic deviations in these personal documents did not signify errors of standard Italian, but rather expressed solutions to problems emerging in a bilingual environment. Apart from their linguistic significance, however, letters as a form of communication became increasingly fascinating to me. Not only did letters, at the time of their writing, allow people to stay connected despite the physical and temporal distances separating them, but their intrinsically private nature made them an ideal vehicle for future readers to gain a glimpse into the inner stories of ordinary people that are often hidden from mainstream history. The study of migration and letters has interested me for personal reasons as well, as I have sought to understand more fully a past that belongs to my parents, who immigrated from Italy to Canada in the early 1950s. This book underscores some of the interconnections between personal correspondence and migration, and illustrates the links, continuities, conflicts, and negotiating efforts shared between kin and lovers in transnational households living apart.[7]

The scope of this book is twofold. It examines the functional role of the letters and their materiality as objects that served to bridge distances and enable the communication of information, news, sentiments, and concerns across vast spaces. Moreover, it explores a number of social and cultural dynamics operating in the content of the letters, revealing how individuals negotiated their separation from their families, lovers, and communities. This book describes the myriad ways in which people affected by migration exerted mechanisms of social support and control across kin networks, and pays particular attention to how gender relations were reified and reinforced in a context of migration. Finally, this book looks at ways in which experiences and expressions of emotions at a distance intensely influenced the language of separation shared between migrants and loved ones.

A Historiographical Review

Letters of migrants have enjoyed a surge in interest by scholars since the publication of the five-volume sociological analysis, *The Polish Peasant in Europe and America* by William Thomas and Florian Znaniecki (1918–1920). The collection format, as used in *The Polish Peasant* and other studies, published in light of the New Social History movement's advocating the words of ordinary folks to speak for themselves, became one of the signature characteristics of subsequent volumes featuring ordinary individuals' letters written in a context of migration. The contributions and theories advanced by historians Marcus Hansen, George Stephenson, and Theodore C. Blegen of what migration expert Donna R. Gabaccia calls the Minnesota School of

Immigration and Refugee Studies, on the topic of immigrants' letters are considerable.[8] Whether their motivations in casting a more democratic lens on immigrants' letters were personal or political, as David Gerber observes, these three Scandinavian American historians—themselves children of Swedish, Danish, and Norwegian immigrant parents—"created a powerful language… to justify their interest."[9] Their respective works reflect the extent to which they viewed the immigrant letter as "a great spur to mass migration, which certainly transformed both Europe and North America, and linked their histories inseparably."[10]

Three recently published works have contributed significantly to the scholarship by using letters of immigrants and loved ones within a framework of historical analysis, in contrast to the collection format. One book with which *Families, Lovers, and their Letters* is in conversation is David Gerber's *Authors of Their Lives* (2006). In examining the cycle of correspondence exchanged between immigrants and their significant others, *Authors of Their Lives* demonstrates the role of letters in reformulating and sustaining personal identities and relationships that had been disrupted as a result of migration. Through a micro-level historical and thematic analysis, Gerber's book focuses on personal relationships at a distance, and "the ways immigrants used letters to achieve that goal"[11] in the course of the nineteenth century between North America and the United Kingdom. By providing an in-depth historical and thematic analysis of the letters and throwing light on the material, the personal, and the social and emotional worlds inhabited by Italian migrants in Canada and their loved ones in Italy during the postwar period, this book further demonstrates that letters, as historians David Gerber and David Fitzpatrick suggest, "cannot truly 'speak for themselves.'"[12]

Gerber's analytical approach and interdisciplinary perspective is shared by two anthologies published in 2006: *Letters across Borders*, co-edited by historians Bruce Elliott, David Gerber, and Suzanne Sinke, and *Envoyer et recevoir: Lettres et correspondances dans les diasporas francophones*, co-edited by Yves Frenette, Marcel Martel, and John Willis.[13] Both collections examine personal letters exchanged between individuals and families separated as a result of migration. And, while they underscore the heterogeneity of experiences across borders and the transnationality of communication in migration processes across temporal, geographic, and cultural spaces, each collection makes diverse, yet parallel contributions to the scholarship. For

instance, *Letters across Borders* examines the social importance of correspondence, and its limits and opportunities. It also points to observations
on letter-writing conventions and practices, issues around censorship and
silences, and identity formation and the state. Conversely, the essays in
Envoyer et recevoir bring to light the challenges of locating and working with
letters, the dissemination of the medium in relation to Canada's postal history, transnational relationships across kin networks, the involvement of the
Catholic Church, and the relevance of literary and political networks across
the francophone diaspora canvassed through letters.

   Letters across Borders, *Envoyer et recevoir*, and *Authors of Their Lives* illustrate the historical value of letters in the context of migration as fundamental
in providing "access to the immigrant's attitudes, values, aspirations, and
fears as no other source has the potential to do," and "the intellectual puzzles
presented by the gaps, silences, and textual inadequacies." [14] Yet, in order to
delve deeper into the personal, social, and cultural universes of migrants and
their loved ones engaged in a process of migration, a myriad of areas remains
unexplored. My study attempts to fill some of these gaps by bringing to light
the voices of women, men, and children who at various stages in their lives
penned their daily thoughts, concerns, worries, satisfactions, dreams, and
hopes to their loved ones through correspondence.

   A further theme in the historiography of letters and migration is the emphasis on the availability of both sides of correspondence. Social historians'
invitation in the 1960s to examine "the process of migration as a complete
sequence of experiences," [15] in conjunction with the focus of emerging historical and social scientific research projects on migration processes from
the viewpoint of those who remained behind have generated an interesting, albeit limited, range of studies on the narratives of migration from the
perspective of those who experienced migration indirectly. [16] Conversely,
migrants' experiences and their narratives articulated in new worlds have
elicited a significantly larger selection of scholarly studies. [17] However, studies that examine the voices of migrants in dialogue with those who remained
behind have remained a rare find. This point is especially relevant when we
consider that "letters sent to emigrants from Europe are much less represented among surviving documents in archived collections of letters than
letters sent to Europe by immigrants." [18] In recognizing that letters moving
in both directions are equally part of the experience of migration, David

Fitzpatrick suggests that, "we need to discover the relationships of those mentioned by name, the events to which allusions are made, the social and economic contexts in both worlds... and to seek clues to other origins."[19] By drawing from the exceptional availability of letter collections that include letters from both the sending and receiving nation-states, my study speaks especially to Gerber's *Authors of Their Lives* (2006), Fitzpatrick's *Oceans of Consolation* (1994), and Samuel Baily and Franco Ramella's *One Family, Two Worlds* (1988) as historiographical exceptions.[20]

Sources and Methodology

My research on Italian private correspondence written in the context of the second period of mass migration to Canada emerges from the historiographical context described above. By using an interdisciplinary lens, this micro-level study explores the multiple and diverse dynamics affecting the personal, familial, and transnational experiences of immigrants and their significant others in the homeland. I examine the roles of gender, family, emotions, agency, myths, nostalgia, separation, and reunion as expressed in letters of immigrants and their loved ones across the Atlantic Ocean. In addition, I examine a "making-sense"[21] process in which these social actors engaged as they negotiated unfamiliar temporal and spatial realities. The work's conceptual framework, analytical approach, methods of inquiry, and interpretation are grounded in social and migration history and ethnography. Because of its size, the Italy-Canada migration movement is a particularly striking example of the large transatlantic "highway"[22] that moved people, objects, letters, news, information, and networks in the postwar period. Although a number of secondary works examine Italian migration to Canada in earlier periods of history, no other work makes such a sustained attempt to permeate the transnational "wire"[23] system linking Italy and Canada from 1946 to 1971.[24]

The letters studied here were written by both the migrants who left and family members and individuals who remained behind. Unlike other sources such as diaries, journals, or memoirs, personal letters provide written dialogues "with intervening time lags before responses."[25] As documents recorded in the moment, or as events had just occurred, or were about to occur, they were written strictly to meet personal and familial needs. As such, the letters were addressed to loved ones within immediate and extended family networks and, in some cases, to friends and lovers or confidantes. Moreover, unlike census data and personal narratives of public figures, these documents were not intended for analysis or for public use. As a result, in order to bring to light the plethora of human experiences, reflections, attitudes, and emotions involved in this process of migration revealed through personal correspondence, and since no public archive possessed these documents, I searched for letters primarily through fieldwork research. This involved making inquiries with networks of friends, family, and cultural and regional associations in Canada, with a focus on Montreal, home to the second-largest concentration of Italian immigrants in Canada.

Handwritten letters are often difficult to decipher and frequently contain grammatical errors that reflect differing levels of education and literacy. Yet, the defining thread that links these letters is the social circumstance of their origin, for all were written because of the migration of a family member or lover from Italy to Canada in the postwar period. Whether written by individuals who had crossed the Atlantic in search of new opportunities, or those who had stayed behind, all of the correspondence was intended to bridge the enormous spatial and temporal distances that separated kin from each other emotionally, socially, and physically. The letters are a time capsule through which a plethora of themes, ideas, ideologies, norms, advice, dreams, plans and hopes were articulated in the language of their writers' everyday lives. They mirror the individual writers' interior psychological and emotional spaces and their views of the outside world. Moreover, they bring to light a multiplicity and heterogeneity of voices as change and migration were catapulting them to new life possibilities. As Nicole Constable observes in her recent study, *Romance on a Global Stage*, the words and stories of such letter writers are suggestive of a diversity of aspirations, motivations, and experiences of women and men involved in correspondence relationships within a context of migration.[26] The experiences that are brought to light in my study offer a range of vignettes of the writers' universes. And, while these are unique experiences in their own right, they also mirror similarities with migrants who travelled from Italy to Canada in the postwar period as well as across other geographic and temporal spaces.

Historically, since the earliest of civilizations, the letter has served as a fundamental vehicle of communication, enabling individuals belonging to differing social classes to stay in touch while apart. For ordinary folks in particular, letter writing became more readily available through nationwide literacy programs, and the necessity in their everyday lives as a result of local and global migration movements and world wars. Italians turned avidly to letter writing, many for the first time when their men left for the trenches in the Great War. At around the same time, Italians were also migrating to distant parts of the world, and there again letter writing became the vehicle of choice for maintaining ties among family members, friends, and co-villagers. Historian Fabio Caffarena observes, "the activation of writing among common folks is tied to the *fervor* that was stimulated through *movement*: movement that was generated by emigration and wars, especially the Great War."[27] And, it was especially in these circumstances that "we begin to observe progressively the importance of acquiring a sufficient capacity to write in order to simply maintain social ties, and manage one's own affairs, in accordance with a typical peasant [*contadino*] pragmatism that views the practice of writing essentially in functional terms."[28] This observation pertaining to the letter-writing practices of Italian ordinary folks shares common ground with the epistolary practices of their French neighbours for whom "family separations that coincided with the acceleration of geographic mobility in the 19th century multiplied the opportunities for writing."[29] As Martha Hanna observes, the Great War in France generated an enormous need for ordinary folks and their sons, husbands, fathers, and lovers on duty on the Front to turn to letter writing in order to stay in touch and remain emotionally connected.[30] Within contexts of distress, such as war and migration, letter writing also served a fundamental purpose in generating among the writers an opportunity to understand, accept, and explain to themselves the difficult painful situations they were experiencing in the moment, especially those they had trouble reliving.[31] And, as historian Antonio Gibelli observes on First World War soldiers' letters, "in certain respects, the letter presented a form of therapy, it became a means for self-preservation: to write home and to receive mail was first of all a means to alleviate the pain of distance and the horror of the present."[32] Thus, we can explain, suggests Gibelli, the almost obsessive need to receive and send mail, "with an intensity decidedly disproportionate to the habits and behaviours of the protagonists."[33]

The largest migration movement between Italy and Canada occurred from the late 1940s to the early 1970s, and during this time the letter continued its popularity as the single most important and affordable source of communication between migrants and their families, friends, and lovers on both sides of the ocean. Letter writing provided continuity in their relations, and crucial emotional, social, and physical links between them. At the same time, by describing in depth their lives and *pensieri*, writers and those close to them were subject to issues that could bring conflict, misunderstandings, heartaches and other emotional challenges across the chasm of separation. Of course, making a break in the communication through silence was always an option for letter writers. However, for those who maintained a prolonged correspondence, reinforcing ties through letter writing addressed a primordial need to stay in touch that exceeded the dangers of being misinterpreted and misread. Individuals and families who strove to stay in touch in the context of migration endeavoured for the most part to negotiate disagreements and misunderstandings that emerged in the course of correspondence by requesting clarifications and emphasizing their best wishes, love, longing and anticipation with words like: "Dearest son, yesterday we received your letter, and we learned of your good health, as the same follows for us. This is the most important thing. Gianlorenzo, in reading your letter, both your mother and I felt like crying" (28 July 1954). "The letter asserts its claims on its own emotional terms," David Gerber suggests.[34] Indeed, not only is the letter's materiality an intimate artefact, the letter, itself, and related elements like the language, the reflections, and the handwriting of absent loved ones, also act as sites of memory of the relationship between correspondents, and of their significant others. While it was hardly a substitute for an absent family member or lover, a letter embodied the presence of that person. And, in fact, for these actors, it became the closest approximation to "an intimate conversation."[35]

Working with letters of a private nature created both opportunities and challenges. Not everyone whose letters were considered for this study is represented here, because not all letter writers or recipients in Canada could be reached, nor were all letters that were delivered saved by correspondents on either side of the Atlantic. Moreover, those who by necessity or choice did not write letters or stay in touch, or did not write descriptive letters beyond a few lines to kin and loved ones, are also absent from the analysis. Other problems emerged, in reading the diversity in handwriting, in the fragmentary nature of the documents, in the wide range of letter writers, contexts, and subject matter, and in making linkages among themes that were often difficult to identify. At the same time, however, the rewards of working with intimate documents of this nature are extraordinary. We know much less about the interior worlds of migrants and their loved ones, as revealed through these letters, than of the public world in migration, such as policies, statistics, and migrant incorporation and communities.

When I began this inquiry in 2001, a few letters became available to me through a personal network of friends and family, individuals who themselves or whose parents had migrated to Canada in the postwar period. I naively believed then that letters would be fairly easy to locate, since the time period I was interested in was not anchored in a distant past. I asked friends and family members if they had kept their families' letters of the postwar period; however, while they were supportive of my inquiry, few had letters to offer. Many admitted to not keeping the letters they had received after first reading them, while others had discarded them over time. In other households, letters had been thrown out by the children of migrants following the death of their parents. One exception was Gianlorenzo Colonello, a family member who had stored his correspondence in his *valigetta*, a small, worn heavy carton brown suitcase tucked away in the crawlspace of his house.

Having exhausted my network of kin and acquaintances, I proceeded to contact Montreal's Italian regional and cultural associations to further my inquiry on family letters. At the same time, I contacted individuals who had loaned me their letters for my master's thesis research on the language of the letters. Eventually, I was invited to give public lectures and describe my research project to members of several Italian cultural groups in the Montreal area: the Italian Women's Centre of Montreal, the Centro Donne di Laval, the Centro Donne di Madonna di Pompei Church, the Centro Donne di Notre-Dame-de-Grâce, the choir group il Coro Alpino, and the Bocce Club of Kirkland. Although I gave most of these presentations to mixed groups of women and men, women in particular responded very positively to the project. At every presentation, the response from the audiences was enthusiastic and encouraging. Several individuals expressed pride that the daughter of Italian immigrants, one of their own (*una di loro*), was interested at a formal, academic level in their stories and experiences as migrants in Canada. Many of the people I encountered regretted having disposed of their letters over the years because they had moved, or lacked space in their homes, or simply had wanted to break with the past. In addition to engaging in field research in the Montreal area, I travelled to Italy in the summer of 2005. Consistent with the transatlantic process of exchange, field research in Italy allowed me to interview Italian-based family members of correspondents whose letters I had located in Montreal.

In fact, out of the approximately one thousand individuals I addressed during my initial exploratory fieldwork of locating letters, only eighteen letter collections—in sizes ranging from a handful of letters to over one hundred documents—surfaced. Once I had identified "family archivists" of letter series, I organized meetings with potential participants. At these initial meetings, I explained the objectives of my research and emphasized how important their letters were as historical documents specific to the experience of migration. While these meetings were carried out informally, they were extremely important in helping to foster trust and a friendship between participants and myself, and usually ended with the participants entrusting me with their letters for a few weeks in order for me to photocopy and digitally scan them. Most of the meetings took place in participants' homes. The conversations were generally open-ended relating to themes, content, and context of the letters. Most of the interviews were carried out in Italian and sometimes in English, lasting between forty-five minutes and several hours.

The Letter Collections

When I first met Maddalena Franchi at an annual event hosted by the Centro Donne di Notre-Dame-de-Grâce in Montreal, she remarked with soft-spoken demeanour that when she had emigrated to Canada in 1960 to join her husband, whom she had married just two weeks after meeting him in Ascoli Piceno, she had been deeply melancholic for her mother and brothers. The only means for them to stay in touch and remain connected—especially in the early years—was through their constant correspondence, which Maddalena has kept discreetly tucked away in a bedroom drawer over the years. "*Quelle lettere mi facevano compagnia* [Those letters kept me company]," she reminisced to me. Indeed, as our conversations moved from her early experiences as a young woman in Ascoli Piceno to her personal difficulties in the first years in Montreal as she struggled to live in a multifamily household while working in the factories and having children of her own, it became clear to me that the letters she had tenaciously held on to for all these years were fundamental to her life story, just as much for what the letters said as for what they didn't say.

Since her parents' passing, Anita Losanto has held on to her parents' and other kin's letters, keeping them in a little brown jewellery box safely stored at her older brother's home. She first produced these wafer-thin, almost translucent rare documents in her office in May 2003. The paper had yellowed significantly, and the writing had bled through both sides of the paper. These documents inspired our conversations to turn towards her grandmother's extraordinary life story, her parents' and siblings' migration experiences to Canada, their economic and social difficulties as they settled, and their desire to continue to nurture close ties with their family in Ripabottoni, despite the distance between them.

From the moment I first approached Maurizio Trevisan and his wife, Clara Renzi, they have continued to share with me their personal letters for my research. On the occasion of our meeting in June 2003, we met in the sunroom of their home overlooking a carefully tended garden of bright-coloured flowers and legumes. Much of my early conversation with Maurizio centred on his experiences during the Second World War, until he reached for a large yellow envelope in a dark closet of the room. From that envelope, countless letters emerged. Many were still inside their original red-, white-, and blue-rimmed envelopes, some with a stamp from the Allied Control Commission in 1946. This package of filed letters dated from the early years of Maurizio and Clara's courtship in the mid-1940s to the 1980s. During subsequent meetings, Clara would also join in the conversation, and volunteer her experiences; for instance, meeting her father for the first time when she was twenty years old. Her father had emigrated to Canada, specifically to Montreal, in the early 1920s, prior to the rise of Fascism in Italy in 1922. Some of the letters date as far back when Maurizio asked her father in Montreal and her mother in Ampezzo Carnico for her hand in marriage.

The letters of Giordano Rossini were a rare find, not only because of the intimate nature of the letters—strictly confidential expressions of love for Ester di Leonardi—but also because they were made available to me through the generosity of her husband. Ester had recently passed on after a battle with cancer, and her husband, an old family friend, casually mentioned to me one day that he had some letters that might be of interest to me. Ironically, Ester had wanted to dispose of them over the years, but her husband convinced her to keep them. So for many years, these letters remained hidden within the walls of a cellar, until he showed them to me. From that point on, the letters of Giordano Rossini have constituted an intriguing part of my research.

The letters of Dante del Moro and Sara Franceschetti were an equally unexpected and exciting find. I had presented my research at a cultural organization's annual meeting, and among the audience members was an individual who later spoke to me about his family's migration history. The letters in this collection complement the selected series and serve as important testimonies to a family's epistolary life story engaged in the moment while in a process of change, mobility and separation. Paolo del Moro's letter collection led to ongoing conversations in the course of the project, both in person and over telephone and email communication.

Gianlorenzo Colonello always referred to his brown *valigetta* in close association with his arrival in Canada on the night of 24 December 1951. For the first time in his life, at just nineteen years of age, Gianlorenzo was leaving not only his parents' home but also his homeland, his *patria*, as many of his fellow kin had done since the turn of the century. As he recalls, in the contemporary-styled home that he and his wife, Elsa Contini, designed and built in Montreal in 1981, he left his hometown of Spilimbergo for many reasons: he was young, he wanted adventure, he needed to work, and he had learned from his aunt visiting from British Columbia that he would make good money in Canada. Gianlorenzo enjoyed reminiscing about his youthful years, illustrating with photographs and letters from friends and family in British Columbia, Ontario, and Quebec. His cousin, whom I interviewed over the telephone, remembers well her childhood in Spilimbergo and the years when, as a young woman, she enjoyed attending parties and helping newly arrived Italians settle in the coal-mining towns of Michel and Natal during the 1950s.

Given the disparities in the size and scope of the collections of letters, however, and the need to create an empirical base adequate to the purposes of analysis and comparison, I focused on six collections, each of which included a minimum of thirty letters and, in approximately half the cases, both sides of the correspondence exchanged between Italy and Canada. In all cases the collections included letters that spanned several years and sometimes decades. Taken together, the 400 letters selected from the original 800 letters offer a snapshot of the migration experience in the twenty-five years immediately following the Second World War, from 1946 to 1971. However, in order to analyze these letters from a micro-level perspective, I established a pragmatic set of criteria for the project to be achievable. As a result, only about half of the letters originally collected were selected for analysis. For instance, letter collections containing fewer than thirty letters in number were excluded. While even just one letter can tell a long and beautiful story, collections containing more than thirty letters would likely provide further opportunities for learning about the contours of migration and separation of individual letter writers and their loved ones. As Gerber notes, "if we are to understand immigrant letters, we must begin with individuals and the significant others with whom they corresponded."[36] I endeavoured to provide a plausible socio-historical context for the letters, and to allow for important insights into subjectivities of different authors and the kinship relations between letter writers, especially within immediate family members and lovers.

Similarly, because their chronological scope comprised the immediate postwar years, with a special focus on the first years of the correspondents' migration, these collections enabled a longitudinal analysis of the emotional and personal trajectories experienced by the letter writers. Letters whose dates extended beyond 1971 or earlier than 1946 were excluded from the analysis. This decision allowed me to focus on the letters of these immigrants as they arrived in Canada, which they wrote in a context of mobility and early settlement and adjustment. Arguably, of the writers who remained in Italy, especially those who planned to join shortly their fellow kin in Canada, the selected letters allowed for an analysis within a context of mobility as well, as they wrote while preparing to leave for Canada. This is especially illustrated in the letters of Sara Franceschetti. The letters of those who remained resolutely in Italy allow us glimpses into their psychological and emotional worlds within a context of adjustment to separation, as we witness especially in the letters of Giordano Rossini, Maurizio Trevisan and his family, Daniela Perini, Carmela Losanto, and Marianna Domenica.

Three of the six letter series include dialogues between migrants who had recently arrived in Canada and their loved ones in Italy. Through this dynamic, I was able to provide important evidence on the bi-directional flow of communication between kin and lovers in a process of migration. Because the letters originated from a variety of locations across Italy and Canada, including small urban centres, agrotowns, agricultural households, and major cities like Rome and Venice in Italy, and resource towns in British Columbia and large cities like Montreal in Canada, they allowed me to examine a multiplicity of locations on both sides of the Atlantic Ocean. Finally, as a result of the intensity and frequency of correspondence between family members and lovers in the selected letter series, I focused on a diversity in relations between correspondents within immediate family networks and lovers (thereby excluding letters from extended kin and non-kin in the original collections): the exchange of letters between parents, children and siblings, and between married, betrothed and courting couples.

Oral interviews were also part of the research. On several occasions, I held formal and informal interviews and conversations with letter-participants and, in some cases, with the letter writers themselves, in both Italy and Canada, from 2003 to 2009. Not only were oral methodologies key in locating and archiving the letters in the hands of private individuals, they were also important for providing context that was not available through the letters themselves. As a result, oral interviews were conducted in Montreal, Toronto, and Fernie, British Columbia (by telephone) in Canada, and in Rome, Mogliano Veneto, Trieste, Vicenza, Pordenone, and Spilimbergo in Italy. Fieldwork research in Italy during the months from May to August 2005 also enabled me to visit archival centres and gain a firmer grasp on the significance of individuals' private writings as historical documents.

Designing a database that would allow me to make sense of the material in the letters according to a number of specific themes was the next challenge. While this task was particularly demanding because of the range of subject matter in the correspondence, I was struck by the intensity with which the correspondents spoke about their experiences of migration. In sharing personal and familial concerns, and emotional highs and lows, they passed on knowledge and advice about practices and procedures for migration in voices that expressed gendered and social codes of behaviour. The letters were also remarkable for what they revealed about family and kinship ties, including not only the function of kin in mediating the physical distance between family and friends, but also the extraordinarily intimate communications between lovers separated by time and space.

I created a database that was composed of thirty-seven categories of information, including letter dates, information about the letter writers and letter recipients, the relationships between correspondents, the letters' place of origin and destination, and the material condition of the letters (ink and paper). In addition, I made a thematic inventory of the letters' contents that focused on specific expressions but also dealt with larger, repeated themes such as kinship, gender, emotions, labour, *paesaneria* (relations between townsfolk), and myths of America.

As I performed the tasks of reading, deciphering, understanding, and finally analyzing the content and context of the letters, I focussed particularly on the broadly overarching topics of kinship, gender, and emotions. These topics became the central themes in the development of the book, in part because they were so common to the sources. As private forms of expression and communication, the letters provided glimpses into areas of human activity that are often obscured by, or invisible in, more public historical documents and that have seldom been explored in the previous literature on letters and migration.

Just married! And soon leaving for Canada… Ascoli Piceno, Italy, 1960s

CHAPTER ONE

"Excuse the errors, I'm writing at night by oil lamp..."

Postwar Italian Migrants and their Letters

My dearest brother and sister-in-law Lucia, I am answering your dear letter, in which you give me news and advise me of your good health. With regards to you, sister-in-law and the terrible stomach pains you are having, I agree these troubles are a problem. But let's hope you recover soon... Please excuse the errors, I'm writing at night by oil lamp.

—Carmela Losanto to Domenico Losanto and Lucia Valessi,
6 May 1963

IN THE DAYS IMMEDIATELY FOLLOWING the announcement of Italy's liberation and the end of the Second World War, some of the recurring images on the newsreels of the time were jarringly contradictory. Footage at the Italian national archive, Archivio Luce, shows Italians excitedly waving white handkerchiefs in the crowded streets of Milan, Rome, Venice, and Naples, juxtaposed with images of the devastating destruction of the cities' buildings and long lineups of haggard-looking Italians waiting for rations of flour, soup, and bread. Other footage shows Italian soldiers wearily returning home from battle and the concentration camps, in contrast to Allied soldiers distributing rations of canned meat, chewing gum, and cigarettes to villagers of the Mezzogiorno. The violence, disruption, and fear resulting from the Second World War had enormous repercussions for the Italian state and its citizens. But the immediate challenge of the postwar period was to reconstruct the nation from the material destruction and the political and psychological disasters that twenty years of fascist rule had caused.

Most contemporary historians—from Paul Ginsborg to Tony Judt, Anna Maria Torriglia, Patrick McCarthy, Christopher Duggan, and Christopher Wagstaff—agree that the mood in postwar Italy was one of deep ambivalence.[1] The victory of a Christian Democrat-led coalition in the 1948 elections ushered in a long succession of centre-right governments which, despite the frequent crises and the chronic instability that ensued, would be largely responsible for the political, economic, and social orientations marking the country for the remainder of the Cold War era. Eventually—mostly in the late 1950s and early 1960s—these policies would trigger what most observers have termed "il miracolo economico," during which rates of growth increased progressively and Italy's economy became competitive with that of other Western European countries.

Yet, the newly born republic had inherited from the previous regimes a country that was marked by sharp regional inequalities, where industrial development coexisted with vast areas of economic stagnation and dire poverty. Italy's industrial sectors, predominantly circumscribed by the triangle of Milan-Turin-Genoa, restarted the engines of production and boosted the employment rate with the aid of the Marshall Plan, largely funded by the United States. At the same time, southern Italy and parts of the northeast remained mired in poverty and chronic unemployment. A 1954 parliamentary inquiry found that of all the families living under the poverty line, 85 percent were in Italy's Mezzogiorno, with a southern region such as Calabria exhibiting a per capita income that was less than one-third of that in some northern regions such as the Piedmont.[2] Compounding the rampant poverty and misery characterizing postwar Italy was the question of literacy among its people. A regional assembly organized by the Communists in 1949 revealed that in the region of Calabria, "49 per cent of the adult population were illiterate."[3] As socio-economic development progressed throughout the late 1950s and early 1960s, nationwide literacy efforts were underway. However, even as late as 1971, according to Italy's national census (ISTAT), 32.4 percent of the Italian population had no formal schooling, and less than half of the adult population (44.2 percent) had completed elementary school. As Italian linguist Stefano Gensini observes, these ratios "are a sign that over thirty years of democratic life were insufficient to make a serious effort in compensating for the sharp cultural fractures of the country."[4]

Major reform of the agrarian economy (such as facilitating land ownership for the peasantry and favouring the consolidation of an independent farmers' class) was often a key feature of postwar electoral promises. But little ever came of these reforms other than stopgap measures designed to deal with special local conditions and to resist the powerful landowners' lobby.[5] Consequently, most of the southern regions and several northeastern provinces continued to exhibit economic stagnation and unemployment well into the 1950s.

As in previous periods of Italy's history, these regions resumed their role as major exporters of labour both for the Italian industrial triangle and for the economies of Europe, the Americas, and Australia. For many struggling Italian men and women, migration became not an option, but a necessity. As a result of Italy's proximity to Europe, nations such as Germany, Belgium, France, and Switzerland became primary destinations for thousands of Italian seasonal migrants who returned home at some point during each year to tend to their domestic affairs.

Canada's Sponsorship Program

For many Italians, the dream of "going to America" that had first surfaced in the nineteenth century was reactivated. Although restrictionist quota laws passed in the 1920s had virtually closed the door to Italian migration to the United States, because of its geographic proximity, Canada quickly became identified as part of "L'America." Indeed, the postwar period witnessed the largest movement ever of Italians to Canada.[6] Migrants and their families who followed originated predominantly from the southern and northeastern regions of Italy. As historian Franca Iacovetta observes, in some cases, entire clusters of villages or towns in the southern regions were mobilized and linked across the ocean.[7] Facilitated generally by the Government of Canada's sponsorship program (a family-based migration policy introduced in 1947), a chain migration of single and married men followed by their immediate and extended families began to arrive in postwar Canada.

Not long after the return home of Canadian soldiers overseas, followed by thousands of war brides, Prime Minister Mackenzie King delivered a statement on migration to the House of Commons that would open a window into what Canada was willing to do in the wake of "the world situation as a whole."[8] The immediate purpose of Mackenzie King's statement was to define Canada's role in helping to alleviate the global, predominantly Euro-centered problem of a burgeoning number of refugees and displaced persons following the Second World War. As an active member of the United Nations, Canada felt a moral obligation to help Europe's devastated peoples in the immediate short term, and in fact, over 160,000 displaced persons from the war entered Canada between 1946 and 1952.[9] At the same time, however, King made certain to emphasize in his statement the benefits of immigration to Canada, observing that migration would serve to increase the country's population, protect its territory, and help develop its resources.

Economic and population growth was characteristic of the postwar period in Canada, which "emerged from the war as fourth amongst the world's industrial and trading nations."[10] In the 1950s, Canada's economic buoyancy compelled politicians to invest in new infrastructure (roads and electrical power facilities), the building of schools and hospitals, the Trans-Canada Highway, the St. Lawrence Seaway, and the Trans-Canada Pipeline, among other major projects.[11] Unskilled labour was in high demand in mining and mill towns across the nation, including Michel and Powell River in British Columbia. In cities like Montreal and Toronto, workers were in demand for the construction and road-building industries as well as in the manufacturing and service sectors. Immigration played a key role in ensuring economic progress and national and civic development, with the population and labour flow from Italy proving to be particularly significant.[12]

As King argued, "A larger population will help to develop our resources. By providing a larger number of consumers, in other words a larger domestic market, it will reduce the present dependence of Canada on the export of primary products."[13] All of this would be possible as long as immigration to Canada mirrored the nation's "absorptive capacity," meaning that the number of arriving migrants would "vary from year to year in response to economic conditions."[14] In what became a historic policy statement, King also stressed that, "Canada is perfectly within her rights in selecting the persons whom we regard as desirable future citizens. It is not a 'fundamental human right' of any alien to enter Canada. It is a privilege."[15] King also assured nativist British- and French-Canadians that, "the people of Canada do not wish, as a result of mass immigration, to make a fundamental alteration in the character of our population."[16] According to historian Robert Harney, in an effort to appease both ordinary Canadians and industrialists at the helm of Canada's railway, mining, and timbering companies, four forces shaped the recruitment choices articulated in King's statement:

> (1) the racialist or cultural assumptions of officials and many politicians, (2) the ethnic lobbies in Canada, (3) the availability of potential migrants of certain nationalities because of wartime and aftermath displacement, and (4) the voracious hunger of Canadian heavy industry for workers who could stand up under strenuous, dangerous and dirty work in remote and unhealthy places.[17]

Yet, despite King's efforts to address the economic needs of Canada, his statement generated its share of protest. The policies it elicited, including the Immigration Act of 1952, were highly debated, especially after 1957, when John Diefenbaker's Conservative government moved to stem the tide of immigration from postwar Italy. In 1967, new immigration regulations were enacted that would change the course of Canadian public policy by focussing on prospective immigrants' skills and education. These regulations would significantly reduce the number of migrants coming from Italy.

King's statement of 1 May 1947, and the ensuing immigration policies that lasted until 1967, offered an important gateway to Italian men and women who were looking for a way out of Italy's postwar economic misery. While thousands still harboured the dream of going to "America," the 1921 and 1924 restrictive quotas imposed by the United States remained firmly in place in the immediate postwar years, forcing Italian nationals to rethink the geographies of their dreams. One viable option was the reactivation of kinship networks of Italian migrants who had arrived in Canada during the first wave of mass migration prior to the First World War. Despite the interruption resulting from the Great Depression and the Second World War, the link in chain migration was restarted. The migration of Italian nationals was further facilitated by the passage of new immigration policies that widened "the categories for admission of relatives in 1946, 1947, and 1949, since there was an urgent need for this on humanitarian grounds."[18] Finally, the classification of Italy as an enemy nation was lifted in 1947.[19] As a result of these policy changes, recently admitted landed immigrants and foreign-born Canadian citizens could now sponsor their Italian relatives.

With new immigration regulations in place, thousands upon thousands of Italians began completing applications either for their own migration to Canada, or for that of their loved ones. The number of applicants was so high that one migration expert has defined the Italy-Canada postwar migration movement as a large transatlantic "highway" of people and networks moving across the Atlantic.[20] This movement proved to be a major episode in Italian migration history. The sponsorship program had enormous significance for the Italian mass migration movement, to the point that Italians became the single most important group to benefit from the policy. As Iacovetta observes, over "90 per cent of Canada's postwar Italians were sponsored by relatives."[21] This is an extremely high ratio, especially when we consider that the average for all nations was 47 percent.[22]

While Canada provided economic opportunities for migrating Italians and their families, it is also true that Canadians benefitted enormously from the sponsorship program. Historian Bruno Ramirez suggests that the program greatly facilitated the integration of the newcomers into the economy at a minimum social cost; for, much of the burden in gaining access to the labour market was placed squarely with the receiving family or household. In addition, it was the immigrants' own responsibility to learn one of the two official languages if they wanted to exploit the job opportunities open to them; it was their responsibility to find ways of upgrading their skills; it was their problem to look after themselves in case of work accidents or unemployment. [23]

And, while the Italian migrants busily adjusted to their new lives in Canada, the sponsoring immigrant families or households functioned—at least for the initial period of settlement—as both a unit of service and reproduction, not to mention as shock absorbers for other migrant workers, their spouses and children.[24] Moreover, similarly to the migration experiences of French Canadians in New England and other ethnic migrants settling into Canada,[25] the selected letters in this book demonstrate how immigrants assumed the responsibility for their kin's early adaptation to Canada, in addition to contributing transnationally to the economic well-being of their families and other loved ones who remained in Italy.

Migrants and Letter Writers

As the collections of letters in this book show, migration transformed in numerous ways the lives of migrants and their dear ones who had remained behind. The letters of fourteen women[26] and men are the focus of this study. These collections of personal correspondence prove insight into the letter writers' life experiences in relation to migration to Canada, and allow us to explore some of the factors that influenced the choices made by the letter writers and their families. Much of the correspondence was exchanged between two generations of letter writers, namely, parents, and children. In other cases, the letter writers exchanged correspondence with siblings, lovers (including spouses), and other kin within similar age groups.

Sara Franceschetti and Dante del Moro

One letter writer was thirty-two-year-old Sara Franceschetti, who lived in a multiple-family agricultural household in the outskirts of Arcugnano, Vicenza (in the Veneto region), with her two children, five-year-old Paolo and two-year-old Elisabetta. A small family inheritance and a loan from his cousin enabled her husband Dante del Moro to emigrate to Canada. Within the same year, he had set aside enough earnings to finally send for Sara and the children to join him in Powell River, British Columbia. Nonetheless, those nearly nine months of separation between Sara and Dante were difficult. For Sara, her husband's departure for Canada meant making do with his missing daily presence, and the support and care he had provided while at home in Arcugnano. It also signified shouldering the enormous responsibility of caring for their two young children and dealing with her loneliness. She writes, "Dear Dante I feel your absence, I try to encourage myself because I hope your absence is short, but I tell you honestly if it would be for an extended time I wouldn't be able to do it, believe me first for the responsibility of taking care of the children and another reason is that one feels terrible living apart even if for a brief period" (25 March 1956). Similarly, for Dante del Moro, who had emigrated to Canada where his cousin (who had arrived in Canada immediately after the First World War) in Powell River awaited him with a home and work, separation from his wife and children had harsh implications. Even though the experience of leaving home for a temporary period was not foreign to him, as he had been stationed on the Russian Front during the Second World War, the experience of leaving behind a wife and children proved extremely trying on his morale, as he repeated in his letters to Sara: "I am happy to hear that all three of you are in good health, for me good health and steady work, but I miss your presence very much, more and more with each passing day" (9 August 1956). Upon arriving, Dante lived for several months with his cousin and his family in Powell River's town site— immediately outside the gates of the pulp and paper company's sawmill. In this period, Dante worked first as a cement worker and mason with a co-villager, and soon after, became employed with the Powell River Company as a labourer. He was also busy looking for suitable housing for his family, who were to join him soon, and finally settled on a house located within walking distance to the mill.

Upon leaving Arcugnano in March of 1956, Dante had made arrangements with his brothers to provide for his wife and children in his absence.
Sara, the youngest of the women married to a Del Moro, was expected to do
many of the household chores in the family unit. Once her husband had left
for Canada, her part-time work in her family's business ceased and she dedi-
cated herself to taking care of their children. In her letters to Dante, which
date from March to November 1956, Sara frequently described the economic
hardships she experienced. She was acutely conscious of the social pressures
to nurture her image as a well-kept migrant's wife: "as you know, I am being
watched more carefully than before, this means that if I dress well, you are
earning good money, if I dress poorly, it means that you are struggling ... you
know how our world is, appearances mean everything" (c. June-July 1956).
When her husband sent her five dollars for their wedding anniversary, she
replied how important it was that she and the children appear well-dressed
to the townsfolk. Sara sporadically made reference in her letters to tensions
in the household regarding Dante's family's desire to purchase various household items she would be leaving behind, or the food and wine rations that
had been agreed upon between Dante and his brothers before his departure.
Another source of tension was the financial support that Sara was required
to receive from her brothers-in-law for the daily subsistence of the children,
as agreed upon prior to Dante's departure. Sara urged Dante to write to his
brothers in Arcugnano and resolve the issues for her. It is clear that her relationship with her sister and brother-in-law, who lived just a short distance
away, was paramount to her daily survival. In references to Sara's sister and
her family, we learn of the extensive support and care that they provided
to Sara and her children, especially as a result of Dante's absence. There is
mention of frequent visits to their home, of their lending money to her,
and providing support and solace, including accompanying her to Rome to
obtain her visa for Canada. Paolo attended elementary school administered
by the nuns and Elisabetta attended a children's nursery nearby. Their father, however, was never far from their thoughts, as Sara wrote: "Paolo and
Elisabetta everyday ask me, 'Did we receive mail from Daddy?'... They ask
me to read your letters aloud, they are not happy with just receiving your
greetings and kisses, they want more, ... they are unhappy when you don't
include enough money for them to buy watermelons, pears and cantaloupes"
(6 August 1956).

Daniela Perini

A collection that especially emphasizes an adult child-parent relationship
are the letters of Daniela Perini, who, along with her sons Davide and Fabio,
faithfully wrote to her daughter Maddalena Franchi in Canada, a young bride
who had left her hometown to join her husband in Montreal in 1960. As a
young woman, Maddalena had attended the church-run Collegio delle Suore
until she was eighteen years old. She followed two years as a hairdressing
assistant with work in the local service industry. Her father had died when
she was still a child, but she and her mother and brothers continued to live
in the family home in the city centre of Ascoli Piceno, located at the southern tip of the Marche region. For Daniela, the most important thing for her
daughter was to get married. When a cousin of Maddalena's introduced her
to Giuseppe Martino, a young Italian immigrant on vacation from Canada,
Maddalena accepted his courtship and married him just two weeks later,
on the eve of his departure for Montreal. Shortly after, Maddalena joined
him in Montreal, where she and Giuseppe began their lives together in the
household of his parents and siblings. As we read in the letters, Maddalena's
mother had difficulty accepting her daughter's departure. Maddalena had
been her mother's closest confidante, and while her migration left an enormous void in her mother's heart, she supported her daughter's decision to
emigrate to Canada. Nonetheless, the loss was both physical and emotional
for both of them, and to help cope with the emotional emptiness, Daniela
and Maddalena wrote frequently to each other.

   Their correspondence began in November 1960 and continued for over
twenty years with varying levels of intensity and frequency until the late
1980s, when Daniela joined Maddalena and her brother—who had emigrated in the mid-1960s—in Canada, leaving behind Davide with his young
family in Rome. In 1961, widowed Daniela Perini had been living with one
of her sons in a small apartment in Ascoli. However, despite the company
of nearby friends and kin in her apartment building, and her son working
nearby, the departure of her daughter left an indelible mark on her everyday
life: "you, my daughter, are always in my thoughts and in my heart, because
a mother cannot forget a daughter. I hope, as you tell me, that the day of our
reunion is not far away, only this hope gives me the strength to carry on [*solo
questa speranza mi da la forza di vivere*]" (5 December 1960). Her eldest son,
Davide, was living in Rome and employed with the city's police force. Not

long after Maddalena's departure, her younger brother Fabio was drafted into the military for one year of mandatory service, from which he wrote often to Maddalena while stationed in various posts in northern Italy. As the letters suggest, Maddalena's departure for Canada was partly offset for Daniela by daily visits to friends in her apartment building and to kin nearby, whether to reminisce about Maddalena or to watch television together in the evenings. Daniela often writes about praying to her favourite saint or to God, "from morning to night... for your good health, your happiness and that God may guide you always towards your prosperity" (3 July 1963). Occasionally, she would travel to Cisterna to visit extended kin and her son in Rome. From these locations, she would include news about the family, for example, "I'm now giving you some good news, Assunta is expecting a baby" (6 June 1963). As we also observe in the other collections, news of kin always represented an important part of the letters.

Carmela Losanto

A letter writer whose correspondence included exchanges between siblings was a lively blue-eyed woman named Carmela Losanto. Writing in the years from 1958 onwards, she was immersed in the struggles of postwar Italy. For generations, her family had lived in the town of Ripabottoni, Campobasso—a region that contributed enormously to the migration movement to Canada, especially Montreal, both before and after the Second World War. In fact, both of Carmela's brothers and her husband had migrated to Canada at various intervals in the postwar years. The archived correspondence of Carmela Losanto dates from 28 March 1958 to 6 October 1972, and is addressed primarily to her sister-in-law, Lucia Valessi, and her brother, Domenico Losanto. The letters describe her responsibilities in overseeing the renovations of her brother's home adjacent to the house she shared with her in-laws on the main *piazza* of Ripabottoni. We learn of Carmela Losanto's long days of work with rudimentary farming tools in the parched fields of the Molisan hills, and of her work at home as mother of two sons whose father had migrated to Canada following the Second World War. On rare occasions, words of her husband appear in the collection as a result of his temporary return to Ripabottoni. Many of the letters describe local town events, especially those of a religious nature, and changes unfolding in the town. As we read in a letter of 28 March 1958 addressed to her sister-in-law, towns like Ripabottoni were prime targets for out-migration, as were other parts of the Molise region in the postwar years: "soon there will be no one left here and nothing will be used. In March and April in Ripabottoni alone, 40 persons are coming there, and I don't know how many are leaving for Milan."

With determination and hard work, Carmela and her in-laws managed yearly to extract some good crops of wheat, corn, figs, tomatoes and other staples from the impoverished lands of Molise.[27] With her departure for Montreal in 1967 came a break from this hard agricultural life. Nonetheless, the decision to permanently leave her hometown entailed personal dilemmas, some of which she confided to her sister-in-law upon receiving her visa for Canada:

> My head is heavy. I don't know if what I'm doing is good or bad.
> How much I would like to talk with you, but on paper I can't
> say everything. I'm sorry to leave my home and other things,
> but the world is made for travelling... with God willing, I too
> will come to America, but now I feel sad and have little desire
> to leave, as the old proverbs say, my native hometown [*paese
> nativo*] (14 January 1967).

Despite her hesitation, however, Carmela made the leap with her adolescent sons.

During her years in Ripabottoni, Carmela had been subjected to enormous kinship pressures, primarily as a result of her in-laws' strict codes of behaviour and high expectations. Unlike the majority of land tenants (*affituari*) in Ripabottoni, they owned several hectares of land—and yet, they lived under marginal economic conditions, as Anita Losanto recalls her aunt telling her. As the youngest daughter-in-law in the family, and because her husband was away, Carmela was expected to follow the orders and dictates of her husband's family, including her older sister-in-law. While Carmela spent long hours during the planting and harvest seasons working on the farm, which was located several kilometres away from the town and did not have electricity, she nonetheless managed to write frequently to her family in Canada. Reaching out to them was a source of comfort in coping with the disciplining glances of her in-laws. Her brother and sister-in-law in Montreal, who had migrated to Canada in 1957 following the departure of their eldest son in 1953, were sensitive to her efforts to oversee their home's renovations in their absence, and frequently thanked her, as we can infer from Carmela's letters to them. Carmela, on her part, took great care in reporting to her brother and sister-in-law on the state of their land, their home, family remaining in Ripabottoni, local labour-related conditions and changes in the town itself. For instance, about their property, on 28 July 1958 she wrote, "the vine is exactly as you left it, no one went to turn it, and now nobody knows if it's still a vine or just a field." In many of the letters, whether through her reporting on the house, the village, their family, or herself, we witness Carmela willingly offering—beyond the call of duty—to help her migrant brother and sister-in-law, and reinforcing bonds of affection and support between them. Despite her desire to be reunited with her family— "my heart longs to be near all of you" (16 August 1963)—her letters show that physical distance did not impede the offer of genuine support and care between kin.

Giordano Rossini and Ester di Leonardi

A fourth set of letters belongs to a young man in Rome writing to his lover in Montreal. Among other factors, these letters demonstrate unequivocally that migration and the separation that ensued especially between couples was no obstacle for love. The love story woven through the tightly written epistles of Giordano Rossini to Ester di Leonardi begins on 10 March 1957, just one day after Ester boarded the steamship liner heading for Halifax, and continues, until 10 March 1958, with the last archived letter of 18 August 1960. From the first letters, we learn that Giordano was a young man in his early twenties who lived with his grandmother (*nonna*) in Ostia, and was employed for a time as a salesman in a store (*negozio*) in Rome. His mother had died when he was very young, and his father had been absent for a part of his life. In a few letters, he describes the infrequent presence of his father and the ambivalent relationship the two shared. Giordano's immediate circle of support included his grandmother, his two best friends, a female cousin of Ester's, and his extended family of aunts and uncles, as well as Ester's aunt and uncle—most of whom had approved of his relationship with Ester. We learn of his leisure activities, like the walks (*passeggiate*) he would take, going to the beach, to the movies, and occasionally, dancing with his friends. We also learn about his dreams for a future with Ester, and his ardent desire to be near her. In his letters—written like a diary—Giordano writes profusely about his state of mind and heart in his separation from Ester: "dear Little one [*cara Piccola*], do you still think of me always? I do!! Even when I go dancing, like I did today, I think of you always, and I think back to those few times we danced together" (20 October 1957). With breathtaking literary agility, he describes emphatically the emotional highs and lows of missing her, his relationship with his grandmother with whom he lived, his personal struggles, his economic difficulties, and his hopes for better employment and days to come, when his beloved would return to Rome and finally marry him, as he confided on 4 April 1957: "here life is hard, especially for me, living under difficult economic and emotional conditions, alas, things will get better, especially when I will have you here with me, I'll feel like a different man." Unlike in the other letter series, however, there is no mention of a desire on his part to join Ester in Montreal. Instead, his hopes remained focussed on her return to Rome.

No sooner had Ester arrived in Montreal than she, along with her sister, became gainfully employed in the city's clothing industry. From Giordano's responses to Ester, we also learn that her brothers disapproved of the relationship she and Giordano maintained by correspondence, resulting in heated discussions in her household. These dynamics, which we can assume were described in Ester's letters to him, caused Giordano to worry about losing Ester, to wonder who was opening her mail, and whether she was receiving all of his letters.[28]

Clara Renzi and Maurizio Trevisan

Correspondence between lovers predominates in a fifth set of letters, exchanged by an engaged couple between Montreal and Venice in 1948 and 1949. Prior to her departure in September 1948, Clara Renzi had already been corresponding with Maurizio Trevisan, a young man from Venice. As it became increasingly clear in 1946 that Clara and her mother would join her father in Montreal immediately after the war, Maurizio wrote to both her mother in Ampezzo Carnico and to her father in Montreal asking for their daughter's hand in marriage. He received a favourable reply from Clara's mother with the words: "I have faith in your loyalty... I am pleased that even your family is in agreement of the relationship" (9 September 1946), and Clara's father's consent: "I am not opposed," on 21 November 1946. As Clara's departure for Montreal loomed near, she and Maurizio remained determined that the distance that was about to separate them would in no way impede their relationship or their commitment to each other: "remember me and love me forever, that your love be always deep and sincere, and never do anything to make it less, know that I love you so much" (15 January 1949). In fact, less than a year after Clara's arrival in Montreal, Maurizio joined her, and within a short period the couple was married in the city's Italian church, Madonna della Difesa.[29]

A second set of letters from the same collection, which begins in 1963 and ends in 1982, is written by a different cast of authors, namely the parents and siblings of Maurizio, who remained in Italy. In 1962, Maurizio and Clara had returned to Italy with their two young daughters to start a new life and take advantage of the work opportunities that had materialized as a result of the country's economic miracle. They proceeded to live in Mestre, a short distance from Maurizio's family in the Venice area. In the summer of 1963, however, when Maurizio's job required him and his family to move to Milan, Maurizo and Clara decided to return to Canada and resume their lives in Montreal alongside Clara's parents. With her son once again a continent away, Laura Adaggi wrote frequently to him, even while her hands became increasingly frail and unsteady: "Maurizio my Love, Yesterday afternoon I received your dear [letter] that made me cry... for the affectionate and reassuring words" (22 March 1968); and, "I love you, I love you! Your mother embraces you and blesses you" (22 April 1969). Both earlier and later letters of Laura underscore a maternal affection undaunted by the physical realities of distance.[30]

Luciano Colonello and Marianna Domenica

Finally, a sixth letter series takes place in a town only a few hours from Venice. Parents Luciano Colonello and Marianna Domenica were maintaining a correspondence with their young son in Canada. Gianlorenzo had first migrated to Michel, British Columbia, at the encouragement of his paternal aunt, leaving behind his native town of Spilimbergo, located on the west side of the Friuli-Venezia Giulia region. The correspondence between son and parents dates from 1951 to 1986 and begins with a postcard written by Gianlorenzo Colonello—the only surviving epistolary document by him—while onboard the *S.S. Argentina* on 14 December 1951 on his way to Halifax: "Dear papà, the sea is calm and we are doing very well and in my cabin, we are three *Friulani* and one *Trevisano*. On this ship there are many *Friulani* and we have fun playing cards. I send you my greetings and say hi to all of my friends [*Io vi saluto tutti e saluta tutti i miei amici*]. I am your son Gianlorenzo."[31] The volume of letters back and forth intensified in June 1954, when Gianlorenzo was in the process of making arrangements for his move from Michel to Montreal. In their rural-based, working-class household in Spilimbergo, several generations of the Colonello and Domenica families lived together and shared responsibilities. Gianlorenzo's father was a day labourer (*bracciante*); however, the job market offered few work possibilities, and as a result, he devoted his hours to working as a land tenant (*affituario*) in the farm fields nearby. While the labour of both husband and wife yielded some good harvests, the agricultural economy was precarious and the land was "relatively poor, turned mainly to subsistence production."[32]

The memory of his mother waving her white handkerchief as the steamship liner moved away from the docks of Genoa was an image that Gianlorenzo preserved in his mind as he departed for British Columbia, where his paternal aunt and her husband awaited him. When his aunt had visited him in Spilimbergo in 1950 and witnessed the economic difficulties her family was facing, she had suggested that Gianlorenzo join her and her family in Michel, where steady, well-paying jobs were available. Gianlorenzo remembers being paid two dollars per hour (equivalent of 1500 lire per hour) in the coke ovens of Michel's mines. This was in sharp contrast to the rare work opportunities available in Spilimbergo, the most lucrative of which paid 1000 lire per day. Once Gianlorenzo agreed to join his aunt and uncle in Canada, she proceeded to complete the papers for the "*atto di richiamo*" (the application for sponsoring a relative as a result of the sponsorship program), and Gianlorenzo was soon on his way to British Columbia.

As the only male offspring of the family, Gianlorenzo needed good earnings to repay his debt for the transportation to Canada, send savings home to his family in Spilimbergo, and pay his living expenses for rent and food to his aunt of approximately one hundred dollars per month. The money Gianlorenzo sent home to his parents was indispensable to their economic well-being, as Marianna Domenica writes to Gianlorenzo and his wife, Elsa: "we always need to wait for your help [*noi dobbiamo sempre aspetare il vostro aiuto*] and we are sorry for that because poor you, you too need to work a lot" (11 November 1960). In the years following Gianlorenzo's migration, his father, Luciano, developed significant eye problems that would eventually lead to blindness and which prevented him from earning an income as an *affituario*. However, in later years, Gianlorenzo managed to purchase a house for his parents to live in rent-free for the rest of their lives. Gianlorenzo's sister had also emigrated to Canada. She lived with her brother for a few years until she returned to Italy in September 1961 to marry and remained there.

A stonemason (*muratore*) by training, Gianlorenzo learned quickly the arduous work involved in the hot coke-producing ovens of the coal mines in the Crowsnest Pass. However, following a number of years of work in the dust-infested, back-breaking labour of the coke ovens and mines, Gianlorenzo decided in the summer of 1954 to sell his car and other personal belongings and move to Montreal, where he lived in a boarding house with other townsfolk. Motivated by the prospect of finding a well-paying job, Gianlorenzo was encouraged to move east by his paternal uncle, who had arrived in Montreal in 1953. One evening in 1958, through the match-making skills of his sister, who had joined him in 1957, Gianlorenzo met Elsa Contini, whom he married on 25 July 1959 at the Madonna della Difesa Church in Montreal's Little Italy. Finally, in September 1961, Gianlorenzo, accompanied by his young wife Elsa, returned home to Italy for a visit after a ten-year absence.[33]

The anticipation of Gianlorenzo's return home was such that when the family in Spilimbergo learned that they had booked their flight several months before the actual departure, Gianlorenzo's mother wrote: "we are very happy that you have already prepared your luggage. We are all very happy and are now counting the days [*Siamo stati tutti felici e ora stiamo contando i giorni*]. Let's hope that God gives you the grace of good health so we can see each other soon, as we wish very much to see you and meet dear Elsa" (4 February1961).

In addition to revealing the letter writers' motivations for out-migration and the emotional connection that was maintained through the correspondence, these letters provide important insights into the materialization of public policy in the lives and life choices of ordinary people. Several letters show how the Canadian sponsorship program enabled chain migration and influenced the life choices made by ordinary individuals. For instance, a letter written in 1948 shows an Italian immigrant woman's awareness of the new Canadian legislation that would enable the migration of her fiancé. Clara Renzi advised Maurizio Trevisan that "now they have issued another law, which allows a fiancée to sponsor her fiancé provided the couple marry within 30 days of the man's arrival in Canada" (14 November 1948).[34]

Sara Franceschetti offers a rare glimpse into the experience of a hopeful migrant interviewed by immigration officers at the Canadian visa office in Rome. In an exceptional document, we read about the trials that Sara experienced as she answered the immigration officer's probing questions. We also read about her sense of relief when her passport was finally stamped with the visa that would allow her and her children to join her husband in Powell River. However, her challenges were not yet over: "I won't be embarking on the day of October 12 because the ship is fully booked... I'll have to wait until October 31 and hopefully there will be space available because it seems that even that ship is booked" (20 September 1956).

Once the papers were approved and the tickets for passage were secured, enormous sighs of relief were breathed as prospective migrants left the visa office with their new, highly sought visas. These individuals could now book their tickets on the *S.S. Saturnia*, the *S.S. Argentina*, the *S.S. Homeric*, and other steamship liners charting their courses for Halifax.

The abundance of work in Canada contrasting with the dearth of employment opportunities in Italy in the immediate postwar period, in addition to the reactivation of transnational kinship networks, were some of the forces driving Italian migration to Canada in record numbers. Additionally, the political-economic climate in both nation-states provided an ideal climate for the "highway" of individuals and families on the move to influence and bring about life-changing experiences for hundreds of thousands of Italians in their homeland and overseas. The life stories as revealed in the six letter collections suggest more than a heterogeneous and complex series of realities anchored in the migration experience. They provide important personal insights into individual and familial circumstances that compelled people to migrate or stay behind. Moreover, the words of migrants and loved ones articulated as events and experiences unfolding in the moment over fifty years ago, whether at points of departure, arrival, or in-between, offer a glimpse into the state of minds and hearts, the worries and concerns, the joys and satisfactions, and the dreams and hopes experienced within a process of international migration.

Friends and co-workers playing bocce in Michel, British Columbia, 1952

CHAPTER TWO

"*Even though distance has now kept us apart...*"
Kinship Across Networks

If it wasn't convenient for you working in the ovens, you did well to change jobs. Besides, the job wasn't even healthy. I advise you to hold on to your money, and make something for yourself now that you are young [Solo ti dico tieni da conto i soldi di farti qualche cosa addesso che sei giovine]. Don't go after cars, and don't get sick while you are away in a foreign land. It's always good to have some money in your pocket, don't you think so? Because as you remember, when you left, you said that you were going to make something for yourself, but instead, if you run after cars and other things, you will get nothing out of it, not even for yourself?

—Luciano Colonello to Gianlorenzo Colonello,
18 August 1954

IN HER ARTICLE, "The Traffic in Women," feminist anthropologist Gayle Rubin argues that "the exchange of goods and services, production and distribution, hostility and solidarity, ritual and ceremony, all take place within the organizational structure of kinship."[1] Rubin also observes that through kinship concrete forms of sex/gender systems are made up, reproduced and reinforced, and that kinship systems have their "own relations of production, distribution, and exchange, which include certain 'property' forms in people."[2]

This chapter examines the "traffic" of kin in migration through an analysis of the personal correspondence that flowed between six kin networks in postwar Italy and Canada. It explores the daily concerns, overarching themes, and ongoing dynamics that affected the members of these networks. The chapter has three main axes of discussion. First, it examines the flow of words, objects, and persons to kin across borders, including dynamics related to the transportation of these items via "personal courier."[3] Second, it looks at kinship in its supportive role of those who migrated. Finally, it explores how kinship's controlling function served to remind kin of their obligations and duties toward family members near or far. A brief discussion on the salience of kinship in the lives of Italian migrants and their loved ones concludes the chapter.

This discussion draws on a broad historiography that has emerged since the 1980s. How families responded to and negotiated the impacts of migration in their households and communities is explored across a myriad of geographies and temporalities throughout the historiography. My analysis is informed by Tamara Hareven's study on French-Canadian families in the early twentieth century, *Family Time and Industrial Time* (1982),[4] and Micaela di Leonardo's ethnographic study on the diverse ethnic experience of Italian-American families in California, *The Varieties of Ethnic Experience: Kinship, Class and Gender among California Italian-Americans* (1984).[5] The theme of change and continuity in migrant households, drawn from Donna Gabaccia's *From Sicily to Elizabeth Street* (1984) and Colleen Leahy Johnson's *Growing Up and Growing Old in Italian American Families* (1985), has helped me to identify specific behavioural dynamics of support and control in Italian families engaged in processes of acculturation and incorporation.[6] The question of what happens to kinship networks and kin members when one or several family members migrate abroad was elucidated through

Fortunata Piselli's work on kinship and emigration, and the changes and continuities that occurred within a small Calabrese community in postwar Italy.[7]

Early traces of the conceptual framework of transnationalism appear in
Robert Harney's scholarly production of the mid-1970s onwards, which examined a continuum that transpired in migration movements between Italy
and North America.[8] In the broader historiography of migration, the theoretical concept of transnationalism has been especially useful to historians
and anthropologists. While, as Donna Gabaccia argues, "transnationalism
is no invention of a late twentieth-century or postmodern world,"[9] in recent
years, the notion has engendered much discussion on the limits and opportunities it brings to the study of migration. In anthropology, transnational
analysis has been especially relevant to studies on Mexican, Portuguese,
and Filipina migration.[10] In his study on Mexican migration, Roger Rouse
analyzes the transnational interconnections of communities of migration as
the "continuous circulation of people, money, goods, and information."[11] In
their collaborative research, Nina Glick Schiller, Linda Basch, and Cristina
Szanton Blanc refer to transnational migration as "the process by which
immigrants forge and sustain simultaneous multi-stranded social relations
that link together their societies of origin and settlement."[12] More poignantly,
however, as Glick Schiller, Basch, and Szanton Blanc argue, "when we study
migration rather than abstract cultural flows or representations, we see that
transnational processes are located within the life experience of individuals
and families, making up the warp and woof of daily activities, concerns, fears,
and achievements."[13]

The Flow of Words, Objects, and Persons between Kin

Letters provided correspondents with information, news, personal reflections, money, and other objects. They were integral to the communication
of emotions, cultural values, norms, and practices of kinship. As material
objects, letters moved across international borders while simultaneously
crossing complex social, political, and familial boundaries. According to
Gerber: "immigrant personal correspondence was an early type of
transnational social space... a social location for the staging of relationships, in which... through the medium of writing, immigrants and their

correspondents surmounted conventional borders and organized their ongoing connections in order to solve the practical as well as existential problems associated with separation."[14]

The "wire" of communication sustained through letters illustrates the movement of kinship networks unfolding in a context of migration. Perhaps the primary function of letter writing for people was to provide a flow of life course news about members of the kinship network. Overwhelmingly, the well-being of migrant kin or loved ones who remained behind was the first topic to be addressed in the letters. Sometimes the news about kin was dispatched with formulaic phrases like, "we are happy to hear that you are all well, as the same follows for us in this moment" (14 June 1954),[15] or the more personal, "today I received your letter of the 17th, in which I am pleased to hear that you are well, and that even Nina is feeling better, as the same is for me as well" (24 July 1956).[16] Depending on the nature of the relationship between the writers, news of kin in the network often centred on major life course events, such as births, deaths, weddings, or illnesses. Typical in this respect is the following excerpt sent from Spilimbergo to Michel, British Columbia: "Gianlorenzo, I am advising you that Dario del Nero, the friend of your uncle [*zio*] Domenico from Gradisca has died sometime around mid-May, and that at the end of May, Santino Menotti, husband [*marito*] of Sandra Tasini, has died" (14 June 1954).[17] Of course, news of the death of a kin member who had previously maintained correspondence within the network carried a particularly grave sense of loss. Carmela Losanto's words, "now, all hope is over" (September 1963), illustrate this point. In one of her letters written in Ripabottoni, Campobasso to her brother in Montreal, we read how Carmela came to terms with the death of a cousin in Pittsburgh: "now, it's over with the relatives of PittiSburga [Pittsburgh]. Those who remain have never written. We never met them in person, nor in writing. They only know how to write American and they don't know Italian, and I can't write American. We are close relatives, and we don't even know each other" (17 August 1959).

The news of a birth, on the other hand, was greeted with elation throughout kin networks and had the effect of creating celebrations in multiple households well beyond the geographic boundaries where the birth took place. We read this in a letter Daniela Perini wrote to her daughter upon hearing that she had just become a grandmother: "You cannot imagine my happiness in becoming a *nonna*... as soon as Giuseppe gave me the wonderful news, I invited everyone in the building to celebrate the little Isabella... I even went to Stefania's and almost got her drunk, as well as Filomena and *Signora* Iannucci, all of whom send you their very best wishes" (8 September 1961).

News of a migrant's son or daughter getting married was greeted with excitement as well, especially if kin members approved of the choice of spouse for the kin member in question. Kin approval could be measured by the level of cooperation exhibited in organizing the sending of official papers that had been issued by the town's local parish about a wedding. Carmela's message to her brother concerning his daughter's wedding illustrates this point: "I'm sending you the papers for Marina's wedding. The high priest asked to be paid £1500 for his troubles in preparing the documents. I already have the money here, so don't worry" (8 July 1963). Approval for the wedding was expressed throughout the network as: "I was very pleased to receive the photograph and meet Marina's groom [*sposo*], and I send her my best wishes" (16 August 1963). Wedding gifts sent from kin in the town to the bride and her family in Montreal were also an indication of shared excitement and solidarity between kin across borders. Carmela writes, "Lucia, Giuseppina is bringing you a box of cloth handkerchiefs that I'm sending for Marina as a gift that she can use. I would have sent her other things, but I don't know what the custom is in America" (5 December 1963).

By contrast, revelations about a kin member's illness often induced readers to empathize with the pain as they struggled to acknowledge its impact at a distance. How separation accentuated the sense of pain and helplessness is reflected in the words of Dante del Moro in a letter to his wife Sara regarding his daughter's illness: "My dear wife [*Mia cara moglie*], Today I received your letter of the 6th and I really don't know how to express my pain in reading the news about Nina, I don't know if I should write, or cry. I don't know what I can do other than keep you deep in my *pensiero*... I hope that by the time you receive this letter, everything will be all right. Don't give up [*Dati coraggio*]" (13 July 1956). Similarly, as noted in the epigraph of Chapter 1, Carmela Losanto wrote to her sister-in-law in Montreal and advised her: "with regards to you, sister-in-law [*cognata*], and the terrible stomach pains you are having, I agree these are a problem. But let's hope you recover soon. I am so sorry to hear about this wretched illness of the stomach, my dear *cognata*" (6 May 1963). Carmela translated her concern over her sister-in-law's health into action by buying the medication requested by her sister-in-law from the local pharmacist and sending it to her through a trusted co-villager who was heading to Montreal during this period. In the same letter of 6 May 1963, Carmela wrote:

> Lucia, I understand everything and I will let you know. The medication is available here. I bought it already. It costs five thousand two hundred and twenty lire, I have already paid for it with the money you have here. So, don't worry. I'm also advising you that I wanted to send the parcel via the post office, but they told me that the package of medication would be opened along the way. For ground delivery, it costs £3500, for air mail, it costs £6000...I spoke with Tonino Cerone who is in charge of preparing packages and he has also told me that the parcel would probably be opened enroute. There is also the risk that the medication would not pass customs. Matteo Manfredi is coming to America with his wife and son [*moglie e figlio*] and they will be leaving on the 23rd of this month of May. He is arriving to America by ship on the 5th of June. He will be bringing the medication for you. Here is his address, you can telephone him when they arrive, so you can go and pick it up (6 May 1963).

The local pharmacist's instructions were included in the letter with the words, "the pharmacist has told me that there are two types of medication and that you need to chew them at the same time" (6 May 1963). Carmela reiterated her concern over the delivery of the medication in a letter she wrote once the personal courier had left the town. She advised her sister-in-law that the person bringing the medication had left on "the 23rd of May and will be arriving in America on the first of June. Call them to check if they have arrived, so you can go and pick up the medication" (24 May 1963). Clearly, the distance separating kin in a migration process was not necessarily an obstacle to direct action.

Receiving news and greetings from kin signified that despite the physical separation imposed through migration, relatives were not forgotten. Carmela's letter to her brother on 18 January 1959 provides an example: "I am letting you know that I have also received the letter that includes the Christmas wishes from Marina, Anita, and Sandro, and I was so happy to see that my nephews and nieces [*nipoti*] have not forgotten their aunts and uncles [*zii*]."

Missing letters, on the other hand, had the effect of producing concern over the lost words and written thoughts or concerns (*pensieri*) articulated by kin correspondents. While some of this concern was mitigated by communications with other members of the network, the frustration over lost letters highlights the resilience of the kin wire in migration, and demonstrates an intense desire to keep the connection alive with loved ones across networks. The feelings expressed by Maddalena Franchi's brother in a letter written from Rome to his sister in Montreal are a case in point:

> Dearest sister [*Carissima sorella*], you tell me that you wrote me a letter while I was away on leave. Unfortunately, I don't know what happened to the letter because I never received it. I was very worried and I often asked about you at home to know how you were doing. Just a few days ago, I received a letter from home, and among other things, *mamma* tells me that it's been some time since she received news from you, and that she too is waiting for some pictures of Isabella. I hope that by the time you receive this, you will have already written to her. She tells me, however, that she is not so worried because I wrote to her telling her that you are in good health, and that I received a photo of the little one (27 September 1961).

Similar feelings were expressed in a letter of Carmela Losanto written on 29 January 1962 to her sister-in-law in Montreal:

> Lucia, the letter that was lost was mine. I had written to you and was waiting for your response, the days were passing and my *pensiero* said to me, what happened? Instead, on Saturday, January 27, I received your letter from my *fratello* Mario... you see, when letters are lost, so are the discussions and everything they say. We would need a book, or if we could at least be together for one day, so we could talk in person [*a voce*], and we would have greater satisfaction in understanding each other.

In addition to the letters themselves, a plethora of objects and gifts were sent back and forth by kin members. These items, which were delivered either through the postal service or with the assistance of a personal courier, fulfilled two purposes. They answered requests by kin to be supplied with items of personal necessity, or they were sentimental gifts sent to mark a life-course event or simply because a courier was travelling in that direction. How these objects were viewed as sites of memory by kin on both sides of the ocean is another question with which I am concerned.

A careful reading of the letters reveals that money, photographs, clothing, shoes, jewellery, thread for embroidery, and other local specialty items were routinely sent as gifts between kin in Italy and Canada. The bank cheques of eighty dollars that Gianlorenzo Colonello frequently enclosed with his letters to his parents in Spilimbergo, for instance, were gratefully acknowledged, as we read in a letter to Gianlorenzo: "I am letting you know that on the 11th we received the money for which we are so grateful to you" (15 September 1954). Sometimes, along with the letter and cheque, Gianlorenzo included lightweight gifts that a friend or kin member travelling to the same area would deliver. Gianlorenzo's father advised his son that he had been visited by a friend and received "everything that you explained in the letter" (15 September 1954). Similarly, his mother, in addition to thanking him, itemized all the goods that had been delivered by his friend in order to prove that everything was in order. Marianna Domenica wrote: "*Caro* Gianlorenzo, we are so grateful to you for the money, and the stockings that you sent me, Teresa and Gina, the socks for your *padre*. *Nonna* Teresa thanks you for the two dollars as does *nonna* Luigia" (15 September 1954).

The desire to reciprocate was part of the gift-receiving dynamic, although circumstances did not always enable such an exchange to occur. In the following excerpt, Marianna Domenica describes this yearning but explains why it was not possible for her to send something in return to her son and his wife. On 1 May 1961, she wrote, "Arcangelo came over and brought your greetings [*saluti*], I would have liked to send you something in return through him, but since he was travelling by airplane, I didn't dare ask him. You always remember to send us something via anyone who comes this way, and you have always had a big heart for your parents [*genitori*]."

Inevitably, the exchange of gifts was influenced by life-cycle events, such as an imminent birth in the family or a birthday, or wedding, as I noted earlier. These exchanges were important because they represented attempts to sustain normal family practice in spite of distance. Here, Daniela Perini wrote to her daughter, Maddalena:

> *Cara figlia*, with regards to what I need to send you... I am sending you something [made by *Signora...*], because as you know she makes beautiful embroideries. It isn't finished yet. If, when your *zia* Rosina comes to visit me, it's ready, that's fine. Otherwise, I will prepare a parcel myself because even *la comare* Stefania and Filomena want to send you something. Don't worry, when that special moment will arrive, everything will be in order. *Cara figlia*, a few days ago *la comare* [godmother] Anna came to visit, and brought me everything you sent me. Thank you so much for your thoughtful gifts, and thank Giuseppe for the two dollars, and the dollar that you sent me (17 June 1961).

While Maddalena's own words of thanks are not available in the collection, we can surmise the meaning these gifts held for her. As we read in her mother's letters, Maddalena was deeply melancholic for the home she had left behind. Moreover, with the birth of her first child approaching, she was very concerned about going through the process in a foreign country with a family she barely knew nearby. It seems safe to assume that the gifts her mother and her godmothers were sending her served as important sites of memory. The "tangibility" of these objects, as anthropologist Loretta Baldassar suggests, "which might be described as their 'emotionality,' that is, their ability to be 'felt' or at least to be used as a conduit for emotion and feeling by proxy, is in many instances more important than their content."[18] Gifts, cards, and letters received in times of need were "special 'transnational objects' that are important largely because of their tangibility—they can be touched and held and thus take the physical place of the longed for person or location. They represent, or more specifically, 'stand for' the absence of being."[19]

The letters reveal how migrants were also solicited to help fund local religious festivities in exchange for public recognition of the family's contribution to the festivities. This recognition worked to demonstrate to local townsfolk that migrants who had left the town had become economically successful elsewhere yet had retained their connection to it. Indeed, it was important both to the townsfolk and the migrants to ensure that travellers retained their connection to the town and remained part of its social memory. As the letters of Carmela Losanto show, while migrants were not obligated to help fund their native town's social or religious events, they were encouraged to do so by co-villagers in both Montreal and Ripabottoni, where a list of donors' names and the size of their donations were on public view. Many co-villagers in Montreal generously helped fund events honouring patron saints back home and targeted their support to the entertainment provided by a local band on the town square or the evening's fireworks. Some were especially keen to preserve their names as good citizens with the community in their native town, and to demonstrate to co-villagers in Montreal that they had not forgotten their roots. In this sense, the public exhibition or acknowledgement of migrants' gifts signified their "virtual co-presence"[20] in the community. In the following letter, Carmela Losanto wrote to her brother and relayed the information from the town-feast organizer on the subject:

> My dear brother [*Mio caro fratello*], I'm now advising you on this matter. Don Mario Filippi is the organizer of the *Festa di San Rocco* and he told me these words with regards to the *Festa di San Rocco*, "write to your *fratello* and to your *marito*, have them send ten dollars each directly in my name. I will place the banknote on the Saint when the procession starts." This is what Don Mario told me. But you, my *fratello*, if you are pleased to donate something to the Saint, let me know immediately. The day is set for August 16, the *festa* day has not been decided yet. So, I tell you again, if you wish you can give the money directly from the savings you have here. In this way, you don't have to trouble yourself with sending it. You can send £500 or £1000... to the Saint. It could help us by giving us strength and good health (3 August 1965).

In addition to gifts, other objects also flowed between kin across networks. Some items, including money, official documents, photographs, liquor, clothing, jewellery, a hair-cutting machine, a pasta-making machine, medication, medical instruments, and family recipes were specifically requested by migrants and loved ones. As we observe in the following excerpts, requests were fulfilled efficiently and great care was taken to ensure prompt and safe delivery of requested items. When we look again at Carmela Losanto's efforts in obtaining and delivering the medication required by her sister-in-law, we observe the strengthening of ties through material exchange. Her words of response to her sister-in-law's gratitude for sending her this much-needed medication are revealing: "Lucia, you tell me that you care only for me. The same is for me. You are always my *cognata*. How much we care for each other even though distance has now kept us apart" (24 May 1963).

In a letter from Sara Franceschetti to her husband Dante del Moro, she wrote:

> *Mio caro* Dante, I'm writing to you in response to your letter of August 9, in which you indicate a second list of items that I need to bring. I know what you need, including the hair-cutting machine. I spoke with Nando and on the first Monday that he is free, we'll go shopping for these items… I received the money from your brother. I needed it… I am starting to shop for the trip and everything else (18 August 1956).

Nine days later, as the preparations for her departure were underway, Sara reassured Dante that, "I have taken note of everything that you are telling me, including the liquor, I understand what you want" (27 August 1956).

In this letter series, we observe both the material nature of requests and the expanding web of contacts that gift-giving produced as some migrants increasingly became merchandise suppliers to their home communities. The list of items to send or bring expanded continually, not only because of the emerging needs of one household, but because members of other households of kin nearby were making their requests as well. For example, Dante wrote to Sara: "Do you remember those two beige woollen undershirts that I had bought last year?… If you find them, you need to buy four more for me, and Angela wants 6 for Elio" (5 August 1956). In other letters, he added, "See if you can find two thermometers for fevers, one for Elio, and one for us" (9 August 1956), and "Angela here is asking you to remember to bring the recipe for the *focaccia*" (16 September 1956).

Not to be overlooked in the network of exchange was the role of the friends and relatives who acted as couriers, bearers of news, and go-be-tweens. As the travel plans of kin, friends, and acquaintances became known, families often made a special effort to write a letter, prepare a parcel or send greetings with the traveller. Likewise, letter writers made special efforts to locate personal couriers who could be entrusted with delivering papers, gifts or news that had particular importance.

Yet, not all items could be delivered. Partly, this depended on whether the personal courier's mode of transportation was by ship or airplane. Sometimes, all the personal courier could bring was a letter or even just *saluti*, as Marianna Domenica wrote to Gianlorenzo: "on Tuesday the 23rd, Dario of Fanna left. We asked him to bring our *saluti* to you. He too could not bring anything with him. I would have liked him to bring something for you, but since he was travelling by plane, he could not bring anything" (25 May 1961).

Letters and *saluti* from a loved one or a fellow migrant often had a profound effect on recipients. Their resonance was such that the personal courier could be seen as embodying the sender in flesh and blood (*in carne ed ossa*), "the internalised presence of transnational kin and country *by proxy*."[21] We witness this phenomenon in Marianna Domenica's letter to her son written after she had been visited by his fellow friend, who resembled him and also lived in Montreal: "It was like seeing you here [*Mi sembrava da vederti te*], she wrote, adding, "*Caro figlio* Gianlorenzo... thank you [*grazie*] for the dollars that you sent us through the hands of your friend... What I would pay to see you" (8 August 1956).

Nor did the ties between personal couriers and loved ones end the moment that a parcel or letter was delivered at its destination, for the relationship between personal courier, sender, and receiver was also based on reciprocal obligations of caring. This kind of reciprocity is apparent in a letter written by Luciano Colonello to his son: "So you advised us that a young man from Casarsa has arrived in Italy and that you gave him ten dollars, so he brought us the money a few days ago with his cousin they came by motorcycle, however he said he will come back to visit us on the day of *San Rocco*" (8 August 1956).

When personal couriers made round trips to and from a destination, they also had an obligation to relay fresh news from abroad back to the families or individuals who had dispatched them in the first place. It was expected by all parties involved that the personal courier would take the time to discuss how things had gone upon visiting the migrant's family back home. Marianna wrote to her son upon hearing that friends had returned home, and had given news to him: "We are happy that Berto and Maria came to visit you and give you our *saluti*. We are also pleased that they told you many things" (23 August 1960).

Although the letter "was always the place in which information was shared on what was needed or desirable, on the best means for its convey-ance, and on when and where it could be expected to arrive,"[22] the medium had its limits. To be able to speak in person (*parlare a voce*) even through a proxy, was viewed in some cases as more effective than writing letters. This was especially true for individuals whose literacy skills presented a challenge. Relaying information that was difficult to explain or open to misunderstand-ings on paper was viewed as less complicated when done through a trusted personal courier. A letter that Carmela Losanto wrote to her brother in Montreal regarding the arrival of her nephew demonstrates my point: "We are talking on paper, you brother [*fratello*], can't understand me. When Sandro returns, he will explain everything to you" (11 August 1964). The next day, Sandro and his wife wrote to his father in Montreal advising him that all was well and that "when we'll be there, we'll speak in person" (12 August 1964). The expectation that the personal courier would relay in person all of the news obtained back home is reiterated in the following words of Carmela upon learning that her nephew had, in fact, forwarded her news to her brother in Montreal: "*Caro mio fratello*, I understand everything, and I am so pleased that Sandro has told you everything about this place" (19 October 1964). Clearly, Carmela was delighted that her nephew had, as accurately as possible, relayed all the news she needed her brother to hear in person.

Support Strategies of Kinship in Migration Networks

As a number of migration studies suggest, kinship networks provided vital forms of support to loved ones and migrants across borders. Tamara Hareven notes, "'Long-distance' kin, like those nearby, were sources of security and assurance in times of crisis and often served as a refuge."[23] Moreover, kin networks that were engaged in a process of migration "stretched to sev-eral locations and these links were mobilized as the local community went through periodic difficulties or during waves of migration."[24] Letters played a key role in maintaining communications across these networks. Indeed, as Loretta Baldassar argues, "the ritual exchange of greeting cards… are a visible sign of enduring relationships."[25] Yet beyond maintaining base levels of contact, letters could also activate strong emotions across different parts of the kin network.

One of the most striking features of kinship support we learn about in the letters is the extensive care provided by kin in Italy for loved ones who, as a result of their own kin's migration, felt abandoned. This phenomenon is reflected in all six of the letter series. Some of the more significant examples include Marianna Domenica's words to her sister-in-law in Montreal concerning her mother's well-being, in which she wrote: "Your family at home is well, and even your mother is doing fine. It's just that, poor her, she can't walk too much, but she is still strong and eats well. Nives, don't worry about her, she has everything she needs. Alba, your *cognata*, and everyone else, love her very much. I often visit her and spend a few hours with her" (18 August 1954).

While Maddalena Franchi was initially urged by her brother to write often to her mother because "she has practically remained alone," as a result of "the empty days she feels since you left" (22 November 1960), both her brother and her mother later reassured her that her mother was fine. And, ten months later, Daniela Perini confirmed her well-being by writing to her daughter: "Dear daughter [*Cara figlia*], don't feel sorry for me, I am never alone in the evenings. Sometimes I visit with Graziella, or *la Signora* Quarini and watch television at her home" (30 September 1961), and "Don't worry about me, because every day and every night, I am at *Signora* Sistini's, like when you were here and we used to visit *Signora* Panetti" (10 December 1961). Even several years later, Maddalena's brother reassured her that their mother was well taken care of: "Don't worry about *mamma*, because either I or Assunta, now more than ever, we are close to her, and we'll do our best to help her enjoy these days as serenely as possible" (c. 1966). In the letters of Carmela Losanto, this kind of support provided by loved ones who remained behind was equally explicit. In the following, she described to her sister-in-law in Montreal how her mother was doing, and some of the difficulties she was experiencing as a result of being alone: "I went to visit your *mamma*, and on that day, even your *cognata* Messalina came with me… your *mamma* is well. She was complaining that she would like to have some company at night. During the day, neighbors and friends nearby visit her, but at night, everyone stays in their homes" (29 January 1962).

Family members who stayed behind were equally active in giving support to arriving migrants. The logic with which kin or friends were solicited to assist arriving migrants, and the extent to which kin assistance was sought, deserves attention here. By weaving the multiple connections between kin across networks witnessed in the correspondence, a circulatory pattern is underscored in the way information was relayed and assistance was recruited. The "circulatory" character of Italian migrations, described by Donna Gabaccia,[26] is analogous to the logic by which information flowed between networks in a process of migration. Here is one scenario that illustrates my point. On 15 September 1954, Marianna wrote to her son advising him that

> Alberto has arrived in Montreal. However, his parents are worried because they don't know if he has found a job or not. Poor them, they too have made many sacrifices to send him away, and now, no one knows where he is. You, Gianlorenzo, see if you can find work for him. Here is his address: Domenica Alberto, Emigration 1162 S.t. Antuine S.t. Montreal QEC. Canada. I beg you, as soon as you know something, write to me immediately so I can right away visit *la nonna* and tell her the news.

Voicing similar concerns, Gianlorenzo's aunt in Michel, British Columbia, wrote to Gianlorenzo:

> Yesterday, I received a letter from home. Everyone is well. Your *mamma* tells me that your cousin, son of your uncle Mario has arrived in Montreal. I know him... Your uncle Beppi and I have been talking about your cousin ... Nonetheless, the mines in Alberta have nearly all closed, and all the jobs here are being filled... I'm very sorry [*mi dispiace proprio*] (3 November 1954).

Three days later, Gianlorenzo's mother in Spilimbergo wrote to Gianlorenzo: "I'm so happy that Alberto is staying with you. Poor soul, at least, he's with someone whom he knows. I hope you can help him find work there, so he can remain near you... All the *zii* here, and *la nonna* thank you for generously helping Alberto. Everyone is happy to hear that he's there with all of you. Give him our best greetings" (6 November 1954). In the same letter, Marianna Domenica included a few words to Gianlorenzo's uncle and aunt (who lived near him): "From the bottom of my heart, my family thanks you for your interest in Alberto and for taking care of him. They are so happy that he is staying with you." Soon after, we learn that Gianlorenzo's cousin had indeed found a job in Montreal: "We are happy that Alberto has found work" (8 December 1954), and that the family back home was wholeheartedly grateful to Gianlorenzo and his uncle and aunt for helping him. Luciano Colonello wrote, "Even today my *cognata* Maria, *mamma* of Alberto, has asked me to write to you, as she is deeply grateful to you and Gianlorenzo for everything you have done for Alberto. Please give him our best greetings" (8 December 1954).

This vignette shows how inquiries on the whereabouts of an arriving migrant often extended through several households within a kin network that was spread over thousands of kilometres. Moreover, it demonstrates the importance of work-related inquiries that were made on behalf of migrants (sometimes even without their knowledge), as well as a form of control—elaborated in the next section of this chapter—that kin exercised on this young migrant, despite being an ocean apart. In this way, they were assured that he continued to behave as they expected him to.

In addition to advocating on behalf of migrants, letters served as important instruments of moral support to family and friends who were coping with their new surroundings in Canada. They encouraged them to take care of themselves and their families, to seek out other kin, and to develop kin-like relationships so that they would not suffer the loneliness and nostalgia that often accompanied leaving home. In the letters of Daniela Perini we observe words of encouragement that inveighed her daughter to take care of her family, and to seek comfort from other kin nearby: "*Cara figlia*, I am very pleased to hear in your letter that you and Giovanna are getting along so well and that you care for each other. Try to always be there for each other like sisters. I urge you to love your father [*padre*], your mother [*madre*], your husband [*marito*] and everyone at home" (1 May 1961). These words of encouragement from mother to daughter are evidence of the expectation that personal happiness revolved around the family. As the letters of kin show, family was paramount to the survival and personal well-being of its members. The dearth of attention in these letters to issues related to personal aspirations and autonomy indicates that little, if any, importance was placed on self-realization and individuality in the life script prescribed by the letter writers and their universe.

Loved ones back home were also engaged in taking care of the houses migrants had left behind upon departing for Canada. The letters of Carmela Losanto illustrate this point as the discussion of her brother's house in the village occupied centre stage in much of the correspondence. As Carmela explained to her brother, she had willingly accepted the task of taking care of his house because that was an essential part of sustaining the family: "*fratello*, you're concerned that I have a lot to worry about with regards to your matters here, but for me, it's nothing, because we care so much for each other... My heart is always with you, my *nipoti* and my *cognata* Lucia, for all the love that we share, I think of all of you" (3 September 1961).

Kin in Italy served as an enormous resource in locating and negotiating the purchase of housing for a migrant and her family who wished to return home, either temporarily or permanently. For instance, Davide Franchi wrote to his sister Maddalena: "Regarding the apartment... The other day I was in Ostia at *Zia* Maria's and out of curiosity, I visited an apartment with Luciana, even just to see what the market value is estimated at in the area" (10 May 1963). Not long after, Maddalena's mother described her excitement about the apartment in Rome that was purchased for her daughter by proxy, and what it meant in terms of family reunification: "Davide told me that he has rented out your apartment. You cannot imagine how happy I am of your home, so that we can all be together. Davide has described to me how he is renovating it. It's a real gem. You should be happy about it, so that when you'll be returning to Italy, you'll find a home in perfect order as it should be" (26 November 1963).

The letters illustrate that family members on both sides of the Atlantic offered experiential knowledge on matters related to migration procedures. They provided arriving migrants with much-needed advice on travel arrangements, as well as what a travelling family member could expect to find upon disembarking the ocean liner in Halifax. In this letter, Dante del Moro urged his wife Sara to begin preparing for the trip to Canada: "I spoke with the notary here, and he told me briefly that I don't need to send you anything,… all you need to do is go to the travel agency… and explain everything" (7 April 1956). In terms of travelling arrangements, he suggested, "ask for tourist-class cabins, even though it's a little more expensive, it doesn't matter. The most important thing is that you are comfortable, I don't want you to stay in the large sleeping hall because it makes for difficult travelling" (7 April 1956). In August, when the date of departure was approaching, Dante wrote: "Keep in mind one thing: you must send the wooden trunks over directly to Powell River, otherwise you will be forced to open them at customs in Halifax. Instead, if they arrive here, you'll need to pass customs here… Buy your train tickets for Vancouver instead. I'll give you more instructions on this later" (5 August 1956). For their arrival in Halifax, Dante advised Sara,

> At the customs office in Halifax, there are a few shops in which you'll find everything you need, bread and canned foods, whatever you like that you can eat on the train. On the train from Montreal to Vancouver, if you still need something, ask one of your travelling companions for help. There is always someone getting off at various stations [to buy items]. Don't try to get off the train yourself, because you risk missing it, as it happened when I came over (16 September 1956).

Migrant kin also sent official papers to help loved ones facilitate the procedures for them to migrate quickly to Canada. They actively linked up individuals within their networks who would be travelling in the same direction and could accompany a loved one travelling alone. A letter from Clara Renzi to Maurizio illustrates this point: "I have here with me your ticket for embarkment. I'm just waiting to telephone *Signor* Frattini tonight in order to know how I should proceed at this point, after which I will immediately send you the papers" (18 July 1949). Clara also encouraged Maurizio to travel through France for two reasons: "my *padre* would be pleased if you travelled via France, so you could meet and bring *saluti* to his brothers." And, because a family friend was travelling along the same route at roughly the same time, she advised Maurizio that this person, "will also be arriving here, and it seems he will be travelling along the same route… we would be so happy if you could travel together." She urged Maurizio to "write to him and make

arrangements together so that we can come together to meet you in Quebec"
(18 July 1949).

In addition to providing general travel information, the letters from migrants who had settled earlier in Canada offered advice on how best to take
advantage of the new sponsorship program. For instance, in September 1955,
Elio Santini, Dante del Moro's cousin in Canada, explained briefly in a letter
to him what the sponsorship program required of sponsors and prospective
migrants. Elio's words of encouragement serve as an important insight into
the kind of support kin promised and realized in the process of chain migration across borders. Elio advised Dante that

> I have read and reread your letter, and it feels like a dream that
> you too are thinking of coming to these lands.... The informa-
> tion I received is that you need to write a well-written letter
> [*una lettera ben scritta*] to the Canadian Consulate in Rome,
> stating my name and address of where I live... you can tell
> them that I assume full responsibility of you upon entering
> Canada... I hope you can come. The advice I have for you is
> that you come alone... when you will see what life is like in
> these lands and if you like it, then you can call your wife and
> children (4 September 1955).[27]

Indeed, the moment Dante arrived in Vancouver on 23 March 1956, he
was so impressed with the welcome and reception he received from his godmother and his cousin that he immediately wrote to his wife telling her that,

> At the station, I found someone waiting for me, someone I was
> not expecting, my godmother [*santola*] Lidia Prusani. And, I
> must tell you, *cara moglie*, that I have no words to describe my
> joy.... She took me out, got me into a car, and there we were
> heading to the ferry boat station. In ten minutes we were home.
> Here, I can't begin to tell you the kind of welcome that awaited
> me. It was as if I were the president of Vancouver. There was ev-
> erything and anything imaginable to eat, all to my heart's con-
> tent. Then, she took me to visit her brother Marco at the Hotel,
> and there too, what a welcome! We then visited several Italian
> friends in their homes.... Imagine that they had already found

a job for me…. Last night, we immediately called Elio on the telephone, which he has at his home, and as soon as he heard my voice, he didn't know whether to laugh, or cry. For now, we said "hello" and arranged a meeting. He's expecting me on Sunday night. I wanted to head that way earlier, but my *santola* would not let me go at any cost, because, as she said, "you are tired, first rest and then you will go up." Perhaps that was best, since I was extremely tired. Imagine that *la santola* missed two days of work, as she waited for me. Now, as I write to you, I'm at Lidia's house... and I'm here alone. I just prepared for myself a nice morning snack, fried eggs with butter, and strawberries in syrup, pastries, and so much more. I tell you this, never before in my life have I found myself in these circumstances. Last night, Elio called, and … I may start working on Monday (23 March 1956).

Not surprisingly, kinship support was also integral to sustaining romantic relationships disrupted through migration. Messages from parents or grandparents living in the same household as the letter writer were included in letters in order to send greetings and to demonstrate that the relationship at a distance was approved by kin. This was a significant consideration for the couple when plans for reunion or marriage were being made. At the same time, however, the practice of adding notes to letters between love correspondents compromised to some degree the privacy of their written words. In the passionate letters of Giordano Rossini, for instance, we witness the occasional participation of his grandmother adding a few words of *saluti* at the end of his letters to Ester. We can surmise that this transgression of privacy stemmed from his grandmother's approval of their relationship. Kinship approval of romantic relations at a distance is further underscored in Giordano's recapitulation of conversations with his grandmother concerning Ester:

Today when I got back, *nonna* showed me 3 cups of Japanese porcelain…. As she showed them to me, she said, "This cup is for Ester, this one is mine, and this one is yours." She kept the most beautiful cup for you. It has golden butterflies on the face of it, mine is completely violet, and *nonna*'s is white with flowers and it has two handles. You see, *Cara*, even *nonna* thinks of you always. She loves you so (18 April 1957).

In the letter series of Clara Renzi, we observe her effort to include the words of immediate family members in her letters to Maurizio as an indication of her desire both to acknowledge the importance of these individuals in her fiancé's life and to expand the web of approval for their relationship. When, for instance, Clara did not receive for some time a word of *saluti* from his family in his letters to her, she inquired directly about the silence by addressing his mother and father:

> *Mamma e papà cari*, some time has passed since I read your writing, why? I greatly enjoyed reading your writing—How are you? Do you remember me? I too think of you often with much affection—We are all well. *Papà* asks me to send you his *saluti*, as does *mamma*. Here, it's already getting very cold. *Signor* Francesco, are you familiar with the cold weather of Montreal? *Saluti* to the whole family, and to you, infinite *baci*, yours Clara (14 November 1948).

In her appeal for a response from them, Clara emphasized the bonds between her and Maurizio's parents in order to underscore their mutual affection. Significantly, she also referred to them as mother and father, even though she and Maurizio were not yet married at the time. Soon after, Maurizio's parents responded, as Clara's subsequent letters reveal.

Forms of Control and Discipline of Kinship in Migration

While kinship networks functioned on many levels to provide support for families experiencing the realities of migration, they also produced a coercive counter-effect by placing significant emotional and social pressures on migrants and loved ones to "stay the course." Just as kinship support was deployed across borders through the language of patriarchal values and norms in personal correspondence, mechanisms of social control and "family discipline" also "transcended national boundaries and bridged continents."[28] The observations of anthropologist Fortunata Piselli on the operations of kinship in migration specifically point to kinship as "the most important form of interaction that, as a conditioning structure, becomes an object of manipulation."[29]

In this context letters played a crucial role in reminding—both explicitly and implicitly—kin members about their duties and obligations, and in providing a vehicle for the voices of authority of parents, spouses, siblings, lovers, and so on. The "naturalness" with which social duties and gender obligations were assumed and reproduced by kin across migration networks exemplifies the culturally constructed notion of "common sense" defined by Antonio Gramsci as the "traditional popular conception of the world."[30] At the same time, the seductiveness of "common sense" knowledge rests in its invisibility as an expression of "traditional" forms of thought, ideologies, expectations, and roles that are viewed, as Clifford Geertz writes, as both natural and practical.[31] The inherent qualities of common sense as "natural and practical," and "taken for granted," as Pierre Bourdieu also observes,[32] are precisely what make familial duties and obligations seem inapparent yet resilient. These structures of conformity operated strongly in postwar Italian families, especially where parental advice and what Colleen Johnson calls "reminders" were concerned.[33]

The letters from parents to children, for instance, repeatedly offered evidence of the social control and family discipline that parents attempted to maintain. By offering advice and encouragement, they directed their migrant adults and children to stay in touch and to maintain their duties and obligations. Upon learning that his nineteen-year-old son had decided to leave the steady work in the mines of Michel, British Columbia, and venture to Montreal, Gianlorenzo Colonello's father reacted as follows:

> Gianlorenzo, as we read your letter, both your *mamma* and I, we were on the verge of tears while reading the words in which you say that you are young and that you want to enjoy yourself. We thought that you went to Canada to make some money for yourself, some savings for another day. Isn't that so? It's fine to enjoy yourself a little bit, but moderately, don't you think so? You are in a foreign land, and it's always good to have some money on you. Another thing, when you answer our letters, read them carefully and think over the words that we're telling you.... Listen to us, you are young, and if you're earning good

money, hold on to it, because money does not come easily. Look at Silvio of your *Zio* Mario. He lives in Belgium, is now married and this year he bought some land on which he will be building his house in Belgium.... You tell us that if you leave from where you are now, you'll be going to Montreal. You do what you think is best, because we just don't know. All I can tell you is that in the city you earn more, and you spend much more... your *padre*, Luciano[34] (28 July 1954).

In the same letter, Marianna expressed her disappointment about her son's desire to leave his aunt's home in Michel. She wrote:

Gianlorenzo, I am very sad to read the words you wrote in your letter.... I had thought you would stay with your *zia* as long as you would be away. In that way, you could buy yourself a house, as you had written some time ago. That was really a good thing for you. But if you are thinking of changing place, think it over carefully. If you move to the city, you could end up without a job. You do what you think is best, but think it over a thousand times. Not I and nor your *padre* can say more than that. You have to do what you think is best for you. And, if you have a good job there, why are you changing now? You need to do what you think is best for you. Don't be angry over what we are telling you. Send us news right away, as both of us as your *genitori* as well as everyone else at home are always happy to hear from you.... Gianlorenzo, take care of yourself. Don't get sick, because we need your help, and if you get sick, it's bad for you, and worse for us. Go visit your *zia*, and listen to her advice. She is a good woman, and she is like a *mamma* to you. Ask her what you should do.

By reminding their son of his initial objectives, both parents were urging him to stay true to his "migration project."[35] By referring to the migrant success stories of other kin they emphasized the benefits of listening to their words. And by reminding him of how much they depended on him financially, they underscored his responsibilities to them.

In her study of Italian-American families, anthropologist Colleen Johnson argues that interdependence in families "is associated with the patterning of affection and authority."[36] The parental authority being exerted in the example above also illustrates the potential for coercion that operated in transnational households.

Gianlorenzo's parents continued to voice their authority by admonishing him not to spend his money on cars, and urging him to save his money. By expressing their economic difficulties and making their dependence on him known, they added considerable weight to their argument. The following words of Marianna are a case in point:

> Gianlorenzo, I would like to ask you for a favour. Only if it's possible. I would need to buy myself a coat, but I don't have the money. If you could send it to me, otherwise, it's okay. The days are getting colder and it's good to stay warm, but if you cannot send it to me, I won't buy anything. Coats are very expensive, and I will just make do. I would also like to buy one for Gina, but if you can't, that's okay. I send you my dearest *saluti, baci...* *mamma* (18 August 1954).

Johnson concludes that interdependence, nurturance and social control underlie children's conformity to parental expectations.[37] The letters received by Maddalena Franchi illustrate the point by revealing how much her experiences were tied up with the fortunes of the family. She was expected to make her migration experience a fulfilling and successful event, socially, personally, and emotionally, in order for her happiness to radiate throughout the network of immediate and extended kin. From the first letter that Daniela Perini wrote to her daughter, the seemingly benevolent words of advice, encouragement, and maternal love translate also into duty, obligation, social respectability, and emotional pressures for a "good"[38] daughter to respond to, and enact:

> *Carissima figlia,* I received your *cara* letter and you have no idea how happy I was to hear such good news from you, for since you left, I did nothing else but think of you and cry. Now, I am comforted and pleased to learn from your letter of the pleasant trip you had, and the warm welcome you received from your

parents…. I pray to the Lord that He grant me the good fortune to hold you in my arms again. I will never stop praying for you, for your *marito*, and the whole *famiglia* there, as well as for your happiness, good fortune and good health. I urge you to write to your *zii* at least one letter for the first time, followed by postcards. *Cara figlia*, perhaps you forgot to send your *saluti* to our dear ones in our building, but I gave them just the same, because everyone here asks for you. I ask you to be good and kind like you have been with your *madre*, and to respect your *genitori*, and to love your *marito*, because happiness in life comes only through loving each other (22 November 1960).

The pervasive requests by correspondents on both sides of the Atlantic to keep writing also deserve attention. The desire to stay in touch extended beyond that of the correspondents to read in a few lines if family members were well or not. It also signified an urge to make kin part of their daily lives despite their physical absence. Ironically, by sharing knowledge about themselves and their families some correspondents left themselves open to criticism from family members who had previously exercised authority over them. Often enough, therefore, one finds mixed together with the well-meaning words of advice and encouragement a different language of proscription and authority as expressed through sermons, reprimands, and other reminders of discipline and control.

The letters offer hints as to what happened when a correspondent's desire to know more was not fulfilled. For instance, in a letter from Gianlorenzo's father, we read his reaction to his son's news that he is no longer living with his aunt in Michel, British Columbia: "We were surprised to hear that you are no longer living with your *zia*, and that they told you that they are old, and wish to be alone. Did you not respect them? Why don't you explain yourself better? When you write, do you always have so little to say? ... We are very worried about this, write to us immediately the reason, because we want to know" (9 July 1954). The letters that follow in the series indicate that Gianlorenzo did eventually report to his parents' satisfaction the events unfolding in his aunt's household in Michel, for at some point, the issue was no longer a concern and their correspondence had shifted toward providing advice and encouragement relating to his move to Montreal.

Maddalena's correspondence also suggests that she fulfilled her duties and obligations as a "good" daughter, because the requests to keep writing or to write more often were predominantly encouragements to write to extended family members. For instance, soon after Maddalena's arrival in Montreal, Daniela Perini once again reminded her daughter to write to kin: "I beg you to write a couple of postcards to your *zii*, because they are always asking for you, since the postcards you sent them have not arrived yet" (5 December 1960). Daniela then proceeded to reassure her daughter that

> you must not be afraid of writing to your *zii*, let me assure you that you write quite well, even Filomena in reading the letter that you wrote to Stefania was impressed to see how well written and structured your letter is. Therefore, try to write a first letter to them, and then follow up with a written note in your letters to me addressed to each of them (5 December 1960).

An additional reason for Daniela's insistence that her daughter write to her uncles and aunts is likely linked to saving face with her extended family in Italy. However, when Maddalena's younger brother later became a similar target of his mother's pleas, it became clear that expectations of a daughter differed from those of a son. In a letter written soon after his arrival in Montreal, Daniela advised her daughter: "*Carissima figlia*, I know that Fabio is a little lazy in writing to me. I beg you to tell him not to make me suffer for his mail" (c. 1966). In this letter, Daniela also indicated to her that she did not expect Fabio to write often: "I am not asking him to write every week, because I know that once he starts working, he will have little free time available, but at least, if he could write once a month" (c. 1966).

To be sure, the frequency and intensity of the flow of correspondence between mother and daughter was astounding when compared with the infrequent letters the son was expected to write. The gender dynamic seems to be an inherent reason. Indeed, if we carefully compare the exchanges between Gianlorenzo and his parents with those between Maddalena and her mother, the gender issue is inescapable. The greater obligation for daughters to write, as opposed to sons, illustrates another difference in the kinds of duties, obligations, and emotional pressures that kinship induced, sustained, and exacerbated in correspondence of migration.

In the letters exchanged between women and men in a transnational love relationship, forms of control and discipline can be observed through the kinds of advice and encouragement that were given. In his first letters to Ester di Leonardi, for instance, Giordano Rossini responded to the possible threat of disruption that her migration could eventually cause in their relationship:

> My love [*Amore mio*], you must return—so much so that the other day, I threw a coin in the *Fontana di Trevi*. As you can see, I'm always thinking of you. Tell me what you've seen, what you're doing. Are you enjoying yourself? Write to me, tell me everything. I feel so alone, and I miss you terribly. I cannot live without you. Don't leave me!!!... Reply to everything I ask you [*Rispondi a tutto ciò che ti domando*] (16 March 1957).

As Giordano prepared to close his letter, he advised her, "*Amore mio*, love me forever and one day you'll see that your perseverance will be crowned by complete happiness. Don't let yourself be convinced by... Maria Luisa. I get shivers just thinking of the possibility that you could change your mind. Remember this, 'no one will ever love you the way I love you'" (16 March 1957). Over and over again throughout Giordano's correspondence with Ester, we hear words of possessiveness, and general emotional insecurity due to the distance between them. For instance, on 21 March 1957 Giordano wrote, "write to me, tell me about everything that you do; do you already have many admirers? Don't allow yourself to be deceived, remain faithful to me. I'm sorry if I write this to you, but you must understand that I love you so much, and because of this, I'm jealous, and more than being jealous, I'm so afraid of losing you." Just three days later, Giordano reflected on similar worries and wrote again:

> My Love, you are still my little Ester, aren't you? Or do I not exist for you anymore? Maybe I hurt you when I ask these questions, but my imagination works very hard and sometimes, I worry that you may fall in love with someone else. Just thinking about it makes me nervous, sceptical, jealous, because I want you to be mine and mine alone, I want you to be my woman. You have no idea how much I love you and will love you for all my life!!! Tell me that it's the same for you!! (24 March 1957).

Even several months later, the insecurities of the relationship continued to punctuate his thoughts with words like, "be careful that you don't fall in love with a Canadian guy!!!" (31 August 1957), "did you receive other marriage proposals??" (1 September 1957), and "what about you, have you met someone for whom you have special feelings?" (4 October 1957).

Discipline in the form of gentle reprimands and requests to keep writing were also voiced in the love letters between the married couple, Dante del Moro and his wife Sara. For instance, following a long interval of silence on Dante's part, Sara wrote: "Today I received not one, but two of your letters, and I see that you have not forgotten these poor souls who live just to hear from their beloved *marito*. Even Paolo and Elisabetta ask every day, 'did we receive any mail from *papà*?'" (6 August 1956). Conversely, when Dante had not heard from Sara in what seemed to him a long time, he also expressed reprimands. Dante searched for reasons for Sara's silence, and in the process, he emphasized the importance of her letters to him:

> *Cara moglie*, since your last letter that I received this past Monday, to which I answered right away, I have not received any other news from you. I don't know why, and I hope everything is fine. I'm in good health, as I wholeheartedly hope the same is for you, my dear ones [*miei cari*]. I'm still wondering why you're not writing to me at least once a week. I don't think it's because you don't have time, it seems to me. I know that you are constantly preoccupied with the children and meeting their needs. However, with a little sacrifice you should think that you also have another little one here, whose needs also wait to be satisfied. *Mia cara*, you must think that despite my good fortune in being here with the cousins, I have no other gratification. I beg you then, try, if you can and want to, send me news more often. Even if they're just two lines, they will be enough for me to feel encouraged and to keep going. It's not that I'm feeling discouraged. But, you know, to hear you say that you are fine is enough to keep my spirits up (2 July 1956).

In another instance, Dante responded to Sara's lapse in writing with a different kind of reproach: "*mia cara*, not even in this letter did you tell me if you received the money. I don't know why that is. You remember to ask me for it, but somehow forget about letting me know once you have received it. Not for nothing, but you need to understand, that I am here in total darkness of everything that's going on. Therefore, try to be a little more understanding" (28 July 1956).

The threads of control, authority and discipline in the letters exchanged between parents and children, as well as between lovers, were interwoven in the dialogues of love and care that flowed between kin across oceans. Lines of kinship were clearly demarcated in migration correspondence. Encouragements to stay the course and stay in touch in light of the enormous physical distances separating kin were part of the dialogic exchange of the letters.

A young couple in love, before their separation due to migration, Venice, 1947

CHAPTER THREE

"My dear, you will have nothing else to do but..."
Gender Relations and Dynamics

My dear... I hope you will be happy here and thankful.... Think that all you need to do are the groceries, bring the little ones to the nursery or school, and everything else.... Just think that while I will be at work, you will have nothing else to do but prepare the meals, the best you can, and patiently wait for the return of your loved ones to gather at the daily table.

—Dante del Moro to Sara Franceschetti,
24 July 1956

THE LETTERS I HAVE EXAMINED reveal a highly gendered universe. As Franca Iacovetta observes, the migration movement from Italy to Canada during the second postwar period was characteristically family-based in that women and children either travelled together with their husbands or fathers, or joined them later, once the husband or father had settled with a steady job and found lodging for them.[1] In this chapter, I show how gender and migration were closely interwoven in the personal correspondence and the transnational lives of the women and men who wrote the letters. I argue that gender norms and gender roles were not only reified, but also reinforced by the letter writers, and subsequently reinscribed in a rigid division of transnational labour that was upheld by both women and men in the kinship network and the personal worlds of the writers. The gendered norms and behaviours I examine were rooted in the letter writers' experiences of the woes and fruits of migration. This study looks at how gender worked both discursively and prescriptively in the mental universes of transatlantic migrants in the postwar period.

More to the point, this in-depth analysis examines the inner, subjective workings of gender evident in the private letters of working-class, urban, and rural-based women and men across social fields between Italy and Canada. As Sarah Mahler and Patricia Pessar argue, "the people initiating, and receiving these flows [of material objects, including remittances] are not situated equally within the gendered geography of power, and the flows both illustrate and reproduce these disparities."[2] The letter writers' thoughts and concerns, which orbited around the pain of separation, fears of the unknown, worries over loved ones, longings for reunification, hopes for the future, joys at being reunited with loved ones, and desires for the completion of the migration project, were inevitably shaped by normative gender behaviours and attitudes.

In the discussion, I show how the productive and reproductive gender roles that existed within the postwar kin context were prescribed, negotiated, and reinforced in letters, which served as the crucial form of transatlantic communication. The study's focus on the productive and reproductive spheres is influenced largely by feminist literature and the claim made by Joan Scott that "the 'origins' of patriarchy are located in family and kinship systems, including relations of household production and reproduction."[3]

This chapter is divided into two parts: one deals with the world of work and the images and ideologies of masculinities and femininities in the workplace; the other explores the domestic sphere of social reproduction and the recurring images of the controlling, yet supportive roles played by Italian mothers at a distance. According to Candace West and Don Zimmerman, "Gender is a powerful ideological device, which produces, reproduces, and legitimates the choices and limits that are predicated on sex category."[4] Indeed, as sociologist Judith Lorber argues,

> Gender is a human invention, like language, kinship, religion, and technology; like them, gender organizes human social life in culturally patterned ways. Gender organizes social relations in everyday life as well as in the major social structures, such as social class and the hierarchies of bureaucratic organizations. The gendered microstructure and the gendered macrostructure reproduce and reinforce each other. The social reproduction of gender in individuals reproduces the gendered societal structure; as individuals act out gender norms and expectations in face-to-face interaction, they are constructing gendered systems of dominance and power.[5]

In 2006, the *International Migration Review* published a series of multidisciplinary articles assessing the state of the literature on gender and migration that has burgeoned in recent decades.[6] These articles trace the development of related studies that progressed from neglecting to "see" gender as fundamental to human activity to acknowledging the multifaceted dynamics of gender as key mechanisms for determining how migration was experienced differently by women and men. If, as Joan Scott suggests, "seeing is the origin of knowing,"[7] the scholars participating in the working group of Gender and Migration Theory of the Social Science Research Council determined that migration and gender are inexorably interconnected. They concluded that while the state of the field of the past two decades was relatively healthy, a number of challenges in further identifying and dislodging the moorings of gender in migration remained.

In short, they rightly argue that, "future scholarship must take seriously the insistence of gender theorists that gender structures all human relationships and all human activities."[8] In order to penetrate the pervasive nature of gender in human activities, specifically pertaining to migration and its multiple chronological and spatial fields, scholars of gender and migration argue that future research must be grounded in methodological diversity and interdisciplinary dialogue so as to effectively "see gender at work."[9] My analysis of the private correspondence arising from postwar migration builds on this research.

Recent studies examining the intersections of migration and correspondence have neglected to point to the intersecting, multi-layered, shifting

gender dynamics that operate on a micro-level in the correspondence between migrants and loved ones.[10] Feminist anthropologist Nicole Constable's
study, *Romance on a Global Stage* (2003), is an exception. In addition to
looking at the wider historical and political-economic context of relationships developed through correspondence, courtship and marriage between
Chinese and Filipino women and US men, Constable's analysis focuses on
the views and experiences of these women and men "who are contemplat-
ing correspondence, in the process of correspondence, recently married,
or about to be reunited."[11] More specifically, her study explores questions
about gender and power in correspondence courtship and marriage.[12] It
provides a "critical rereading of correspondence relationships that illustrates
how they are situated in relation to history and political economy, without
robbing people of their individuality, emotion, or sense of personhood."[13]
Feminist anthropologist Rhacel Parreñas's work has also provided a model
for analysis. She examines how gender works across transnational spaces
(affecting individuals, families or households who migrated and remained
behind) and the emotions that are experienced differently by women, men,
and children in transnational households and labour across global spaces.
While Parreñas's analysis in *Servants of Globalization* (2001) and *Children
of Global Migration* (2005) do not draw on private letters, they are based on
anthropological fieldwork and are grounded in the gendered voices of individuals caught in the throes of migration.

The World of Work

Work in the textile and garment manufacturing factories in cities like
Montreal during the postwar years was physically and mentally demanding
for women like Clara Renzi. For thousands of Italian immigrant women
who arrived in Canada during the postwar period, wage labour entailed long
hours of back-breaking work under dire conditions that included speed-ups,
close supervision, dust, and foul-smelling fumes.[14] Not long after arriving in Montreal, Clara joined the throngs of Italian women in the garment
manufacturing industry, and described to her future husband, Maurizio, how
discouraged she felt about working in the factory even as she persevered in
her attempt to look for a better way to handle the work:

Since Tuesday, I've been working in this large workshop…
I was hoping to continue working happily… to deserve the
praises of my department supervisor, a French woman. I
wanted to work, I wanted to succeed at it because I felt I was
doing something for our future happiness. But I can't… the
work is too demanding for me, and I am not that strong, I had
to stay all day continuously sitting at the sewing machine without a minute's break… I feel discouraged, but what can I do? I
was hoping to get used to the deafening noise of the machines,
to the assiduous work, but I come home every day more tired
than ever. Tonight my *papà* scolded me for not quitting my
work [*lavoro*], but really, I cannot take it any longer. Maybe it
would be better if I worked at home with *mamma*. Tomorrow
papà will buy me a sewing machine so I can continue to work
(8 October 1948).

Work in the garment manufacturing industry was itself hard, but for a
young Italian woman who had recently arrived from a small town in northeastern Italy, managing the cold winter temperatures in the foreign spaces of
a Canadian metropolis contributed to the difficulties she faced. For Clara, it
resulted in fatigue, leaving little desire for anything but rest at the end of the
day. In the following excerpt, Clara described to Maurizio her daily drudg-
eries of going to work while recounting how her dream of a future life with
Maurizio helped her to

forget this insignificant and boring life I lead every day and so,
my adored one [*mio adorato*], don't think that it's an exciting
life. I need to be at work at 8 o'clock in the morning. So, I wake
up at 7, sometimes even earlier, since it takes me over half an
hour by tram to reach the factory. The streets are impossible to
walk on. They are covered with ice and snow. Now, I leave it up
to you to imagine how tired I am at night and how much I feel
like going out to enjoy myself (1 February 1949).

Clara felt compelled to work and earn a wage that would allow her to contrib-
ute financially to the realization of her future life with Maurizio. Yet, implicit
in her correspondence was the option that once she was married she would
no longer be required to engage in waged work.

Although many women in postwar Italy and Canada were engaged in working outside their domestic roles, the prevailing image that their income only supplemented what the male heads of households provided suggests that, despite their contribution to the workforce, women continued to be identified as belonging to the domestic sphere. The secondary status of Italian women's wage work stemmed, according to Elson and Pearson, from "women's role in the family" as caregiver of children, men, and the elderly.[15] A woman's secondary status was further reinforced by the lower wages women's work brought to the household. Indeed, as a single woman living with her parents, Clara's wage work in the garment industry was viewed as entirely supplementary to her family's needs, which perhaps explains why her father was unhappy that she was tiring herself out rather than staying home with her mother. Yet Clara persisted and continued to work in the factory. She managed to renegotiate her salary, and despite her father's opposition, went back to work. In the same letter in which Clara described her work day, she expressed her satisfaction related to her work and salary:

> *la padrona della fattoria* [the factory owner] called me several times to tell me that she has found a girl who is willing and hard-working. I caught the fish by the hook and do you know what I did? (It's obvious that she needed me.) I asked her for a raise, so that I now make 6 dollars more per week, I'll let some time pass, and then ask for another raise. Otherwise, I'll change jobs. Here, there are lots of jobs available. There is something for everyone. I'm sure she won't fire me, she needs me too much. So, before I was paid 45 cents per hour, now, I'm paid 55 cents. It's good, no? And if you come down, I'm willing to keep working. Here we work, but we also get lots of satisfaction from our work (1 February 1949).

Clara's shift in this letter, from total exhaustion to satisfaction in her work, is linked to her missing Maurizio, as she wrote earlier in the letter: "You see my Maurizio…I am not able to enjoy myself, it makes sense, you're not here and without you, what can possibly be appealing to me? I bet that if you were here, I wouldn't even be tired in the evening!" (1 February 1949).

The concept of women's work and wages as supplementary was reiterated in Giordano Rossini's letters to his love Ester di Leonardi, who in March

1957 emigrated with her sister and brothers to Montreal. In order for Ester to return to Rome where Giordano lived, Giordano needed to find a regular, well-paying job that would enable him to provide for her when they were married. Responding to Ester's description of her daily work in the textile factories, Giordano, while sympathetic to the fatigue caused by her work, viewed her experience as little more than an "extra" to her capabilities as a woman. It seems he did not view easily wage work for her as a measure of self-fulfillment, nor as a fundamental component of their lives together as a married couple. We witness this in Giordano's letter to Ester on 31 May 1957: "learn the art, and put it aside. So that when we'll be married, you will know how to make *una cosa in più* [something extra]." The expression *una cosa in più* suggests that Ester's wage work was in fact, viewed as secondary. In the household envisioned by Giordano, he would be provider and breadwinner, and she would be nurturer, confined to the reproductive sphere—an ideology that was not uncommon in postwar Italy.

So, what was a man to think when he received some money from his working "girl" in Canada? In Giordano's case, the money Ester sent was a kind token of generosity, a pampering of her beloved. His vision of married life with Ester took for granted his role as the main, if not the only wage earner in the household. The fact that he was not yet able to provide for her economically before she left for Canada was the reason, he believed, they were now apart. However, instead of underscoring the opportunity for Ester to put some money aside for their future together, he believed the onus to provide for their family was left to him and that it was impossible for them to marry until he had steady employment. When Ester sent him a dollar in the mail, he replied: "*Cara* Ester, when I returned home this evening, I found your letter of the 15/4 in which there was the dollar for me. Dear Love [*Caro Amore*], only a heart in love could send this *pensiero*. And so, I thank you wholeheartedly, *grazie Amore*, but as a good wife [*buona moglie*], you shouldn't spoil your *marito* (even if he is your future *marito*)" (20 April 1957).

While a large percentage of Italian women in Canada was gainfully employed in the 1950s and 1960s,[16] Italian women continued to identify themselves (and be identified by others) primarily according to their reproductive roles. As Maila Stivens observes, kinship is central to social reproduction and relegates women to domestic units.[17] The valorization of women's contribution to domesticity and reproduction over wage-earning Italian kin was a factor in women's subordination. The more women confined themselves to the domestic and reproductive sphere, the more important their husbands' breadwinning capacities became. Ironically, as Stivens points out, women's solidarity in kinship played a contradictory role in this asymmetrical balance of power. While kinship provided logistic and emotional support for women to improve their position, it also encouraged the sustaining of "ideological coherence of kin structures," thereby increasing women's submission to male control.[18] By contrast, Italian migrant husbands' roles as main breadwinners entitled them to social and economic power, and identified them as representatives of the family both in the public sphere and within the kinship network.

Significantly, for young women like Clara and Ester living with their families, life in Canada—despite the physical exhaustion caused by work in the garment factories—also included opportunities for leisure and freedom (*libertà*), such as going to the movies and dance halls, attending language classes or going fishing, and visiting places. For Giordano, who read over and over again Ester's letters and tried to make sense of the details of her descriptions of life in Canada, Ester was living a life of *libertà*: "I'm happy that you're doing well. It must certainly be different from the life you led here. I imagine that you have more free time, and *libertà* than here, and so, enjoy it to the utmost, because you don't know what the future holds for you. Don't forget that a good housewife [*una brava donna di casa*] must know how to face unfavourable circumstances" (30 March 1957). Giordano's curiosity about her life in Canada was not easily satisfied, as his inquiries into her new life deepened over time: "Other than what I wrote to you, there is nothing new, and you, dear future Wife, what will you write to me in your next letter? I'm always eager to read your letters" (5 October 1957). His desire to know if she was seeing anyone else compelled him to write: "Dear Precious, I write to you after one day's break… I was asking you if you had met anyone you liked or that you like now?" And, a few lines later, he added: "My Love, I so want to see you, and hold you tight against me. I feel so lonely, I found the woman of my life. In you I found the person with whom I intend to share my life, always be near her, perhaps you cannot imagine how much I love you!" (5 October 1957). Giordano's desolation and loneliness are expressed frequently in his letters, especially in his descriptions of days that amounted to "not much or nothing" (25 April 1957). From his responses to her, we can assume that she provided a rather sparse description of her social life to him beyond going to work, fishing or visiting touristic sites of Montreal. However, we can also speculate that an attractive young woman like Ester would have had opportunities to socialize with friends (male and female), as Giordano imagined: "What will you do tomorrow? If you have good weather, I bet you'll be going for a ride, if the weather is awful, you'll stay home or go to the movies" (5 October 1957). However, with Ester's side of the correspondence not available, an interpretation of her responses is observable only through Giordano's letters. In view of Giordano's description of his monotonous and lonely life, coupled with the enormous void he claimed to have experienced since her departure, it seems likely that Ester had a kind of "pacte épistolaire"[19] with her lover. Because she loved him, it seems clear that she endeavoured to provide details and information that had less potential of causing him hurt or confusion.

Despite the desire and enthusiasm of both Giordano and Ester, their relationship was not on solid ground, as it was based entirely on the thread of epistolary communication at the initial stages of a romantic relationship, when the couple was particularly vulnerable to doubts, fears, misunderstandings, and confusion. Some of this unease is apparent in Giordano's uncertain reaction to the news that she was working outside her home:

> *Tesoro mio*, I was already worried about you since I hadn't received any mail from you. I have been anxiously waiting for 17 long days for news from you. And finally, yesterday I received your letter of 12-4/57, in which I learn that everything is proceeding normally. There's only one thing that surprises me, and that is, from what you are telling me, you don't work from home, but somewhere else. Where do you work? Can you tell me? Does Maria Luisa work there too? I am so happy to hear that you love me always so much. This is an enormous source of comfort for me. I too love you so so much [*Anch'io ti amo tanto*]!!—I wish we were already married!! So that I wouldn't need to worry about losing you (18 April 1957).

One of Giordano's greatest fears was of losing Ester. Even though in nearly every letter he offered reassurances of love and devotion, some letters include a defensive response to the fact that she was now actively engaged in the productive (public) sphere. For instance, when Giordano learned that other men enjoyed her company, he offered her some "well-meaning" advice on how to keep the trappings of fate (*il destino*) and other men at bay. He wrote:

> *Amore mio*, with regards to those who surround you, try to ignore them. If you can, avoid them altogether. I think it's pointless for me to advise you. I'm certain you know exactly what you need to do. By now, you are a girl who knows about life, and who will not let herself fall prey to the first man she meets. I tell you this because I am so afraid of losing you one day. It's not because I'm not convinced of your love. It's *il destino* that worries me because it's so cruel. I can expect any of its dirty tricks from one moment to the next. We just can't trust it! That's why, *cara* Ester, let's try to break free from the temptations, flatteries and promises, as these can be trappings of *il destino*. I don't want to bore you with this small talk, I'm just begging you to be careful!! Don't trust men!!! (9 June 1957).

The excerpts above illustrate two intersecting factors that contributed to Giordano's fears of losing Ester. First, the fact that Ester worked outside the home in an environment that was not socially controlled by kinship or other women caused Giordano to worry about the possibility of other men courting her (and the possibility that she might have responded to these flatteries also did not escape him). Second, the fact that Ester exhibited freedom and agency[20] (perceived by Giordano through her descriptions of her new life in Canada, her work, her outings, and her gesture of sending him money) may have rested uneasily with him. We can infer that changes in her social and discursive environments were not synonymous with his image of her as a gentle, accommodating, submissive, domestic woman, but rather, of a woman empowered by her wage-earning capabilities, who exercised free will within the social limits imposed on her. While Giordano admitted to having been seduced by her personality, her determination, and her agency during their time together in Italy, now that they were apart those personality traits became a source of constant anxiety for him. As a result, his letters contained not only words of devotion and longing, but also conveyed a rigid gender ideology of how he envisioned their life together. In these dreams, Ester would not work outside the confines of her domestic world, but would have babies and be waiting for her husband when he came home at the end of his work day.

A man's fear of losing "his" woman is also evident in the letters of Dante to his wife, Sara. The following excerpt shows how susceptible long-distance relationships were to miscommunication, and how jealousy could be provoked even between a husband and wife of many years. The tensions that unfolded began innocently, with Sara's letter describing their daughter's return to good health:

> Your lady boss [*padrona*], think about it, weighs 60 kg, and is as fresh as when she got married. She even receives a few compliments (from the male sex). I tell you this to make you feel a little jealous, even though these comments make no difference to me. Especially, when I think that Paolo is nearly as tall as I am, and soon will be doing his First Communion, I feel old, but not for my old man (6 August 1956).

The letter fuelled a sarcastic "masculine" response from Dante:

> *Mia cara Signora*, I'm pleased to hear about your weight, your youthful freshness, just like I can't help feeling flattered by the compliments you receive, and I hope there's something left over for the poor emigrant. I also need to ask you a favour, 'if you can,' when you'll have someone else, can you let me know? so that I too can take a few steps forward… Forgive me, I too have gained some weight, not in terms of fat. My muscles are now like steel. So you think about it, instead of writing to me the letter that you wrote, it would be better if you told me in person, and then, what would happen?… I want to see if you are able to tell me (15 August 1956).

Sara did not retreat submissively in her response. Instead, she spun the discussion from initial enthusiasm to dry pragmatism, and ended the letter by reciprocating the furies of jealousy, by turning the table around and threatening to exact revenge should she find out about *his* infidelity. She wrote:

I have no time, nor any thoughts for any compliments that
I receive here or there as an indication that I'm well. For no
other reason did I write this to you, and if I find out that you
took advantage of my being away, and became acquainted with
other women, God help you when I come down, hopefully
soon! Upon Sara's word, that you know very well, when she
pulls out her claws, then we'll see. And about those muscles,
we'll see who collapses first, and then we'll see about talking
(25 August 1956).

Following Sara's response, Dante backed down and tried to make amends:

Dear complainer [*Cara brontolona*], I see that you are quite
wicked. You don't accept a word any more, not even when I'm
joking. Don't worry, as far as I'm concerned you won't need to
use your claws on me. Of this you can be sure, even though the
temptations are many, yours truly doesn't lose his head over
this. I close this letter with my best wishes, as I hold you close
to my heart. See you soon, I tell you (31 August 1956).

To quell the tensions between her and Dante, Sara responded: "regarding
the reproaches that I made to you... I say them in answer to you, based on
what you're telling me. But, don't take it personally, I don't think your wife
is so cruel, you should know her, or did you forget her already? I think not.
I close this letter sending you my best wishes, lots of *baci e abbracci* [kisses
and embraces], Sara" (7 September 1956). Finally, the argument was closed
with Dante's more emphatic affirmation of his love for Sara: "I love you and
I never forget you, and You?" (12 September 1956).

The fear of unknown circumstances that could potentially destroy the
dream of family reunification also emerged in the letters. A common source
of anxiety was the need to fulfill the visa requirements of the Canadian government.[21] The following letter from Sara to Dante describes some of these
difficulties:

Mio caro Dante, I've just returned from Rome and I'm writing to let you know that everything worked out for the best,
concerning the trip and the meeting. We wrote to you even
from Rome, but I want to tell you now calmly how it went.

We left Vicenza in the morning of the 25th, and slept in Rome for one night. Once the examination and interview were over, we visited Saint Peter's. At 8:30 p.m. we were already home.... At the meeting, there was the same doctor who examined us at Castelfranco... there was even the consul general who had been at Castelfranco, but I couldn't talk to him, because I was required to speak to someone else. There are three of them who sign the visa. This one was more difficult than the others. He wanted to know every possible detail [*morte e miracoli*]. I answered all of his questions, regardless. But, I was scared out of my wits. Altogether, even this one went well. I cannot tell you what a sigh of relief I breathed, *caro*, it wasn't as easy as at Castelfranco. There were a lot of people, and think that from eight o'clock in the morning to noon, if Luca had not been with me to give me a hand, I don't know how I would have handled it with the children. Though they are well-behaved, they are children and they don't listen to our reasons (27 September 1956).

The examination process for procuring visas was extremely distressing for both women and men.[22] The outcome of these official meetings would determine their fate: they would either stay in impoverished Italy or have a chance to improve their economic well-being by moving to Canada. Inevitably the fears of prospective migrants were compounded by the awareness that within minutes of the interrogation their migration project and all hopes for family reunification could be shattered at a bureaucrat's whim.

Sara's experience at the embassy is an example of the difficulties that faced a married, working-class, agrotown woman when dealing with bureaucracies. Her limited experience in the public sphere, combined with the pressures of travelling across the peninsula with her two toddlers (even though she was accompanied by her brother-in-law) on a very important mission made the experience a daunting one. Like that of other working-class women who came of age in the late 1940s in a small village, Sara's life predominantly revolved around the domestic sphere. As a woman whose husband had migrated to Canada, she tended to her children's material, spiritual, and emotional needs, performed household chores and duties within the multiple-family household she and her children lived in, nurtured and sustained kinship ties around her, kept a close correspondence with her husband in Powell River, and prepared for the imminent departure for Canada. None of these activities required her to frequent or perform in the public sphere, especially in a larger context outside of the town (*paese*) in which she lived. Certainly one can speculate on how encounters such as that at the embassy might have been different for married men. As Lorber suggests, a married man "with recognized interests to protect, he can speak up and expect to be heard in public gatherings. And, as an individual *whose basic needs are provided*, he can devote his time to building the exchange networks that enhance social influence and prestige."[23] Indeed, as Elson and Pearson argue, the man's role as breadwinner was not limited to economic power, but was "also constituted in the process of establishing the connection of the family with the wider society."[24] Consequently, as the public representative of the family, the male breadwinner had social power[25]—defined by Elson and Pearson as "collective power, reproducible through social processes, relatively autonomous from the characteristics of particular individuals"[26]—which in turn facilitated his moving about in the public sphere.[27]

Of course, even when the interview went well and the visa was granted, prospective migrants were still faced with unknowns about the nature of daily life abroad. We glimpse an example of this in a seemingly innocuous exchange between Dante and Sara regarding women's fashion in Powell River. In the years following the Second World War, Italian fashion for women was significantly influenced by American women's dress and way of life, which were seen as "modern" and emancipated. As Penelope Morris, Anna Maria Torriglia, Paul Ginsborg and Victoria de Grazia[28] suggest, *il modo Americano* (the American way of life) had penetrated virtually all facets of Italian life. For an Italian woman who was preparing to migrate to Canada, it seemed important to prepare a wardrobe in *la moda Americana* [American style], in order to integrate more quickly into the new community. In the following epistolary exchange, however, we also witness how a simple inquiry about fashion in Canada brought a number of sexist assumptions to light. In answer to Sara's question about women's dress in Powell River, Dante wrote:

> And now don't laugh, or think badly of what I am about to tell you, always concerning dress and fashion. Here the weaker sex, older women, married women and single women, take care of keeping fit… and expose the two most extreme points of the female anatomy (You tell me what they are…). They also care

a great deal about wearing sleeveless tops, like shirts, blouses, light-colored and quite transparent. I'm telling you this to give you an idea. I'm not suggesting you dress like this. Actually, as far as I'm concerned, you know that I don't care for these things at all, don't think badly about me, but as you know, *l'occhio vuole la sua parte* [looks also count]. This is what I can tell you based on what I've seen (5 August 1956).

Ironically, while Dante explicitly expressed his indifference to women's dress fashions, he also admitted that looks count, and discouraged Sara from wearing those same fashions. To excuse this double standard, Dante resorted to the proverbial expression, *l'occhio vuole la sua parte* (looks also count). Indeed, as anthropologist Stanley Brandes suggests, "the utilization of proverbs is an effective appeal to time-honored sources of authority; hence, whenever talking about sexual matters, men will resort to them as a conscious means to buttress and legitimize their own point of view."[29] However, the exchange on women's dress attire between Dante and Sara did not end there. A little further in the letter, Dante offered his dress recommendations for his wife and children during their transatlantic voyage:

trousers are ideal for everyone, including you, they are less cumbersome than slips, especially for going up and down the stairs on the ship. They are also safer from keeping prying eyes away from your things to the curiosity and maliciousness of the others. You think that I'm jealous, right? Yes, that's true, and why shouldn't I be!?... If I'm not jealous of what's mine, what should I be jealous of!? (5 August 1956).

Of course one may wonder how Dante knew that women's private parts were visible when they climbed the stairs onboard ship. But the other obvious question that emerges is: why did he feel the need to tell his wife that she was his private property? The rupture between Dante and Sara caused by migration appears to have heightened his sexual insecurities about her fidelity. Dante felt the need to reinforce his hold on her, otherwise, he felt there was a danger that she might escape him.

Now, how did Sara respond to her husband's claim on her? She replied: "I too thought about sewing myself some trousers, but *caro mio*, Paolo doesn't like seeing me wear them. He says that I'm not a man, and that I look ridiculous" (14 August 1956). She continued: "naturally, I won't listen to him, but you see, he's starting early to give orders, even to his *mamma*, he says 'I'm the boss after my *padre*.' Therefore, don't be jealous, because your son would set me straight, even though he's barely a metre high" (14 August 1956).

Two corollaries emerge from Sara's reply. First, she agreed that trousers were a good thing for her to wear. At first glance, we might be persuaded to observe agency in her decision to sew and wear a pair of trousers (especially, since women's trousers in postwar Italy symbolized a break from women's traditional attire).[30] However, it is difficult to know whether she made her choice voluntarily or in order to follow Dante's prescriptive advice. Second, in her response to his comment, "If I'm not jealous of what's mine," Sara seems to be giving in to her husband's jealousy, by responding that he need not worry and attempting to quell his fears by pointing out that another male in the family, their young son, would be the first to set her straight (*fare la morale*).

Over the next two weeks, Sara busily prepared her wardrobe. As she and her husband continued their discussions on what to bring, and what not to bring, and how much money these items cost, Dante reminded Sara to invest in sturdy luggage and wooden trunks. He also asked her to bring woollen pillows for the train ride, and: "in terms of travelling clothes, long pants for all three of you, for when you arrive, make sure you have a dress to wear upon getting off the train" (19 August 1956). There are several possible reasons why Dante recommended to his wife that she wear a dress upon arriving in Powell River. Foremost, this instruction signals Dante's desire for his wife to embody the aesthetic ideal of the "natural woman" image of femininity in postwar Italy. As Lorber argues, "dress makes personal and social statements. As long as gender categories are socially significant, dress will reflect difference and signal gender identification."[31] Even though in large urban centres, like Rome, Italian women were wearing trousers, as the letters of Giordano Rossi to Ester di Leonardi reveal, the culturally acceptable dress of a traditional Italian woman stood in sharp contrast to the image of a "modern" woman dressed *all'Americana*, and whose trousers signified that she was liberated and emancipated.

One of the curious features of the correspondence between couples is how infrequently the migrants described the work they did. For example, in a majority of the letters written by Dante del Moro, his only reference to his work appears in concluding throwaway lines like *il lavoro va bene* (work is going well). This finding is surprising, especially given the significance that life in the productive sphere represented for a male migrant whose main purpose for migration was earning good wages. Yet, work in the mills of Powell River was extremely demanding.[32] And, for a migrant husband whose loved ones were never far from his *pensieri*, being away from them was mentally distressful as well. Indeed, as Robert F. Harney observes, "The abnormality of life for the migrants came not from promiscuity but from total physical and cultural frustration."[33] Dante's words to Sara illustrate how physical exhaustion was part of the migrant's work experience: "Even my work is going well, it's a little hard, but I am happy all the same, and I work willingly. And my boss is happy, he treats me well, for everything and in everything" (12 April 1956). Several months later, in advising Sara that he had little time to spare, he wrote: "my work is going well. For this second fortnight period in August, I worked twelve days straight, without even one day's break, other than going to mass in the evening" (31 August 1956).

While Dante's letters offer few details about his work, it was extremely important to him, not least because his earnings provided for his family in Italy and would enable them to join him. Yet, as Harney observes, "the phantom that lived with them was, at least in part, created by fear and guilt about how well they were fulfilling family obligations."[34] In Dante's case, fulfilling his family obligations by providing constant emotional, material, and psychological support was the core of his *pensiero*. This was likely the reason why his letters were filled with references to the well-being, concerns, and worries about his wife, children, and other loved ones in Arcugnano, but said little about his own struggles or frustrations. Perhaps the following words best summarize his intentions: "Today as I write to you it is Sunday, and I worked like every other day, I'm a little tired but I'm fine, and I'm happy because I see that with every day's work, I earn money and put it aside for you" (25 August 1956).

In this letter series, we witness Dante's deep sense of responsibility to fulfill his role as the male breadwinner, provider and protector of his family. Husbands, fathers, and brothers who set out for Canada in the postwar years, before their families joined them, sent home their large savings via bank transfers, while smaller cash amounts were usually included with the letters. In cases of emergency, sums like fifty-dollar bills were sent in the mail. This method carried a risk that made migrants nervous, as we read in a letter from Dante to Sara: "You see, now I find myself forced to send you the money, with the risk and danger of losing it … if I send it to you through the bank, as I usually do, the money won't arrive on time. I hope they won't be opening especially this letter. I would be very sorry if they did, it's the fruit of my labour [*è frutto del mio sudore*]" (22 September 1956). While the smaller amounts sent home were perceived by senders as "extra" money, in reality, much of it (regardless of the amount), including gift money, was spent by the recipients on the daily subsistence needs of a transnational household.

Moreover, a migrant's wages earned in Canada heightened his male pride as a good breadwinner and overall provider for his family. This sense of self-realization and pride is crystallized in Dante's words to Sara: "I will immediately send you everything you need, don't worry about it, with the salary that I earn, I can support three families like mine in Italy and not in destitution, but as royalty [*Signori*]." Then he added:

> I paid back my debt to Elio in just two months. Plus, I deposited in the bank $400 for your application, plus a few small expenses for myself, like a smoke, and other odd items of necessity. I'll also tell you something else. If all goes well, I will have found a more comfortable home for us by the water, and it's near my boss's house. It's in a nice quiet location, where there is lots of fresh clean air and sun as it is now. You just need to walk a couple of steps, and you're right on the beach. What do you think of that? (15 August 1956).

This excerpt illustrates a male provider's pride in effectively and efficiently fulfilling his obligations to his family overseas. First, by advising Sara that he was sending her everything she needed, Dante reassured her that she had no reason to worry about the family's subsistence. His earnings enabled him to meet not only his family's material needs, but those of three other families in Italy as well. Further, he believed that in Canada his family's economic and class status would rise to a higher social level. This is an important point, especially in light of postwar Italian society's nearly impermeable class structure. By mentioning that he had repaid his debt to his sponsoring cousin Elio, Dante meant to say that his earnings were significant enough to make him debt-free. He could now concentrate on setting aside money for the single most important goal of his migration project: his family's arrival in Powell

River. As his wife's sponsor, he had deposited four hundred dollars for her migration application to be processed. And, in addition to all of this, he had found a nice little house for his family near the ocean and near his boss's house, hoping it would please them.

While there is no question that the transnational family benefitted materially from the male migrant's fulfillment of his roles, at the same time, his economic gains and power entitled him to make specific requests of his wife. For instance, in preparation for her arrival in Powell River, Dante wrote: "make sure you bring everything [*tutto*] that I told you" (22 September 1956). *Tutto* in this case included men's undershirts (*canottiere*), a thermometer, a watch, liquor essences (*essenze di liquore*), wine-making instruments, jewellery, including a wedding band for himself (which he notes that she had lost), and other special requests from his cousins and friends in Powell River. This additional responsibility could not have been welcomed with delight by Sara, who was already coping with her duties as a mother of two toddlers, running a household within the walls of a multiple-family household, and preparing for the family's permanent departure and settlement overseas.

On 22 September 1956, Dante wrote to Sara: "I see here from your writing how much you worry, and while I expected this to happen, you shouldn't lose sleep over so little. I always told you not to worry, that you have a man who is still capable of thinking for his family and meeting their needs." He then proceeded to give her advice on who in their kin network in Arcugnano could provide her with additional funds in order for her to buy the items he had requested as well as other necessities required prior to the departure for Canada. The husband's role as protector was reinforced by his experience as an immigrant. We witness Dante protecting Sara from "needless" worries by shouldering them himself and emphasizing that his capabilities extended beyond his physical strength into the realm of moral and psychological support. He confidently advised Sara regarding a plethora of issues that had been left unresolved at the time of his departure. Such matters included the handling of large sums of money and whom to talk to about financial assistance, how to secure the children's Catholic education, handle family tensions and townsfolk gossip, and select an appropriate godfather for their son. For the most part, Sara accepted his advice, except on one occasion when she replied: "Don't tell me that I'm stubborn. I too know what I need to do, and how to behave" (7 September 1956).

The economic power gained by male migrants through their Canadian earnings and savings not only reinforced, both privately and publicly, the notion that opportunities for economic improvement were real in postwar Canada, but also that the myth of America was within their grasp. Dante's godfather in Italy, Giovanni Manfredi, wrote to Dante encouraging him to return one day to Italy, "in a beautiful, large car and with lots of money for you to buy at least all the land you and your brothers worked on. But then, you will have others working it, and you'll just be there visiting the land tenants [*affituari*]" (c. December 1956). This image of a migrant returning to Italy as landowner was one of the most sought-after dreams for male migrants whose families had been tenants. As Bruno Ramirez notes, "American savings allowed the returnee migrants [*ritornati*] to refuse to submit again to wage labour or tenant farming under the old landlords."[35] *Ritornati* who returned to Italy to buy land with the intention of renting it out were actively engaged in the change of status that resulted for themselves and their families. They were no longer farm labourers, but rather had become independent farmers and landowners, albeit on a small scale and without the benefit of structural reforms that should have been implemented by the state. Indeed, through this *compare*'s eyes, America signified "the fulfillment of their hopes," [36] as historian Dirk Hoerder suggests. America also represented the dream and opportunity for a man to "make something of himself," that is, to realizing the independent-entrepreneur dream that was encompassed in the myth of America.

We witness evidence of this dream in a letter from Luciano Colonello to his son, Gianlorenzo. As noted earlier, Luciano advised his son to hold on to the money that he had earned in Michel, British Columbia, and not to spend it on cars and other material things: "Because as you remember, when you left you said that you were leaving to make something for yourself [*per farti qualche cosa per te*]" (18 August 1954). We infer from Luciano's words that the male aspiration to "make something for himself" was sustained not only by a show of pride at material gains, but also through the enormous familial obligations he sought to fulfill. For Gianlorenzo, some of these familial pressures were conveyed by his mother's admonishment to "make sure you take good care of yourself, don't get sick because we need your help. And if you get sick, it's bad for you, but worse for us" (28 July 1954). According to the letters, it seems that both Dante and Gianlorenzo did make something for themselves.

Dante's success had enabled him to purchase a home, and to sponsor his wife and children. Within a few years of working in Michel and later, in Montreal, Gianlorenzo had purchased a car and a two-storey house in Spilimbergo for his parents and sisters to live in rent-free for the rest of their lives.

In her analysis of the role of the good provider, sociologist Jessie Bernard observes, "men were judged as men by the level of living they provided."[37] In a migration context, the level of a migrant's economic success was mirrored not only in the money he sent to his immediate family, but also in the kind of life they appeared to be living, in part as a result of his remittances. Nowhere in the letters was this phenomenon more apparent than in those that Sara wrote to Dante about the way in which she and her children had become subjects of observation for the townsfolk. As noted earlier, after receiving a gift of five dollars in the mail from Dante on the occasion of their wedding anniversary, Sara wrote that she would be buying herself a new dress with the money: "because, as you know, I am being watched more carefully than before. This means that if I dress well, you are earning good money, if I dress poorly, it means you are struggling.... You know how our world is, appearances mean everything" (c. June–July 1956). Not only did Dante need to make enough earnings to send to his wife and children for their subsistence, but he also had to send "extra" funds to send a clear message to the townsfolk in demonstrating his success and justifying the sacrifice of his absence.

Dante's absence from the household also gave the townsfolk of Arcugnano an opportunity to carefully scrutinize the kind of life Sara was leading without him. Indeed, as Elson and Pearson argue, "the absence of a husband is as significant as his presence for the establishment of a woman's social identity... 'subject to an overall culture of male dominance.'"[38] In this letter, we observe Sara's frustrations concerning the townsfolk's whispering voices that circulated as a result of Dante's absence: "*Caro Dante*, you ask me how I'm doing. They are starting to talk about me. They are starting to say that now that the husband is away, I'm putting on weight, that I'm turning white and red. They say that when you were here, you overworked me. You know how people are, they're always suspicious of others" (c. June–July 1956).

Not only were townsfolk suspicious, they also exercised control through social discipline and coercion. Implicit in Sara's letters is a sense that the townsfolk were on the lookout for any kind of transgressive behaviour (social, moral, and sexual) on her part. The lines of communication between the townsfolk in the *paese* and the migrant's network of kin and co-villagers in Canada worked with such efficiency and velocity that any negative gossip from the town would have made its way quickly to the migrant's new address.[39] Another reason for Sara to reveal this information to Dante was, we can reasonably surmise, to mount some kind of defensive response should word get to him from any co-villager. Sara's strategy worked because in his next letter Dante wrote: "I'm happy for you, for your good health. Don't listen to that talk. I know in what state I left you, and I also know that even if you were overworked, I don't think I'm to blame. But in any case, let them say what they want" (10 July 1957).

In addition to working for wages and increasing his savings, worrying over his loved ones, and keeping the townsfolk's suspicious voices at bay, there was also an enormous emotional price to pay for a migrant male breadwinner and provider. Already in the gender division of labour, as Bernard observes, the increased onus on men as providers (and workers in the public sphere) had reduced "the amount of time available for spontaneous emotional give-and-take between husbands and wives."[40] For migrant men, this emotional distance was further exacerbated. Not only were gender roles reified and reinforced through migration, there was also an acute awareness on the part of the migrant breadwinners that they would have to endure an emotional loss in order for the project to succeed. We witness this awareness in Dante's letters to Sara, in which his loneliness and desire to be reunited with her and their children were articulated. One scenario in particular encapsulates the emotional cost he experienced as a result of his separation from his family. It concerns their son's much-anticipated ceremony of First Communion:

> I see here from your writing your news about Paolo. And to tell you the truth, I don't know how to tell you how happy I am. I would only want to be there with you on the day in which our young man receives the Divine Grace.... I can't help telling you that despite my immense joy, I am jealous and I envy you, and your good fortune to help our little one on that Holy day. On the other hand, I think that as their *madre*, you have the right to help them in their sorrows and joys of life. It means that as always, I will be there with my heart and my love that is stronger than ever (28 July 1956).

To compensate for his absence, Dante emphasized the importance of a mother's presence in her child's life. Sara responded with the words: "don't envy me for the good fortune I have in assisting him on that Holy day. It would be best if we were both present" (6 August 1956).

Reproduction and Domesticity

In the months leading up to their family's reunion in Powell River, one theme that frequently emerged from Dante's letters concerned his ardent wish that his wife would be happy there. This desire was captured in the epigraph for this chapter, in which Dante described how easy Sara's life would be, because she would only have to shop for groceries, cook, and take the children to school while he was off toiling for wages. Considering that it was completely normal, indeed desirable for a working-class Italian, Catholic wife to devote all of her time and energies to meeting the needs of her husband and children, it is not surprising that Sara did not object to the promise of a quiet, domestic life. Yet, what clearly did irritate her was Dante's teasing reference to the leisure time she managed to find.

"I have taken my place in doing other household chores," she wrote, "so that, *caro* Dante, I have little time to read, even the Gran Ottel [Grand Hotel],[41] an enormous sacrifice, you know (I'm joking)" (14 August 1956). She reminded Dante that because her sister-in-law was bedridden, she had additional household chores and little time to read magazines. In this exchange, we observe both Dante's and Sara's denial of her personal entitlement to reading material she would have normally enjoyed. Instead, Sara's response was precisely to justify herself entirely as a woman tied to her primary roles as nurturer and domestic of the household. The question of self-entitlement, she appeared to say, was not even an option.

Yet, what was Sara's life like in the first months upon arriving in Powell River? Did it conform to the ideal that Dante had constructed in his letter of 24 July 1956? In the following excerpt from a letter to her sister, we observe Sara's description of her situation in the months following her arrival in Powell River:

> Life [*la vita*] here involves eating, sleeping, and doing those
> odd household chores, not too many because the water is avail-
> able inside the home, the laundry machine does the laundry

in half an hour. There is ironing and making supper, while the bread, and groceries are delivered to the home. I don't need firewood for the kitchen, as everything is run by oil, even that kind of work is spared. All day I knit sweaters. I've started knitting some even for others, that's why I asked you for the magazines because I didn't bring any with me from Italy, not even one. I'm also widening my skirts and slips as none of my dresses fit me anymore, and I sleep every day from eight in the evening to nine in the morning. This is my life in Canada (22 February 1957).

Compared to her life in Arcugnano, where she had been busy moving about every day, taking her children to the nursery, performing various chores, visiting friends and family, and riding her bicycle to the town centre for purchases, her description seems like a fairly comfortable existence. Or was it? In my view, her description of life in Powell River also reads like that of a gilded cage. Gone are the agency, decision making, and movement she exercised in Italy in the absence of her migrant husband. While the worries, concerns, and frustrations she experienced in Arcugnano as a result of her husband's departure were numerous, she now faced a life enclosed within the walls of her home, in which her tasks were limited to mostly making supper, doing laundry, and knitting sweaters. The family tensions that distressed her in Arcugnano were now far away, but in the distance she also missed the pleasures that came from daily interactions with her sister and her family in her homeland.

The letter describing Sara's life in Powell River is significant for raising other gender issues as well. The availability of household amenities (*comodità*) such as automatic washing machines along with the household services that were delivered to her door, confirmed to Sara's sister (and her family) that the image of North American households as disseminated on Italian television, magazines, and cinema was accurate. A letter from Sara's niece illustrates the point: "how I would like to see your new little home, everything *all'Americana*, it must be a dream" (6 January 1957). This image of America was reinforced especially by working-class women who remained behind in Italy's agrotowns in the South and Northeast, as it stood in stark contrast to their lives, which were immersed in the daily economic struggles of the postwar period. We observe then how the longing for domestic *comodità* was seen by Italian women as a step towards emancipation. However, these automatic household appliances and home delivery services also had a contradictory effect for an active, smart woman like Sara. While they freed her from endless hours of toiling (and paradoxically, increased expectations and standards of cleanliness), they also restricted her activities, her movement, her agency, and her contact with an outside world.[42] In doing so, her life in Powell River, as she described it in early 1957, had lost an important dimension with the elimination of the possibility for engagement and self-realization outside the domestic sphere. As she told her sister at the end of the letter, with regard to their home's landlords, "they are good people, and they let me do whatever I want of the house" (22 February 1957). Indeed, she could do whatever she wanted, as long as she remained within those walls.

We might be tempted to assume from Sara's latter comment that despite constraints, she was neither passive nor powerless, and was instead able to exercise agency and self-realization through her gender roles as wife, mother, and homemaker (*casalinga*). While there is no question that the private sphere enabled women to exercise agency within the domestic realm, their power as women remained limited to it. The gender division of labour that was actively enforced in a majority of Italian migrant households in postwar Canada underscored the role of women as belonging to the private sphere and those of men to the public sphere. Consequently, as Elson and Pearson argue, women were identified in domestic terms, while men were given access to social and economic power in the public sphere.[43] In a 1974 essay in *Woman, Culture and Society*, feminist anthropologist Michelle Z. Rosaldo raised an important point in relation to women's confinement to the domestic sphere. She argued that "as long as the domestic sphere remains female, women's societies, however powerful, will never be the political equivalents of men's."[44]

Yet, in postwar Canada's resource towns it was inevitable that women would be associated with the domestic sphere. There were no industries that were geared for women's work, as there were in Montreal or Toronto, as Franca Iacovetta documents.[45] In the towns of Powell River and Michel, British Columbia, despite the scarcity of female wage work, women worked as volunteers at the local church and women's associations (such as the Ladies' Pleasant Hour), as staff at the local stores and hotels, and as teachers and nurses.[46] However, these occupations were seen as extensions of women's reproductive roles. For Italian immigrant women whose gender roles, by convention, were even more narrowly defined than those available to Canadian-born women, the difficulties of finding employment (including language constraints) were especially apparent in Canada's resource towns. Their supportive social roles in Italian immigrant benevolent societies and regional associations were an extension of the roles they had "naturally" assumed.[47]

We observe a similar gender dynamic in the scenario in which Gianlorenzo's male friend needed help cleaning his house in anticipation of his wife's arrival from Italy. We learn that female kin and co-villagers were asked to help clean his house. In her letter to Gianlorenzo, which includes news of friends and family in Michel, Anna wrote: "Gabriella and I dropped by to clean Giacomo's house. His wife is arriving on Wednesday this week. He has a nice house, not too big, but really quite pretty, and so Saturday, he'll be having a party with friends" (12 September 1954). She also remarked, "I'm now closing this letter as Giacomo and Mario want to play cards and they won't let me continue writing. They send their greetings [*saluti*], and promise to write to you soon... affectionately, your cousin [*tua cugina*], Anna" (12 September 1954). Several gender dynamics can be observed from these few lines. First, Gianlorenzo's friend Giacomo was surrounded by both male and female friends. Second, the gender of the friends determined what roles they played in the community of Italian immigrant friends and kin in Michel. While Giacomo played cards with his male friends, including Mario and Anna's husband Carlo, Anna wrote and played the proper female role of cleaning.

On the other side of the ocean, the gender division of labour among transnational couples was equally reified and reinforced in postwar working-class Italy. In Giordano's letters, we observe an idealized image of a married Ester, an image that Giordano hoped would be concretized upon her return to Italy. The role that he envisioned for her would require her to focus solely on tending to her husband's needs and on raising children. This image of her cooking, cleaning, and waiting on him stood in sharp contrast to the life Ester was actually leading in Canada as a single working woman. Giordano wrote:

> My love, I love you so very much [*Amore mio, ti amo tanto
> tanto*], I want you to become my *cara* little *moglie*, how it would
> be beautiful to live together forever!! How it will be wonderful
> when I'll be returning home from work and I'll find my little
> Ester waiting for me at the window, or at the door step. Don't
> you think it will be lovely? I promise you an eternity of hap-
> piness. With you, I will be the happiest man on earth (2 April
> 1957).

Here, an ambivalence in Giordano's vision of Ester is observed. While he
envisioned her future as a happily married woman circumscribed and in-
fantilized within the confines of her home, he also imagined his relationship
with Ester involving shared confidences and emotional intimacy:

> between *marito* and *moglie* (even if, future), there needs to be
> an understanding. Don't you think so? You too, if you've got a
> worry or something that's bothering you, write to me about it.
> Maybe I'll be able to give you some advice on it. Try to be more
> open with me. Don't be so shy!! Because one day, when we'll be
> married, we won't be keeping secrets from each other, do you
> understand? (5 April 1956).

In other words, we can surmise that Giordano wanted his wife not only to
serve him, but also to be happy and content while she performed her domestic subservient role. Once again, the rhetorical question arises: What more
could a married woman possibly desire in life, other than to be a "domestic
queen" or *Signora*? Indeed, a working-class Italian married woman could be
a *Signora* as long as she embraced her roles as wife and mother and confined
her aspirations and agency to the domestic unit.

Of course, one way of fulfilling a young woman's dream of becoming a
Signora was through migration and the achievement of economic success
through her husband's breadwinning capacities in *America*. Perhaps the
significance of this dream to young Italian migrant women is best summarized in Vittoria Ranellucci's words from the documentary film *Caffé Italia,
Montréal*: "I wanted to be a beautiful, rich lady, just as I saw the wealthy in
Italy, what I mean is, I too wanted to be like them."[48]

The domestic wife image that Giordano harboured of his Italian migrant sweetheart included having babies:

> I went to visit your family and the little Alessandra. How beautiful she is. I thought a lot about that day when our *figlio* will be the one in the stroller!!! He too will be very beautiful, especially if he'll look like his *madre*!! Think what a lovely child he will be!!... He'll have CURLY hair like his *madre*, or rather like yours! If our first should be a girl, then I hope with all my heart that she will resemble you! Do you know why? Because you are simply beautiful!! (12 May 1956).

The prevailing notion of women as natural mothers, and of maternity as a necessarily central part of their destiny, was also reified and reinforced in the narratives of migration. Migrant women's kin contributed significantly to the reinforcement of women's roles, not only because maternity was viewed as a natural consequence of a happy, married life for women, but also because it was hoped that babies and children in immigrant households would help channel married women's nurturing energies to their "natural" roles. A woman's kin also hoped that babies would help distract her and thus alleviate feelings of nostalgia and loneliness that came with leaving her friends and family behind.

In December 1960, soon after arriving in Montreal, Maddalena received news from her godmother about her family and friends and reassurance that they had not forgotten her. In her Christmas and New Year's wishes to Maddalena, her godmother wrote: "may 1961 bring you many beautiful things, lots of joy and prosperity, and foremost, a beautiful *pupone*" (14 December 1960), that is, a beautiful, healthy baby. Indeed, in the eyes of her godmother as well as other friends and family, there was nothing else a recently married migrant woman like Maddalena could possibly desire—especially in light of the emotional void she had been experiencing as a result of leaving her immediate family behind.

Not surprisingly, this view was frequently represented in the correspondence that Maddalena received from her mother. Upon receiving news from her daughter that she was pregnant, Maddalena's mother was clearly delighted, and immediately responded: "I'm very happy and I send you again my most fervent, joyful wishes, try to withstand [*sopportare*] the troubles you're feeling to the best that you can, because to be a mother [*essere mamma*] brings enormous satisfaction" (10 January 1961). Both the mother and godmother of Maddalena reiterated the same message: to be a mother is a natural destiny for a woman. In addition to fulfilling normalized feminine desires, the arrival of a child would mitigate Maddalena's nostalgia and loneliness.

Women in transnational households also played a key role in helping to make up emotionally for the absence of their children's father. As Rhacel Parreñas observes, in the absence of a migrant father, forms of "intensive mothering" became normalized in the daily lives of transnational households.[49] We observe this dynamic in the letters exchanged between Sara and Dante, as Sara wrote: "I asked for a loan so that I could buy some sweets for them [Paolo and Elisabetta], not for me, but for them. I'm not ashamed of saying it. I have spoiled them, I know that, but don't reproach me. They are without their *padre*, and therefore, it seems something is always missing" (25 August 1956). Indeed, while the presence of both parents was seen as important in a child's life, the implication is that, in the context of migration, the mother's presence was more necessary to the children's emotional and psychological well-being than the father's. In the absence of other forms of communication between the children and their father, treats and sweets would, at least, keep the children in a positive frame of mind.

Gender roles for women in transnational households were occasionally reconfigured in order that women might serve especially their male kin. The expectation that an older daughter would serve as mother to her younger adult brother, for instance, is emphasized in the letters between Maddalena and her mother. On the eve of the departure of Maddalena's younger brother Fabio, their mother wrote a letter to Maddalena, with the request that Fabio bring it to Maddalena upon arriving in Montreal. She wrote: "*Cara figlia*, I entrust you with Fabio, as *fratello, cognato,* and as *figlio.* Try to guide him in every way and advise him as you know how" (5 February 1966). The request to be a mother to her brother was nothing new for Maddalena. In a letter from Fabio, written a few months prior to his arrival in Canada, we observe how Maddalena had accepted and welcomed the prospect of seeing her brother in Montreal, while asking her mother to ensure that Fabio would listen to his older sister. In the process of planning his migration to Canada, Fabio wrote to Maddalena, reassuring her that he would work at the same location where she was working and that, "with regards to what you're telling *mamma*, I will do whatever you ask me to do, and I can say that even though we are brother and sister, you'll be for me a second *madre*" (16 July 1965). For Maddalena, however, the pressure was felt both ways, as she was also expected to remain a comfort to her mother back home. "Write often to *mamma*, she is usually alone," her older brother implored her, "and even if Fabio is with her for those few hours, they are never enough to fill those empty days she now has since you left" (22 November 1960). The special responsibility thrust on women for the care of their parents was also reflected in a brief exchange between two sisters-in-law in the Colonello/Domenica household, one in Italy, the other in Montreal: "don't worry about your mother, she is well taken care of, and everyone loves her. I visited her to give her my best wishes... There is always a family member with her" (25 April 1961).

The reconfiguration of women's roles within kinship is also evident in other contexts of migration. For instance, in the following scenario a migrant's aunt is asked to be like a mother to him. In a letter from Marianna Domenica to her son, Gianlorenzo, she described her reaction at his decision to break free from his aunt's maternal protection: "no kinder and more caring woman exists. I tell you the truth, Gianlorenzo, I thought you would stay with her for as long as you would be away" (28 July 1954). Although Gianlorenzo had, no doubt, mentioned to his parents in Spilimbergo that he would be living near his uncle and his family in Montreal, the message that resonated most strongly, especially with his mother, was that he was leaving the safety and nurturing care of his aunt in Michel. By contrast, the realities that Gianlorenzo would still be under the care of family in Montreal, that he would gain higher earnings through his new job in the construction industry, and that he was leaving behind a dangerous mining job, were not emphasized to the same degree.[50]

Canada's postwar immigration policy, specifically through the sponsorship program, played a large part in shaping the gender construction of postwar Italian migration. Given the cultural-historical context of the time period, the norm that a wife would necessarily follow her husband wherever he migrated to is not surprising. Although it would be misleading to ignore the agency that women enjoyed in helping to influence the decision-making process of their husbands' migration projects, the prevailing message in the letters demonstrates that the social and cultural expectations placed on wives gave them very little choice in such matters.

We read an illustration of this dynamic in a letter from Silvia Franceschetti written soon after her sister Sara had left for Canada. In describing the void she felt as she looked around her empty home, Silvia wrote: "I imagined this would happen from the day Dante left, the *moglie* follows her *marito* even to the end of the earth, as I always told you" (13 November 1956). This message was also strongly conveyed to Maddalena Franchi by both her mother and her godmother soon after she arrived in Montreal. In her first letter to her daughter, Daniela Perini described her happiness and relief at knowing that her daughter had arrived safely (despite her evident sorrow in being separated from her daughter). Towards the end of the letter, however, she gave Maddalena some motherly advice, and suggested that now that she was married and surrounded by a new family: "*Cara figlia*... I ask you to be good and kind [*buona e brava*],[51] like you have always been with your *madre*, and to respect your parents [*genitori*], and to love your *marito*, because happiness in life comes only through loving each other" (22 November 1960). Similar to Dante's words of encouragement to his wife in the first letter, excerpted at the beginning of this chapter,[52] the sentiments articulated by Maddalena's mother can be seen as benevolent and well-intentioned. However, when we examine them through a gender lens, the message is quite simple: personal happiness for an Italian woman was attainable only through the fulfillment of her gender roles performed within the institution of marriage.

Her mother was not the only person to encourage the development of affective bonds between Maddalena and her new family. In her Christmas letter, Maddalena's godmother wrote: "try to make them love you more with each passing day, and you will not regret leaving behind your homeland and your family in order to create your own family so far away from your loved ones. Now your place is with your *marito* and his family" (14 December 1960). These words of advice from a mother and godmother could not be easily ignored by Maddalena, especially since letters were her only source of communication with her family. While Maddalena no doubt experienced great loneliness and nostalgia once she arrived in Montreal, we can surmise that many of those feelings remained buried within her as she became aware over time that neither her mother nor her godmother could help her negotiate the sorrows of migration beyond their support through letters. Further, while their advice was well-intentioned, it placed a large part of the responsibility on Maddalena to ensure that positive, affectionate bonds developed between her, her husband, and her in-laws. Finally, these excerpts underscore the significance of kinship in the reinforcing of normative gender behaviour in transnational households.[53]

Private letters of ordinary women and men engaged in the throes of migration mirrored deeply gendered universes, both in the productive and reproductive spheres. Individuals on both sides of the Atlantic were forced to negotiate new ideas emerging from political and cultural endeavours moving toward postwar economic stability. This involved some reflection on the part of migrants and of those who remained behind about accepting or resisting—in part or in whole—changes in fashion, work opportunities, attitudes, and responsibilities that migration had forced these women and men to come to terms with.

By responding to the dangers of migration through the reification and reinforcement of gender roles, Italian women and men who settled in Canada in the postwar period also sought to valorize and entrench within their families a set of socio-cultural conservative values, morals, and behaviours. The anchor of these values was family unity. And, in order to keep their families united under "traditional" values and expectations, Italian families in Canada felt compelled to maintain a firm grip on the morals, traditions, and norms of behaviour they had learned as children in Italy.

In other words, migration had ultimately an indirect yet profound effect on the lives of Italian migrants and their children in postwar Canada. It worked to accentuate and preserve a patriarchal understanding of family life that was difficult to challenge.

A religious procession in honour of the town's patron saint, San Rocco.
Rippabottoni, Italy, 1963

Visiting Rome after several years in Canada, 1961

CHAPTER FOUR

"*My dearest love...*"
Emotions at a Distance

My love,
last night upon returning home, with great joy I found your
lettera No. 4. I didn't expect you to write to me so soon! You see!
I also write to you often. I am so happy when you declare your
love for me. I too love you so so much, and I want to marry you
as soon as possible! ... I can't wait for you to be here with me
forever.

—Giordano Rossini to Ester di Leonardi,
28 May 1957

MIGRATION STUDIES HAVE SHOWN limited interest in exploring the plethora of feelings that have been intrinsic to the experience of migration.[1] One reason for the dearth of studies is the inaccessibility of documents, such as letters, that are most likely to reveal the private emotions of migrants.

According to David Gerber, "the typical archived immigrant letter was to parents, siblings and friends."[2] He explains that

> Immigrants probably wrote love letters, the privacy of which was widely understood to be inviolable, but none of these survives in the archived collections on which this study is based, probably for the reason that they were never intended to be seen by anyone but the addressee... Whatever their wishes in the matter, immigrant letter writers could never be sure that thoughts committed to paper in these letters would not ultimately become public.[3]

John Willis points out that another reason why these documents are seldom used by historians is that their content is deemed to be too personal: "Passion is an extreme example of epistolary communication that is almost too hot to handle."[4] Yet, precisely because they are "too hot to handle," these writings crystallize in no uncertain terms the emotional experiences and struggles of migrants and their loved ones at various stages of a migration process.

This chapter examines the emotional narratives in letters exchanged between parents and children and between lovers in the postwar Italian migration movement to Canada. The paucity of literature on the intersections between emotions and migration has compelled me to base my analysis on studies that included an interdisciplinary approach to the examination of emotions; in particular, studies on letters of ordinary and not-so-ordinary folks in contexts both inside and outside migration.[5] Emotions and the expression of emotions in the letters are situated within a specific context. As Michelle Z. Rosaldo argues, the ways that emotions work, for instance concerning the emotion of shame, often depend "on socially dictated ways of reckoning the claims of selves and the demands of situations."[6] Following the lead of anthropologists Catherine Lutz and Lila Abu-Lughod in noting that, "the sociocultural analysis of emotions is both feasible and important,"[7] this study emphasizes some of the emotional complexities and webs of meaning experienced by migrants and loved ones engaged in a process of migration.

The methodological and empirical concerns about intimate letters raised by historians and other scholars further informed my inquiry,[8] as did Gerber's observation of the "spiritual communion" between friends and the power of letter writing in breaking down the barriers of time and space, even if momentarily.[9] The interconnections between courtship, letter writing, and change and continuity were elucidated through the work of Laura Ahearn (2001), Karen Lystra (1989), and Nicole Constable (2003).[10] The work of literary theorists was instrumental in analyzing abstract notions such as time and love. As Janet Altman observes, the notion of "temporal polyvalence,"[11] a juncture of the present, future, and past in a specific text, reminds us of the ways in which "memory, imagination, and hope make of past and future the only living present for the letter writer separated from the lover, visible in the very oscillation between past and future tenses."[12] Epistolary time is defined by many moments: the actual time that a described event is performed, the moment when it is written down, the differing times that the letter is mailed, received, read, and reread.[13] The dynamic of time in letter writing is referred to by Cécile Dauphin as "le temps épistolaire," namely, the letter writers' attempts to conquer time and space by engaging in time-space compression through the practice of letter writing.

Rhacel Parreñas's *Servants of Globalization* (2001) served as fundamental reading in developing my understanding of the pain of family separation, feelings of non-belonging, gender dynamics, and the personal effects of migration in the daily lives of the letter writers writing across and in between borders.[14] The collection *Families Caring across Borders* (2007), by Loretta Baldassar, Cora Baldock, and Raelene Wilding, contributed to my understanding of the experiences of caring and caregiving within the transnational context of migrant kin and their loved ones across global spaces.[15]

Despite the respect for letter-writing conventions and mutual understandings sustained throughout the correspondences, the letter writers in this study revealed themselves as emotionally connected and affectively expressive individuals. My discussion in this chapter draws from a number of studies across disciplines. The term emotional "energies" that I use in my discussion is borrowed from Altman (1982) to discuss the multiplicity of feelings reflected in the letters. At the same time, I am aware of the dangers in reading these letters as "a pure and unmediated expression of folk consciousness that somehow can speak for themselves," as David Gerber observes.[16]

Emotional Energies and the Notion of Rupture in the Letters of Parents and Children

In the following section, I explore the dynamics and consequences of rupture as reflected in the correspondence of kin members in four family networks: a mother and father in Spilimbergo writing to their son, Gianlorenzo Colonello; the correspondence between two young children in Arcugnano, Vicenza and their father, Dante del Moro, in Powell River; the letters of a mother in Ascoli Piceno to her daughter in Montreal; and a mother and father writing from Venice and Cipressina to their son and daughter-in-law in Montreal.

My focus is on the emotional energies that pervaded the personal correspondence of these four family networks. I suggest that the experience of rupture and separation was negotiated differently in emotional terms based on whether or not the migration of a loved one was perceived as permanent by family members (parents and children) who remained behind.

In the article "Men without Women" (1978), Robert Harney examines the impact of separation on Italian male migrants in Canada. Anthropologist Caroline Brettell followed with life-story descriptions of Portuguese female migrants in France in her study, *We Have Already Cried Many Tears* (1982). The studies of Harney and Brettell both examine the impact of separation from the viewpoint of migrants. On the other hand, Linda Reeder's *Widows in White* (2003) discusses the image of suffering Sicilian women perceived as abandoned in the wake of their husbands' migration.[17] Central to my discussion, however, is Rhacel Parreñas's recent ethnography on Filipina domestic workers, *Servants of Globalization* (2001), in which Parreñas explores the pains of separation experienced in transnational households both by female migrant domestic workers and by their children who remained behind in the Philippines.

While many dreamed and made plans for a return to their homeland, as was the case for the wave migration of Italian families in the early twentieth century, postwar migration to Canada was perceived by numerous families as permanent. Conversely, for individuals whose families remained in Italy, or who did not immediately recreate a "family" of their own, migration was perceived as temporary with an imminent return home, albeit without definite dates. For many loved ones who remained in Italy, this kind of distance signalled a permanent and definitive separation. Part of the reason for this perspective, despite the acceleration in transportation and communication technologies in the postwar period, was the high level of anxiety that migration to Canada entailed for migrants and their families. By contrast, for those who viewed migration as part of a family strategy, like Dante del Moro and Sara Franceschetti, who experienced temporary separation, the departure and absence of the migrant was viewed in tandem with the imminent anticipation of family reunification, even though Dante's migration encompassed its share of anxieties and uncertainties. In this study, I analyze migration emotions in relation to love and nostalgia; emotional dependency; the imagination; time and space conceptions; "bridging" efforts; and the overall meaning of being left behind. Other letter series relevant to the discussion are those of Maurizio Trevisan, Maddalena Franchi, and Gianlorenzo Colonello, which offer windows into sentiments experienced as a result of permanent migration.

Literary historian Marie-Claire Grassi suggests that "between parents and children, a visceral, rather than carnal love, is woven, and the language of emotions captures this."[18] How was this visceral love between parents and children transformed in the face of this kind of separation? And how are expressions of love and nostalgia different in the light of the realities of permanent and temporary separation? For mothers and fathers, the migration of their children was an experience of deep loss. For male migrants who left behind their wives and children, migration was experienced as a temporary rupture that would need to be negotiated over time, whether in the short or long term.

Maurizio Trevisan's mother wrote to her youngest son—the only household member to migrate to Canada—in the days and weeks following his return to Montreal with his family in the summer months of 1963. Although Maurizio had first migrated to Canada in 1949 when he was twenty-one years old, it was not possible for Laura Adaggi to join him, since the remaining four of her children, her husband, and their extended family all resided and worked in and around Venice. For a short time in 1962 and 1963, Maurizio and Clara and their two daughters enjoyed living near Maurizio's home in Italy. The situation soon changed when Maurizio was relocated in Milan. It was then that he and Clara decided to return to their home in Canada and live near Clara's parents in Montreal. The consequences of a second separation from her son, this time together with his family, proved extremely difficult for Maurizio's mother, who eagerly awaited letters from her son to preserve a connection with him:

> *Mio* Maurizio, I have nothing else to say beyond what I told Clara. But to you, *mio tesoro*, I want to tell you how I have felt about *mio Amore*, this torment of mine has not at all been allayed by the presence of our dear ones. There is no one who can fill this enormous void that surrounds me…. At times, I tell myself that it was just meant to be. I beg you, my Maurizio [*Ti prego, mio Maurizio*], take care of your health and your peace of mind. I think of you, my dear, with my infinite love (c. July-August 1963).

Equally compelling is Daniela Perini's first letter to her daughter, Maddalena, who travelled aboard an ocean liner to New York to join her husband waiting for her in Montreal. Maddalena had been Daniela's helper, friend, and confidante, and her departure proved to be emotionally difficult for her mother. Migration to Canada would not be an option for Daniela until much later because both her sons lived either with her or just a few hours away, and she felt they needed her. As a result, Maddalena's migration to Canada was seen by her mother as permanent, even though her daughter for years harboured the desire to return home.

For Maddalena, the separation required her to reach out to her mother as much as possible for strength and support via letters, while seeking comfort with her husband and his family in Montreal. Despite Daniela's efforts to convince herself that Maddalena's departure was a good decision, their correspondence reveals her initial emotional struggles with the separation. Upon receiving news from Maddalena that she had arrived safely, Daniela wrote: "*Carissima figlia*, I received your *cara lettera*, you have no idea how happy I was to hear your wonderful news. Since you left I have done nothing but cry and think of you" (22 November 1960). In light of Maddalena's permanent migration to Canada, and daily absence from her mother's home, it is not surprising that the sorrows of rupture persisted for Maddalena's mother even six months after her departure. In April 1961, Daniela wrote: "For the moment, I have nothing else to say, as I stop writing to you, know that you are always in my heart, and that not one hour goes by every day that I don't think of you. I embrace you and kiss you affectionately with the Lord's Blessing. *Mamma*" (18 April 1961). Her emotional attachment to her daughter was frequently summarized in the letters by the phrase, "*Cara figlia, il mio pensiero* is always with you" (27 February 1961).

In contrast, Dante del Moro's departure from Arcugnano to Powell River was part of a household strategy that would require a temporary separation until Dante could send money for his wife and children to join him. In nearly every letter to Sara, Dante included special words of affection, reassuring his family of his constant love. To his children specifically, he wrote: "*Cari Paolo e Elisabetta*, your *papà* sends you lots of *baci* and tells you that he can't wait to eat with you all the candies that he has put aside for you" (8 June 1956). Within four days of this letter, Dante wrote again to Paolo and Elisabetta. To his five-year-old son, Dante wrote about his difficulties in living without him, and to his younger daughter, he talked about the chocolates and candies that he would be sharing with her soon. Dante's awareness that their separation from him was short term and that family reunification was imminent are evident, and by writing directly to his young children he made them aware that they would be with him soon:

> *Caro Paolo*, my young man, Your *papà* thanks you for your affection, and tells you that he can no longer stand being away from you. He asks you to pray to Our Lady so that She can make you come here soon to your *papà* who loves you so much. *Mia cara* Nina,[19] your *papà* is happy because he knows you are a good girl, and that you always go to the nursery school. If you learn many poems, when you come here, you'll be saying them to me, and I will give you a bag of candies and chocolates that I have put away for you (12 June 1956).

How did the children respond to their father's emotional outreach? In her brother's handwriting, we read one of Elisabetta's responses: "I am your *Nina* and together with *mamma*, I send you lots of kisses and see you soon, my dear old man [*baci e arrivederci presto, caro vecio*]" (9 August 1956). In the same letter, Paolo added, knowing the importance of his First Communion for his father: "*Caro papà*, I'm going to have my First Communion before we leave. Are you happy? Lots of *baci* from your Paolo" (9 August 1956). Paolo's announcement that he would be doing his First Communion prior to leaving was important in light of their separation. First, it signalled again an anticipation of family reunification, as both events (his First Communion and the family's departure) would take place within a short time of each other. We also witness a child's desire to please his father despite the distances between them. This observation illustrates further Grassi's point that "the parent-child relationship is placed along a double axle: to please and satisfy one's parents, and make visible to everyone the markings of a successful education, and consequently, to 'deserve' parental tenderness."[20]

"*Figlia mia cara*, your letter and your wonderful news that I just received is a balm for my heart" (5 December 1960), wrote Daniela to her daughter shortly after Maddalena's arrival in Montreal. Indeed, receiving good news from a migrant daughter helped appease a mother's sorrow and melancholy in light of her daughter's permanent departure. On the other hand, the emotional bond between mother and daughter was such that Maddalena interpreted her letter to mean that her mother was suffering because of her absence. Maddalena's response, in turn, galvanized Daniela to persuade her daughter that she was, in fact, doing well despite missing her terribly, and that she too should not suffer: "*Cara figlia*, don't feel sorry for me, I am never alone in the evenings. Sometimes I visit with Graziella, or *la Signora* Quarini and watch television at her home. And, today I leave for Cisterna to attend Lisa's wedding" (30 September 1961).

In situations of temporary separation, emotional dependencies (especially in the expression of sorrow and loneliness) were allayed by the knowledge that family reunification would occur at some point in the near future. The anticipated reunion of love partners, as we read vividly in the letters of Clara and Maurizio and of Dante and Sara, in contrast to the uncertain reunion of parents and adult children observed in the letters of Laura and Daniela needs to be underscored here as a contributing factor in the letter writers' expression of rupture and connection. However, temporary separation between couples, for instance, also revealed traces of powerlessness experienced similarly by parents, children, and siblings living apart. Indeed, the urgency to respond itself can be interpreted as a manifestation of powerlessness. We read an illustration of this in Dante's words to Sara regarding their daughter's diminished health:

Today I received your letter of the 6th of this month. I don't
know how to tell you how much it hurts me to hear about Nina,
I don't know if I should write or cry. I don't know what I can
do besides think of you constantly. Is it possible that there is no
end to this torment! That we have to keep living like this, I don't
know, I don't know who to turn to anymore, and sometimes,
I think that the Divine Providence has forgotten us… I cling
to the hope that when you will have received this letter, everything will be better (13 July 1956).

Imagination played a crucial role in helping family members overcome
and negotiate separation. In this excerpt, we witness Paolo reaching out to his
father (through his mother's words) in anticipation of their eventual reunion:
"Paolo instructs me to write to you and ask you to send some money for the
train [ticket] he would like to buy so he can join you" (27 April 1956). In a
subsequent letter, as the date of departure for Paolo and his family drew near,
Paolo asked his father for money to be spent not on a train ticket, but on a
bicycle, as his mother writes:

He's still sleeping now, but he said that when I write to you, that
I should ask for some money for a small bicycle, as he has now
learned how to ride it, and he wants to reach you by bicycle because… I had told him that once he would know how to ride a
bicycle, we would be leaving for Canada. So you can just imagine, all day he asks me, "are we going?" (20 September 1956).

Both messages reveal that Paolo very much wanted to see his father again.
Through his imagination and dreams of joining his father, five-year-old
Paolo attempted to cope with and defy the realities of distance that separated
them.

When family reunification was unlikely to occur, however, letter writers
often resorted to other *pensieri* to fuel their imagination. A photograph sent
by Maurizio to his mother acted as a catalyst for her to imagine the life her
son and his family were leading now that they were back in Canada:

I'm replying to your letter and the photo you sent me a few days
ago. Imagine my immense joy and emotion in seeing you both
and looking so well… how much I think of you, and I am able

to see you not only in the photo, but in my imagination as well. And, each day I feel that my little girls are well, and I imagine how much they are enjoying themselves… Dear little ones! [*Care Piccine*!] in Italy, they did not have what they enjoy now (14 August 1963).

In situations of temporary separation, the anticipation of a reunion with family members is evident as a result of its realness and imminence. In cases of permanent separation, however, feelings of longing and hope were necessarily channelled in different directions. The following excerpt from Dante's letter to his children is an example of the former:

> *Mia cara* Elisa, your *papà* knows that you have a terrible cough and prays for you and your sweet *mamma* who is going to help you get better. Always listen to your *mamma,* take the syrup, and say your prayers. You will see that the Virgin Mary has never abandoned those who believe in her. She will help you feel better soon, and then you will be coming to see *papà* who has all these candies waiting for you. You, Paolo, I can just imagine you, what have you been up to? All kinds of things, right!… but listen, if you're a bad boy and you don't listen to your *mamma,* I'll know about it, and then, you won't be coming to see me, and then you will receive nothing. Therefore, listen to your *mamma,* and always say your prayers (2 July 1956).

Dante's words of encouragement and paternal love compelled both children to respond by referring also to the family's imminent reunion: "Elisa tells me to ask you, how many candies will she find when we arrive? Receive *baci* from Paolo who is by my side" (16 April 1956). As the date of reunion drew near, Paolo and Elisabetta could not contain their excitement. Sara described their elation on board the *S.S. Vulcania*: "Elisabetta is all happy, as she sings and dances about because soon she will be seeing her *papà*…. Paolo is smiling from ear to ear. Every day he asks me, 'how much time before we arrive?' Elisabetta and Paolo send you their greetings [*saluti*], and lots of big kisses [*bacioni*]" (November 1956).

In instances of permanent separation, however, other forms of negotiation often occurred before the resignation at being apart set in. The emotional solidarity expressed by correspondents on both sides of the ocean was one effort engaged in by kin, an example of which we read in Daniela's words to her daughter: "You tell me that you would pay anything to see me, and that you miss me tremendously. I leave it up to you to imagine what I would do to embrace you, Giuseppe and *la nipotina* [my granddaughter]" (10 December 1961).

Another form of negotiating permanent separation within the confines of the letter entailed the encouragement to write often, a request that was reiterated in all the letter series of this study. Marianna Domenica's words to her son, his wife, and his sister provide an example: "I send you all my best wishes and thank you for your loving words that comfort me. Write to me often. I enjoy receiving *notizie. Baci cari*" (c. 1960).

Responding quickly to a dear one's letter was also a means of negotiating permanent separation, as we read in Laura Adaggi's words to her son: "Maurizio, *mio Tesoro*, last night upon returning from the party, *Signora* Livi handed me your letter. Can you imagine my joy? It was like the sweetest final touch to my special day" (6 October 1963). In another letter Laura described the urgency with which she replied to her son's earlier letter in order to keep their epistolary dialogue fresh and alive. In this letter, a wide range of emotions, from gratitude, pride and relief to excitement is also observed:

> My most beloved [*mio amatissimo*] Maurizio, I hope that this letter finds you in good health as I can assure you of ours. I have before me your last letter dated January 6. I am delighted to read that all is well... On the next day, I rushed to answer you. I also wanted to let you know that we received your cheque, for which, to this day I am extremely grateful to you. Yes, *mio* Maurizio, my big heart reveals itself always and in every way through the goodness of my *figlio* (2 February 1966).

While letter writers constructed emotional bridges in words in order to negotiate the gulf between themselves and their loved ones, they also resorted to other techniques, such as including photographs or describing how they were leafing through a photo album to achieve a kind of contact with their families. As historian Martha Hanna suggests, "letter writers knew in ways that historians have forgotten that the letter itself was a physical artefact that could cultivate intimacy by making the absent correspondent seem almost palpably present."[21] Lystra also observes, "Though never an adequate substitute, correspondents experienced letter writing as symbolically akin to personal presence."[22] One letter that illustrates this mechanism was written by Daniela Perini to her daughter in Montreal, upon receiving news of the birth of her granddaughter: "you cannot imagine my joy in becoming a *nonna* already, I can't wait for you to send me a photo so that I can meet my *nipotina*" (8 September 1961). While a person-to-person meeting with her granddaughter in Canada was not possible, this did not prevent Daniela from announcing and celebrating the news with her friends and family in Italy, as she told Maddalena: "as soon as I heard the wonderful news from Giuseppe, I invited all the friends in our building in honour of my little Isabella" (8 September 1961). Once Daniela received a picture of her newborn granddaughter, her enthusiasm and joy were boundless: "*Cara figlia*, I leave it up to you to imagine the joy I experienced in seeing my *cara nipotina*. I cried of joy, and all day long, I stood there admiring her over and over again. I must tell you that she is indeed a beautiful girl. Whoever sees her is impressed with how healthy she looks besides being beautiful" (30 September 1961).

In addition to the role played by photographs as markers of recent developments, the action of leafing through a photo album elicited a visual experience of a familial past.[23] Daniela was familiar with this activity, as she confided to Maddalena one day: "*il mio pensiero* is always with you and all of you, every so often when I miss you I open the photo album to look at your pictures and Giuseppe's, and in that moment, I feel you are close to me" (27 February 1961).

While the external devices of photographs and photo albums were bridging mechanisms in their own right, at the same time, they forced individuals to confront the realities of a loved one's absence. For Daniela, once the photo album was closed, she inevitably faced again the emptiness of her home. Even four months later the pain of separation was hard to withstand, as she wrote to Maddalena: "I leave it up to you to imagine how much I would pay to see you again and be near you. But unfortunately, we need to be patient and we need to believe in God who will bring us together again one day. I cannot be near you now, but my heart and my *pensiero* is with you always" (17 June 1961). As sites of memory, photographs, photo albums, and letters possessed a dialectical dimension in that they simultaneously helped to mitigate the absence of loved ones and sustain the bonds of love and affection between kin, while serving as reminders of the loss that was experienced through migration.

In other cases, this dialogic relationship was experienced by proxy, as when parents, for instance, were visited by their migrant child's friend, or a migrant was visited by someone from his or her hometown. Immediately after being visited by their son 's friend from Montreal, Marianna Domenica wrote: "it was like seeing you here [*mi sembrava da vederti te*]. How much I would pay to see you again. But it's no use, the distance keeps us too far apart" (8 August 1956).

Particularly in the cases of individuals and families who stayed behind, the letters show the importance of kinship and community in helping to cope with a loved one's absence. We observe this phenomenon in a letter written by Dante's brother-in-law in Arcugnano: "your children and Sara are well. Every night, Paolo as he returns home from the nursery, passes by to say 'hello'" (25 July 1956). Other correspondents were less fortunate, however, and seemed to experience separation as a factor that further isolated them from their community. In a letter written by Laura Adaggi to her son following his return to Canada, we observe how, in light of these circumstances, kinship support was simply not available: "Everyone thinks of their own things, their own interests, and I remain alone in my sorrow with my memories" (c. July–August 1963).

While loneliness and nostalgia were realities for all migrants and loved ones, these letters suggest that the intensity of these emotions was expressed more profoundly in situations of permanent separation. The absence of a loved one was experienced daily, and even more so during holidays and special occasions, as is revealed in a letter from Daniela Perini to her daughter: "*Carissima figlia*, I am delighted to receive your news, and immediately I am writing to give you news about us... Our Christmas was fine. We had a nice time, but I can't say the same for New Year's Day because I missed you terribly" (10 January 1961). The letters of Laura Adaggi reveal a similar scenario. In the aftermath of her fiftieth wedding anniversary celebration, Laura wrote to her son: "Briefly Maurizio, it was a gorgeous day. Even Marta looked her best. Only you were missing, *mio* Maurizio, and your family. At the table I talked about all of you. The party was beautiful, but my heart was not happy thinking of you, my infinite love [*mio amore infinito*]!" (6 October 1963).

Emotional Energies in Love Letters of Migration

In contrast to letters between parents and children, another form of emotional contact that characterized the transatlantic experience was the correspondence between lovers. To begin with, what is a letter of love, or rather, a love letter? According to Roland Barthes, a love letter "refers to the special dialectic of the love letter, both blank (encoded) and expressive (charged with longing to signify desire)."[24] In a scholarly debate on the contours of a love letter, Mireille Bossis offers the following definition: " The expression, *par excellence*, of sentiment, it transports us to the sphere of the eternal and the repetitious, of the fleeting and the unexpected, but also to the sphere of everyday life with its own codes and banalities." [25]

While definitions of the love letter abound in literary works and epistolary studies written over the centuries, the correlations of the love letter with migration have not been explored. The literature on "romance epistolary," as Janet Altman calls it, or the "lettre d'amour" as opposed to the wider meaning of "écritures intimes" suggests that love letters are the exclusive written expression of unmarried couples at the early stages of their courtship. But what of the married couples who wrote of love and other things in their letters as they reached out across the distances that separated them? Are their letters not love letters as well? As Karen Lystra suggests, the intimate communication of lovers (including letter writing) was enacted by both single individuals and *married* couples.[26]

In this study, the term *love* implies romantic love in a heterosexual relationship. But how do we define romantic love—the emotion that has been the subject of countless novels, stories, verse, proverbs, songs, and other forms of creative works, as well as individual reflection since the beginnings of civilizations? Anthropologist William Jankowiak offers one definition as he equates romantic love with romantic passion: "any intense attraction involving the idealization of the other within an erotic context. The idealization carries with it the desire for intimacy and the pleasurable expectation of enduring for some unknown time into the future."[27] In his research on love and lust in Nigeria, Leonard Plotnicov suggests that romantic love is "the ardent, fervent, and passionate desire for another without whom the lover experiences the feeling of being acutely incomplete, as if a vital part of her or him was lacking."[28] In light of these recent efforts by anthopologists to define romantic love, I argue that whether letters were written by a married couple, a betrothed couple, or a couple in courtship, if the context and content of these letters resonated in a striking way the emotion of romantic love—as defined above—then they are by definition letters of love. In all the cases I examine, the couples engaged in correspondence shared two primary experiences: their love and desire for each other, and their separation engendered by migration.

From Dante del Moro's first days on the *S.S. Saturnia* to the moment of family reunion at the port of Powell River, nine long months of separation had passed. Dante and Sara's intense correspondence of love and longing captures the emotional highs and lows of migration as experienced by a married couple.

The second such set of letters was exchanged between Clara Renzi in Montreal and Maurizio Trevisan in Venice. In 1948, three years after Clara and Maurizio began courting, Clara and her mother left Italy to join her father in Montreal. Prior to her departure, she and Maurizio had written to each other between Venice and Ampezzo Carnico to stay in touch and arrange meetings. Thanks to Canada's sponsorship program, Maurizio joined Clara in Montreal in 1949, and soon after they were married. Their correspondence of nine months—from October 1948 to June 1949—illustrates the emotional woes and joys of a betrothed couple.

The third set of letters contains only one side of the correspondence between Giordano Rossini, who lived in Ostia and worked in Rome, and Ester di Leonardi, the woman he loved, who had emigrated to Montreal with her sister and brothers to join their uncle and brother. Giordano wrote frequently to Ester, and his letters offer a unique glimpse into the psychological and emotional universe of a young man desperately in love.[29]

The power of the love letter rests, in part, in the nature of the document itself, which allows both for a first reading and subsequent rereadings to discern underlying meanings.[30] Indeed, as anthropologists Jan Collins and Thomas Gregor suggest, things that cross personal boundaries, like intimate and revealing words, take on deep emotional significance.[31] Scholars of epistolary studies agree that the process of letter writing in love correspondence hinges in part on dynamics that are specific to the process itself, i.e. waiting, receiving, reading, rereading, writing, and sending a letter, as well as on the specificity of the context, content, and relational dynamics of the correspondents. Such emotional traits and dynamics are both implicitly and explicitly expressed in the three letter series of this study.

In her observations on the *lettre intime*, Marie-Claire Grassi notes that "the body becomes present and the writing marks not only the sign of the self/I but also the excess, the expressions of overflow, the incessant hyperbole that transforms the expression 'I love you' into 'I adore you,' and plays infinitely with the thousands upon thousands, millions of kisses and tender things."[32] The metamorphosis of affective expression in letters of love transpires not only in intimate letters in general, but also, as we witness below, in the specific context of migration and separation between two people in love. We observe how the intensity of the expressions of love—moving from less to more—is subtler in the correspondence between the married couple, Dante and Sara, than in the letters of Maurizio and Clara, or Giordano and Ester, who were not married. Dante wrote to Sara on 22 June 1956:

> You see *mia cara*, every day I live with the hope of seeing news from you. It doesn't matter what kind of news, and today, more than any other day, as soon as I woke up, I went to the post office (two steps away from here) always with this desire nestled in my heart that is with me always. But nothing. All I found was an immense disillusion, and so I started to write to you, with my thoughts pouring out to you [*con il pensiero rivolto a voi*] (22 June 1956).

Within less than two months, Dante wrote again:

> What can I tell you… with every passing day, I feel more and more lonely and the feeling of missing all of you becomes stronger and stronger, as does my wish to have you here with me… So we can talk about us, our daily problems, have someone with whom I can confide in freely; someone I can open my heart to; even though I find myself with *cari* friends, you know very well that one can say everything to them only up to a certain point. And the rest we have to keep to ourselves… I close this letter after sending you many *saluti*. I want to tell you that I love you very much [*ti amo tanto*] and that my heart continues to be with you and our dear children. Everything else (beyond health) is meaningless (5 August 1956).

In contrast, Clara's letter to Maurizio, written just a few weeks after her departure, evoked more clearly articulated affections:

> I think you think of me as much as I think of you, that you love me as much as I love you, and so, this is enough to put my heart at peace and to set aside my worries. I'm not sure why in the past few days I didn't write to you... I'm still working and it's going well... many times the Italian girl who sits with me tells me that I must be truly in love, do you know why? It's easy to guess, because I only speak of you... I remember every song, every detail, and while I am forced to face my reality, my gaze and my thoughts are absent... what can I do but remember the past? And I only know when I can do it. I would like to sleep and dream forever, and only awaken with you here... sadly, I need to wait and open my eyes to reality, and accept whatever fate [*il destino*] sends our way, hoping that it will bring us well-deserved happiness. I dream to see you again soon because, believe me, I miss you terribly (15 January 1949).

Finally, the letters of the courting couple, Giordano and Ester, convey the strongest intensity of affective expressions, likely because the probability of a breakdown in their relationship was highest of the three couples. Here Giordano wrote to Ester within a few days of her departure:

> *Mio caro amore*, here I am again. Writing to you for me is an enormous consolation. Did you receive the letter and postcard that I sent you in Lisbon? I hope so, how are you all? Did you have a good trip? Did you start thinking of your return trip? *Amore mio*, you must come back—so much so, that the other day, I threw a coin for you in the *Fontana di Trevi*. As you can see, I'm always thinking of you. Tell me what you've seen. What you've been doing. Are you enjoying yourself? Write to me, tell me everything. I feel so lonely. I miss you terribly. I cannot live without you, don't leave me [*non mi lasciare*]!!! (16 March 1957).

In a study of young Nepali couples' pursuit of romantic love through correspondence, anthropologist Laura Ahearn suggests that love is perceived as something that "afflicts and torments them... makes them feel like they're going crazy."[33] At the same time, Ahearn notes, "love also empowers them, giving them a sense of agency in other realms of their lives."[34] Similarly, Karen Lystra discusses "emotional power" in romantic love in nineteenth-century America, and shows how "the dynamics of romantic love created interpersonal power through the pleasures and satisfactions as well as the vulnerability of a shared identity."[35] She suggests that while romantic love was unstable in its duration or staying power, it had compelling effects on individual lives.[36]

One of the effects of romantic love is self-empowerment. The love correspondence of the three couples reveals romantic love as a form of empowerment for the writers. We witness this effect on Giordano as he describes his sense of inspiration and optimism after receiving confirmation of Ester's love:

> *Amore mio*, you have no idea how much joy you have given me
> when you wrote to me from Gibraltar... I was eagerly waiting
> for your letter. Any news that would prove to me that you have
> been thinking of me... I hope *il destino* is on our side now un-
> like in the past. And so, have faith and don't be impatient, for
> my love for you will never change... I know very well that you
> love me too (18 March 1957).

Consider also Dante's words of joy upon receiving good news from Sara: "I cannot begin to tell you how happy I am to hear that Elisabetta is feeling better. All I can say is that I feel like a new man" (10 July 1956).

In *Invitations to Love*, Ahearn observes that the active force of love in young Nepali women and men is associated "with being 'developed' and successful."[37] In the analysis, agency through love is associated with becoming financially "successful"—as in the case of Giordano, who wrote to Ester that now all he had to do was settle down economically [*sistemarsi*] so that she could return, marry him, and be happy for the rest of her life: "I cannot give up—I must face up to life, and fight it, fight it for my ideal, overcome the obstacles that stand in my path or rather, our path" (10 March 1957). In other letters, similar messages were invoked with words like: "You'll see that as soon as my finances are settled, I'll make you come back and we'll get married immediately" (21 March 1957), and "I'm willing to work even 15 hours per day, so that I can have a good job and marry you as soon as possible" (26

March 1957), and finally, "when are you coming back? What a silly question, since your return depends on me. The earlier I establish myself economically, the earlier you will come back. Isn't that so?" (4 April 1957).

"Success" was also expressed when one of the parties fulfilled the necessary Canadian migration procedures that would hasten their reunion in Canada. Here the power of love provided both parties with the strength to overcome difficulties and surmount obstacles, including space, between them. Despite their physical absence, migrants and loved ones drew from this love and transformed it into agency on their part.

For instance, on 7 April 1956 Dante wrote to Sara that he had visited a notary in Powell River to try to expedite the migration procedures for his wife and children. He wrote, "I spoke with the notary here in Powell River, and basically, he said that I don't need to send you anything... all you have to do is go to the travel agency and they will proceed with the paperwork using the same file number as mine..." Related to the desire to expedite his family's arrival in Canada was the notion of saving as much money as possible, in addition to sending them funds for their daily subsistence while in Italy: "I intend to follow through like this for the only reason that the less money I send you, the faster I can put up house and have everything you need from top to bottom, and I wish (always with the good Lord's help) that upon your arrival, none of the necessities will be missing, except the linens" (15 August 1956).

Another illustration of the interconnections between love, inspiration and migration procedures is Clara's letter to Maurizio:

> Tonight, I just couldn't resist. For better or for worse I wanted to write to you so that I could also send you these papers that you will find included here, I don't know if you have started the procedure, but I hope to know something about this tomorrow (I tell you honestly that if it wouldn't be the case, my disappointment would be immense), in any case together with the papers you'll be bringing to Rome, I would include even this one, but before going there for the interview, you'll need to be in possession of your ticket for boarding a ship. I will send it to you as soon as I hear something from you advising me of the stage in which you are at with the procedures (8 May 1949).

The fading of romantic love also appears in the letters. As Roland Barthes suggests, fading or fade-out is a "painful ordeal in which the loved being appears to withdraw from all contact, without such enigmatic indifference even being directed against the amorous subject or pronounced to the advantage of anyone else, world or rival."[38] It is perhaps no coincidence, then, that this emotion—in conjunction with a sense of empowerment and the feeling of going crazy—are identified in the love letters of these three couples. Because the expression and feelings of love appear both in single letters and sequentially in correspondences, love in transnational relationships of migration was a kind of dialectic that elicited feelings of both elation and misery.

"I was going crazy [*Ero fuori di me*]" (18 June 1956), wrote Sara to Dante, when she had not heard from him in days. And Dante wrote to Sara that all he did was work and think of her and their children: "When you write... think that your husband, when he returns from work, the first thing that he does is check if there is any mail for him, and only upon seeing your handwriting does his fatigue pass" (12 June 1956). When compared with the other letter series, the expressions of "fading" in the letters between husband and wife appear more subtle. However, they also illustrate profound sadness, as Sara's words to Dante show: "and so the days pass, and our existence diminishes" (13 June 1956).

In the love letters between Maurizio and Clara, and Giordano and Ester, jumbles of feelings often surfaced in the same letter. For instance, Clara wrote to Maurizio:

> *Mio amore.* There is no place for me to find peace. You can imagine why, can't you? Not even today did I receive news from you. I am devastated and disheartened in a way that I cannot describe. Why, tell me, why do you do this? Do I deserve this kind of punishment? Maurizio, I beg you. Please, as soon as you receive this letter, let me know something, so that I can put my heart at peace. Oh! What a life. How tired I am of thinking about one possibility over another. I just cannot take it any longer... and I ask myself if happiness actually exists in this world. Maybe it does, but it lasts for such a short time that we can barely notice it, and when we find it, how much we need to fight for it and sacrifice. You see, tonight I am anything but

optimistic, believe me it feels like everything is against me, and there is no other reason for this but your silence… you know that I suffer enough from your being so far away, why then add these moments of trouble to me? I admit that your silence might be due to a postal delay, but to me this reason is only remotely possible. Nothing but horrible thoughts enter my mind (6 November 1948).

Just ten days after seeing Ester for the last time, Giordano wrote to her, "today was a dark day for me, I had the devil in my hair, I don't even know the reason for my anxiety. All I know is that my nerves are broken. If I continue like this, sooner or later, I will be deep in a depression. I cannot take it any longer. Since you left, I don't talk to anyone, I've closed myself off" (20 March 1957). In a following letter, Giordano confided to Ester what the Easter holiday meant to him: "In two days it's Easter and everyone will be celebrating with joy and happiness, perhaps I will be the only person for whom Easter brings no joy, no diversion. I have become strange. I don't know how to explain it, even in the wake of a surprise, I am indifferent. For me there are no holidays, every day is the same, monotonous and dull" (18 April 1957). Just over ten days earlier, he wrote: "I am so confused in my head, sometimes I'm afraid I'm going crazy" (6 April 1957). And later, he wrote:

> *Mia adorata*, even this holiday has passed like all the others. I did nothing special. It's very strange! At every holiday, I feel so alone. I would like to go somewhere far far away where I can be alone and see no one, I am bothered by these masses of people who laugh and joke. I'm almost envious of those young men who take walks with their girlfriends. I would like to do that too, but *il destino* won't let me!! I am destined to remain away from you, and this makes me almost angry; I would like to see no one. In the meantime, no one understands me. They don't know what's going on inside of me. Maybe you too cannot understand me. I feel terribly alone, abandoned. I thought I had found the person with whom I could confide, and find solace. Instead, here! *Il destino* has taken her from me to faraway Canada (30 May 1957).

In her discussion on romantic love in Victorian America, Karen Lystra observes:

> the emotional highs and lows of romantic love contributed to an intensified concentration on the individual's interior life and added further impetus to the development of a personal identity separate from social obligations and public roles... Both sexes experienced a wide range of feelings and an intensity of emotion during romantic love which not only strengthened individual self-consciousness but also helped bridge gender divisions. After marriage, the emotional response patterns of romantic love were less intense or at least the range of emotional expression in letters was narrower. As long as romantic love survived, however, its characteristic response patterns might be activated within as well as outside a marital relationship.[39]

Indeed, throughout the three letter series, the tone of urgency and desperation also ranges in intensity. While a measure of emotional fluidity is sustained in the letters between the married couple, Dante and Sara, it is striking in the letters of the betrothed couple, Clara and Maurizio, and even more so in the letters of the courting couple, Giordano and Ester.

In the following letter, Clara's expressions of emotion moved from happiness at receiving news from Maurizio to uncertainty and desolation as she sought to understand his silence:

> *Mio amato* Maurizio, if I have delayed a little in sending you news, it's only because I was waiting for a reply from those two letters I had sent you some time ago. I have anxiously waited all this week and I leave this up to you to imagine. I would call my *mamma* every day at my break to find out if I had news, but the answer was always negative. Yes, I received the letter you sent me from Ampezzo (noted) with a 15-day delay from the other letter, and then nothing. What happened? You tell me what I should be thinking. Or maybe you want me to go crazy? Oh Maurizio, you shouldn't do this to me. If you bear a grudge against me for that letter that I wrote to you in a moment of disgust and disappointment, you are wrong, very wrong! You

know yourself that sometimes it's not our reasoning selves that govern us, but our nerves. Even people who are sweeter and less impulsive than me fall for it at certain moments. We need to understand and empathize. As I was telling you earlier, I wanted to write to you this week even because I had lots of little things to tell you, but I couldn't even find the words to tell you what I wanted to say... I want to tell you more about other little things concerning your arrival, but since they are of minor importance, I'll keep them for another letter, when my heart will be happier. I ask you, please, my dear old man [*mio vecio*] write to me, I need to hear from you especially now... I am so happy to hear how much your visit was appreciated by my family back home. Oh! I knew it would be so. They are so fond of you! I couldn't stop myself from crying when I read your descriptions and heard you speak of my dearly beloveds, and my little and dear country, as it is always in my heart! But perhaps it's best not to talk about these things... one thing remains for me, one hope and that is to see you again, to talk to you about everything I have seen and lived, and everything we are living! But, why, why are you not writing?... I'm going to sleep now, hoping that tomorrow is a new day, a day that will bring me your news... *mio amore*, I send you my dearest and most ardent *baci* (8 May 1949).

Arguably the most emotionally volatile of the letter series is the collection written by Giordano to Ester. In nearly all of the close to one hundred letters archived, the message is clear: Giordano was struggling with Ester's migration to Canada and her physical separation from his life. Here is a striking example that illustrates Giordano's mood, fluctuating from hope, nostalgia, and insecurity to curiosity, jealousy, sarcasm, and self-criticism, and finally back to hope again:

Ester, *Carissima*, here I am again sitting at the table writing to you, if I could I would stay here all day to write to you, because when I write, I have the impression that I'm talking with you. It doesn't feel like you are thousands and thousands of kilometres away. *Caro Amore*, if you only knew how much I miss you, I spend my entire days thinking of you! *Cara* Ester, you know what I say? That I love you so much, and that you are my only hope! Do you still love me? How much time do I still need to wait before I can hold you again?? How much I wish that day would be tomorrow. *Cara,* what did you do today? Did you work? Or did you go out with some handsome Canadian guy? No!! I'm joking, I know very well that you would not do this wrong to me (if wrong is what we can call it). Do you know what I did today?... *Signorina*, this is the two million [lire] question... you have one minute to answer it... Think carefully before replying... The question is this: what did I do today?... well, *Signorina*??.... no!! I did not go dancing.... no! I did not go to the movies, nor out with Blondie... I'm sorry *Signorina* di Leonardi, but your time is up, and you lost the two million. The answer was: "A LOUSY NOTHING." *Mio Tesoro*, don't you think I'm an idiot writing to you these things? I think so. Please ignore them, when we'll be together I'll stop doing them!! (25 April 1957).[40]

Emotional dependency is another characteristic of love that is illustrated in the letters between these three couples.[41] It is reflected clearly in the happiness that letter writers described upon receiving good news from their beloved. For instance, upon finding a letter waiting for him as he returned from work, Dante immediately felt the impulse to share his happiness with Sara by writing: "*Cara* Sara, yesterday on Saturday, I returned from work. I was a little tired and my cousin had an intuition. Better than this it could not have been: your letter. As soon as I saw it, I was no longer tired, and my heart leaped with joy. It was like seeing all three of you here. From this, you can surely understand how happy I feel" (22 April 1956).

Although many letters delivered good news, others brought bad news, while silence offered no news or opened the door to negative speculation. As observed above, when this occurred, feelings of sorrow, melancholy, desolation, and even desperation often overtook the letter writers. In this excerpt, Dante responds with apology and sorrow to his misunderstanding of a previous letter his wife had written:

Cara moglie, within a short time from my previous letter, I cannot avoid writing to you, because I just cannot accept everything that you have told me in your letter, and I ask you to forgive me in the way I reacted in my response. But, if you only knew how badly I felt, and how I continue to feel, you would not judge me... Now that I write to you I feel a little better, but the other day, I was beside myself. Even my cousins noticed it as I have never been like this before (18 June 1956).

The following exchange between Clara and Maurizio underscores the dynamic of emotional dependency in love correspondence, as she experienced sadness and melancholy as a result of his sorrow:

Afterwards, when I read your letter the second time, I understood everything, and was immediately sorry, deeply sorrowed as I read your expressions that were replete with sadness and melancholy, I didn't expect such a letter. I thought the holidays would bring you a little joy... This was my wish that I have hoped for you and always will. I wanted you to be happy even if you missed me, that you would have the best memories possible of Christmas... so that you would not suffer, but that's not the way it was for you (6 January 1949).

Clara wrote on the same subject in a subsequent letter:

Some time ago, I received your letter in which you tell me that you are recovering. You cannot imagine how sorry I felt knowing that you were ill, despite it not being serious. This is what it means to be apart from each other, the person you love the most in the world is suffering and you are totally unaware of it. You cannot comfort him. You cannot diminish his pain. It's terrible! However, now that I know that you are feeling better, I am very happy (15 February 1949).

Indeed, after receiving good news in a letter from Maurizio, optimism resurged in Clara's replies: "You cannot imagine how relieved I am to read them and how much happiness they bring to me" (14 November 1948).

The joy that Giordano felt at receiving happy, encouraging news from Ester is reflected in his letters to her, nearly all of which begin: "My dream [*sogno mio*], last night I received your letter No. 6 including the 3 photos. You cannot imagine my joy when I receive news from you" (15 June 1957); and "*Tesoro mio*, yesterday I received your letter No. 7—thank you so much! You make me so happy when you write to me. *Amore mio*, I love you so very much" (16 June 1957). Clara's descriptions of how longing affected her state of mind are echoed in Giordano's words of sadness at missing Ester since her departure. He wrote, "Here in Italy, Spring has arrived. People often tell me, 'Don't you see what beautiful days we're having?' But for me, these things don't exist anymore. Do you know why? Because I miss you" (16 March 1957).

According to Lystra, "simply thinking of the lover"[42] helped to build emotional bridges. Some couples attempted to compensate for the reality of their separation by writing almost daily to each other. For example, in Sara's case the act of writing letters was an important part of her daily existence. In this excerpt, she confided to her husband the necessity of writing to him: "three days that you don't write to me and I am immediately anxious. The more time passes, the greater the difficulty I feel in writing to you, but every day I write to you, later I will tear them up... it's a way for me to release my anxiety" (c. June 1956). As with other forms of personal writing, letters offered a space for reflection, articulation and dialogue, however delayed, for writers. In cases where letters were torn up, before or after delivery, they represented a truncated communication that nonetheless allowed for the self-preservation of the writers without their seeking comfort from a confidante. At the opposite end of the wire, meanwhile, Dante became concerned when he did not receive any news from his wife for several days, and also turned to writing as a form of therapy: "I started writing to you... so that I could calm this anxiety [*calmare questa anzia*] that continues to wear me down" (22 June 1956).

In her correspondence with Maurizio, Clara confided that she was comforted by the words in his letters:

> Last night, I went with *papà* and *mamma* to see an Italian movie, *La Traviata*. Giovanna and Marco came with us as well....
> Oh, what a movie... truly beautiful, and that music, how much it brought me back to you. Did you see it? If you haven't, you

mustn't miss it. It's worth seeing. I reread your two last letters. In them I find so much true love, so much affection... so much comfort for me in these words, that you cannot imagine. They bring me everything I need to continue to love, and to hope, like thousands and thousands of girls (30 October 1948).

For Giordano, writing to Ester was an important source of comfort and solace as well as a necessity for his emotional survival: "I love you very much [*amore mio, ti amo tanto*]. As I write to you I look at your photo, and do you know what I tell you? That you are truly a beautiful girl (and one day, you will be a beautiful lady, *Signora* Rossini, how does it sound to you?)" (18 March 1957). In another letter, he wrote, "when I returned home this evening, I found your letter from Halifax... *Vita mia*, I love you very much, I read and reread your letter, while reading it, it seemed that you were here speaking to me, I could hear your voice and see you near me... as I write to you, your photograph is before me (the one you took in Portugal).[43] You are so beautiful!!" (26 March 1957). And, while at work in Viareggio, he wrote, "I'm taking advantage of a little free time for me to write to you these two lines. If I don't write to you, I feel terrible" (27 April 1957).

"The letter writer," Janet Altman observes, "is always in dialogue with a possible respondent... [and] any letter appears as part of a potentially ongoing sequence."[44] As participants in an epistolary dialogue[45] of love, correspondents exchanged questions and answers in their letters. This strategy of asking questions and providing answers was a way of sustaining dialogue and maintaining active engagement to ensure that the letter writer was not forgotten or neglected.

Giordano Rossini, for instance, even went so far as to give instructions to Ester on how to respond to his letters. In this excerpt, he asked Ester if she could number her letters to him in order for both of them to keep track of their letters and maintain as much as possible an uninterrupted flow of dialogue between them: "*Cara,* you should do one thing, that is, as soon as you receive this letter, the first one that you'll write to me afterwards should be identified as No. I, and then as they follow, do you understand? That is, the one that follows number I will be number II, so that I can keep track of all the letters, do you agree?? This one is my No. I" (2 May 1957). Letters were also action-oriented, as Dirk Hoerder observes, "they demanded responses, an answer, money, information from the recipients."[46] Giordano asked Ester if she could keep his letter in front of her as she wrote to him so that she could address *all* of his questions. Not content with these requests, he also asked her to write to him more often, using tighter, smaller handwriting so she could include more in her letters, and he would thus have more to read about her: "Can you write to me more often? Instead of waiting for my letter and answering it, can you write to me even before receiving my mail; if you have time, of course! And when you write to me, can you write using smaller handwriting so that you can include more in the letters" (7 April 1957). Beyond the understanding that "letters are dialogues with intervening time lags before responses,"[47] Giordano's eagerness to constantly receive news from Ester compelled him to urge her to write often, and tell him everything, even before receiving a letter with questions from him. When it seemed to him that her commitment in writing to him was waning, he wrote: "it seems to me that when you write, you're in a hurry. It seems like you're writing to me without too much involvement on your part. No! *Cara* Ester, please don't be offended. I know it's not as it appears, this is why I said, 'it seems.' Surely, you have a good reason for this" (3 May 1957).

Another way writers made sure that their lovers would respond to their letters was by making an explicit epistolary agreement (*le pacte épistolaire*) to maintain the correspondence, as Clara wrote in her letter to Maurizio:

> You cannot imagine how comforted I am to read your letters
> and how much happiness they bring to me, for this I ask you, I
> beg you to write to me, to write to me: once a week punctually,
> I'll try to do the same so that neither of us needs to suffer... one
> line, one short letter is all we need... but the flow must be con-
> stant, lively and continuous because if one day that disappears,
> it is over (14 November 1948).

Not only was letter writing a practice akin to personal presence, as Lystra suggests, but through love letters, correspondents allowed themselves to "feel" the presence of their lover. For instance, to help comfort Sara, Dante asked her to imagine him with her at night:

> Do you know what you should do?... When the children are
> asleep, and it's late, and you're in bed, turn off the light. Turn
> to one side of the bed. Rest your cheek on the pillow to sleep.

You'll find that after a while you'll feel a tender caress and the
endearing breath near your lips of the man who has loved you
so and who will love you forever (23 May 1956).

The letters of Giordano to Ester further illustrate this observation: "when
I write to you, I feel you close to me. It feels like I'm talking to you, so much
so that I would never want to stop writing to you" (7 April 1957). After visiting a church with his grandmother, and reminiscing about when Ester was
there too, he described to Ester his near-spiritual experience of feeling her
presence: "as I concentrated on praying, suddenly I felt you close to me, like
that Christmas Day!! *Amore mio*, there is no place that does not remind me
of you" (19 April 1957).

The writers' imaginative act of appealing to the heavens to bring a message of love was another quasi-poetic, quasi-religious mechanism for letter
writers to bridge distances.[48] In his letters to Ester, Giordano invoked the
stars to bring Ester his message of love in an effort to reach out to her in
that precise moment beyond the temporal and physical realities that confined him. The following excerpt illustrates a particular moment in which
Giordano felt compelled to reach Ester immediately and his imagination
offered him the only possible means of doing so:

> before I close, I want to tell you that I saw our star tonight and it
> seemed to be saying to me: "Ester sends you many many kisses
> and is always thinking of you" to which I answered: "Dear little
> star [*Cara stellina*], bring many big kisses to my beloved [*ba-
> cioni al mio Amore*] who is so far away from me. Tell her that
> I will love her for all my life. Tell her not to forget me." Until
> tomorrow, *Amore carissimo* (19 April 1957).

In *Six Memos for the Next Millennium*, Italian literary scholar Italo
Calvino writes, "The imagination is a kind of electronic machine that takes
account of all possible combinations and chooses the ones that are appropriate to a particular purpose, or are simply the most interesting, pleasing, or
amusing."[49] Indeed, in the letters of all three series, imagination played a
central role in evoking the absent loved one through the reconstruction of
events from the past, or in describing those in the present and the possible
future. As Bernard Bray suggests, these temporal travels of the imagination
offered letter writers "the promise of the journey, the description of a future

nest or of any other place of happiness. It could also entail the mention of a place of memory that emerges from shared memories."[50]

In their correspondence, Sara and Dante looked to the future and imagined their lives together with their children in Powell River: as Sara wrote frequently towards the end of her letters, especially at the end of a long day away from her husband, "I close these scribbles sending you many greetings, I embrace you and send you many kisses... even though I don't use tender words, think only that I cannot wait to begin my life alongside you; It will be better than ever before" (20 September 1956).

Imaginings of an anticipated daily life led writers to reflect upon their desire and longing for their lover. For instance, in order for a serene life to materialize upon their reunion, Sara wrote to Dante urging him to discontinue his night shift, because "when I will come down I don't want to continue sleeping alone at night, I sleep alone at night now without my man, and I long to feel his arms holding me tight to the point of feeling breathless" (27 September 1956).

Clara imagined what life would be like for her and Maurizio once he joined her and they were married. She wrote that there would be a greater understanding between them, and that neither of them would have to suffer alone for they would have each other: "Oh! We don't live only on bread, as you correctly wrote one day... it's logical that you cannot have everything you want in life. I know this for sure. I know we will have our share of sorrows as well, but we'll be able to overcome them, it will be the two of us then, we won't be alone" (27 May 1949). Moreover, as Clara wrote, Maurizio would participate in the building of their house together with her parents: "the other night we were talking and my father said, 'if Maurizio comes, he'll give me a hand'... I have no doubt about that, since I know how much you enjoy working. Right, Maurizio? And anyway, we're talking about our little house" (15 February 1949).

In his daily entries to Ester, Giordano's reminiscence of his past days with Ester evoked strong images that moved from the past to the future. In one letter he described his feelings when he first laid eyes on her on the beaches of Ostia, and how he imagined his life with her in Rome. In another letter, he described a scenario of their lives together set far into the future:

Last night for the first time, I saw a comet. I went to the terrace and there!! In the midst of thousands of stars, with its luminescent tail was the comet! So that when we'll be old, we'll be able to tell our children, or even our grandchildren. Don't you think so?…When our children will ask us, "*Mamma*, did you ever see a comet? What's it like?" to which you will say, "go to your *papà*, he saw one once. Ask him to tell you all about it." And so, I, with all the patience in the world, will explain to them that one day in the distant past of 1957, I went to the terrace and … so on… (25 April 1957).

Closely related to these imagined scenarios were references to dreams. In many cases, letter writers referred generally, almost reflexively, to the act of dreaming about their partner. For example, Dante wrote to his wife that, "I hold you all close to my heart with enormous love… dream of me, as I dream of you always" (25 August 1956). Simlarly, Clara exclaimed to Maurizio:

I remember every song, every detail, and often reality calls on me while my gaze and my thoughts are absent… Isn't it strange? Not so much perhaps for someone who knows what it means to love, what would I do if I cannot remember the past? And only I know when I can evoke it again, and when that happens, I would like to dream. I would like to fall asleep and wake up only with you near me. Of course that would be too beautiful, unfortunately I have to wait and open my eyes to my reality (15 January 1949).

Giordano often wrote to Ester at the end of his day, when he was ready to fall asleep and hoped to dream of her. In one letter, he wrote: "Forgive me if this letter has no beginning and no end, but I'm very tired. I will write to you again tomorrow. And so, I wish you a good night, and I hope to meet you in my dreams. See you soon, my love—do not forget me [*amore mio—non ti scordar di me*]" (18 March 1957).[51]

The instances when letter writers recounted dreams involving their lovers are of particular interest. According to David Fitzpatrick, the report of a dream was a vehicle through which "immediacy could be invoked, in an imagined present."[52] Giordano was quick to recount the following dream to Ester:

> Last night I dreamt of you. We were together at Nietti's. There
> was a party and you were wearing a black skirt and a light blue
> pullover. You looked beautiful as always. Suddenly, everyone
> disappeared, and we found ourselves locked in each other's
> arms. And just as I kissed you, I woke up. What a beautiful
> dream…it all seemed so real, so realistic. Unfortunately, like
> all dreams even this one vanished into a cloud of smoke. How
> much I would love to hold you and kiss you on your rose-
> coloured lips (20 March 1957).

In these cases, it seems that the act of dreaming functioned both to trigger
the imagination of correspondents and to bridge the distance between lovers
through a recounting of the experience.

Marie-Claire Grassi writes, "As with all those who live apart, to abolish
time and distance is the primary function of the letter—a sort of ephemeral
materialisation of the loved one."[53] The notions of time and space are central
to the practice of letter writing in a context of migration, and according to
Janet Altman the "temporal polyvalence" that is often evoked in letters is
crucial to understanding the way messages about events are perceived. These
oscillations are also evident in love letters of migration, as we read in the
writings of Giordano to Ester:

> *Carissima (futura mogliettina)…* when you return, we'll go
> back to the Colosseum and read again the inscription we left
> on that distant day in 1956, do you remember? It was raining,
> and we had walked around the Colosseum 7, 8 times. I was so
> happy every time I saw you, a strange throb stirred inside of
> me. It was the emotion, the feeling of sublime happiness that
> came with seeing you. *Amore mio,* now when I think of you, a
> sharp pain pierces my heart (4 April 1957).

Some of the temporal oscillations that occurred in letter writing were
a function of the social conventions of what Cécile Dauphin calls "temps
épistolaire."[54] And, as David Gerber shows, time consciousness was also
accentuated by the rhythm of the "modern" postal system.[55] Indeed, time
in relation to separation was a source of conversation in the letters. A common complaint was the writers' frustration with time and the slow passage

of time. For example, Sara wrote to Dante: "*caro*, it was exactly three months since the day you left. It feels like yesterday, and an eternity" (c. June1956). In a following letter, she wrote, "today is September 3rd and it has now been 6 months since you left. It feels like 6 centuries, not 6 months. You can just imagine how eagerly I await that blessed day of our departure" (3 September 1956). In anticipation of his family's arrival, Dante wrote, "at this point for you, my dear ones [*miei cari*], the wait is not a question of months, but days. For me, instead it's just as long, and to tell you the truth, I have been calm and patient until now. But now, I don't know why, a day feels like a month" (12 September 1956).

The experience of the slow movement of time is further observed in the correspondence between Clara and Maurizio, in which Clara wrote: "Nearly two months have passed since we left each other, I don't know how you feel about it. Sometimes it feels like I arrived only yesterday. Other times, it feels like I've been here forever. Oh! If only it were so, how much happier I would be if at least two years would be behind me, then there would be less time for me to wait for you" (14 November 1948). Giordano's letters to Ester are another case in point: "*Amore mio*, this evening I felt particularly alone… Oh!! Ester! How I love you!! How much time needs to pass before I can see you again?? Time moves too slowly, and I miss you more and more every day" (19 April 1957). In an attempt to negotiate further the temporal separation between him and Ester, Giordano went to such lengths as to reconfigure the perception of time so that it did not appear so long: "Now, I don't need to think anymore that we have to wait 2 years, but rather 24 months. It feels like less time. Can you wait 24 months? Or is it too much for you?" (24 April 1957).

Many writers also felt constrained by the limitations of the letter as a means to express their true feelings. Giordano wrote: "*tesoro mio*, I love you, I love you, I love you. These words written on paper do not do justice, they cannot demonstrate their true meaning… when I write to you and say the word 'love,' it comes from the depths of my heart, and I say it to you with every breath of my soul!!!" (28 May 1957). Likewise, Clara referred to the difficulties of keeping alive her communication with Maurizio using only pen and paper: "It is certainly a continuous tribulation to be so far apart. It's hard not to be able to express yourself, and allow yourself to be comforted when there is pain. Let's hope it won't be long now" (27 March 1957).

These excerpts demonstrate the challenges that the letter writers experienced first-hand as they each came to terms with the need to channel all of the elements of their love relationship through the medium of prose. Lystra suggests, "By their own reports, their dialogue on paper felt akin to actual conversations. They told each other that love letters reflected the verbal intimacy of being alone together."[56] The following excerpt from a letter from Dante to Sara conveys the point: "I close this poor writing of mine, as I pretend I have been talking to you, one on one" (2 July 1956).

One tactic that helped letter writers overcome the spatial and temporal limitations of letters was simply to postpone a discussion to a later date when they would be together. For instance, in the wake of a possible misunderstanding that originated in a discussion between Sara and Dante, Sara wrote: "it's better to talk about this in person when we'll see each other... talking about it together leads to a better understanding... Don't worry... I will get by anyway" (3 October 1956). By rereading several times Ester's letters, and pretending to be carrying on a conversation with her, Giordano tried to negotiate their limitations and to seek comfort from her presence through them at the same time. Negotiation of distance entailed both writing to Ester: "*Mio caro amore*, here I am again with you. Writing to you is an enormous consolation for me" (16 March 1957); and receiving mail from her: "Dearest Ester, I wait impatiently for Saturday, the day I usually receive mail from you, this is a happy day for me, happy, because I receive news from you, I learn what you're doing, and especially, I hear your beautiful words of love; *Amore mio*, you are my life" (6 September 1957). By reading, writing, and rereading the letters they exchanged, lovers separated as a result of migration negotiated the limitations of letter writing and found some solace in the process.

Finally, what can be observed about the emotional experiences of migrants and their lovers who remained behind? And, what does a comparison of these experiences reveal about the differing state of minds of these individuals? One of the difficulties in answering these questions stems from the complexities of the emotional stories that the letters offer. However, the analysis has revealed subtle differences and similarities between the two experiences.

A number of the letters illustrate some of the emotional experiences of migrants as they left their loved ones in Italy. For instance, Dante wrote to Sara:

Mia cara, I can imagine your pain… yours is enormous, and mine is even deeper. Because you, at least, are surrounded by our people in our lands that we know, and that somehow you can make it through. But I have no one here I can confide in my sorrows, my pains. Even if I am surrounded by good people who care about me, it's never like having you with me, because you understand what I want to say (2 June 1956).

And over two weeks later, Dante wrote:

You see, *mia cara*… I know you understand these things, but only up to a certain point, because despite everything, you have not experienced yet what it means to be out into the world, away from the affections of your dear ones, away from everything. That is not my case. Against my will, I have experienced this already, prior to now and in other circumstances in which I find myself now (18 June 1956).

In the following letter, Clara reflects on the emotional meaning of separation as a result of visiting Montreal's airport. Her reference to death and rebirth in relation to departures and arrivals of loved ones is analogous to an element in letters of romantic love in which the writers "endlessly refer their passions to the occurrence of death—the supreme separation, but also the blessed occasion for an eternal reunion."[57] Clara wrote:

Last night in fact I experienced something I have already lived some time ago. Visiting the air field at Dorval, I can't explain it… the crowds saying goodbye and others greeting those arriving… My eyes watched and my mind reflected. Departures bring sadness, arrivals bring happiness. You and I can relate to this a lot because for three years we have been living this, that is, this feeling of dying and living again and then dying again! The last time was the worst, and the most painful of them all. It was the last one, let's call it that, so that your arrival will be the happiest ever, and then nothing will separate us, because you'll be here forever [*sempre*], never to leave me again, and I will never leave you. I will follow you wherever you go, even to the end of the earth… If you only knew how I watch other couples,

looking carefree as they walk together and smile at each other.
How I envy them (27 May 1949).

The letters of Sara, Maurizio, and Giordano offer insights into the emotional experiences of lovers who were left behind. Sara wrote: "Not even for your birthday, will we be together, I had hoped we would be but I just don't see any other solution… I tell you the sincere truth, it pains me enormously [*sono tanto addolorata*] because time drags on beyond what we had predicted" (c. summer 1956); and in another letter: "I am so worried. I don't sleep any more… try to help me as soon as you can… as I close this letter, I send you my wishes, and I hope that (once in Canada) I will not have these worries any more, as I have them now" (17 August 1956). After having waited for days for news from Dante, Sara wrote: "I see that you have not forgotten these poor souls who live just waiting for news from my beloved husband. Even Paolo and Elisabetta, every day they ask me, 'did we receive any mail from *papà*?'" (6 August 1956).

Maurizio's letters illustrate how he felt when Clara left:

> Clara *mia cara* and beloved… in this moment, fourteen days
> have passed since your departure, or rather from your arrival.
> How fleeting time is. It passes and moves forward in an ironic
> way, and maybe for us, even with joy. The days pass, and sadly,
> a void remains in my heart and in my brain. No measure of
> time can allay it… how much sadness and melancholy this day
> brings to me (6 October 1948).

Giordano's letter describes the effect of revisiting the places he and Ester had been to together in the past. The sadness of these visits is evoked in his letter:

> Tonight I went back to the school's front doors, and I saw you
> again in my imagination. You were standing there waiting for
> me, like that Tuesday of *Carnevale*. Do you remember? Each
> memory I have of you hurts me—not physically but spiritu-
> ally—I saw you in the classroom again where we danced. In
> my mind I heard the music being played again like the day we
> danced to that magical music that touches hearts and unites
> them forever. *Amore*, love me forever (16 March 1957).

The fear of being forgotten was underscored in all three letter series. Giordano's letters voiced this fear in the strongest terms: "you wrote to me begging me not to forget you, but in this case, I am the one begging you not to forget me. As far as I'm concerned, you can enjoy yourself as much as you like, I only ask you not to forget that here in Italy, there is someone who waits for you and lives only for you" (19 March 1957).

For Giordano, the possibility of being forgotten over time by his lover overseas became a reality. The physical and temporal distance between Giordano and Ester eventually became overwhelming and proved fatal to the relationship. Giordano's letter of *Addio* (final farewell) describes his feelings of being left behind as the love relationship with Ester was broken:

> *Mia cara* Ester, this morning I received your letter hoping to find a solution or some way of resolving our situation. I read it at least 10-15 times, but in the end, I was back where I started. I believe the only solution for me is to bury everything deep inside my heart, and carry this weight with me all of my life. The word that hurt me the most in your letter was your final "*Addio.*" As the last word of your painfully sad and agonizing letter, that "*Addio*" struck me like the final blow!! Now, my beloved Ester, my life is without meaning. At one time, I lived with the hope of a better tomorrow, in which I would finally be with the person that I love. Now, there is no tomorrow for me as I have no one! … I want you to know that I don't hold a grudge against you… In the end, you, like me, need affection. The only difference is that you succeeded in finding someone to share this affection with, and I instead, don't know if I ever will… *Cara* Ester, I have nothing else to say, or rather I could keep writing but it doesn't matter anymore!! I beg you to be there when I'll be back next week. Remember that you would be hurting me even more if you decided not to show up… *Carissima*… see you soon… even if we will be apart and leading separate lives, we can still meet again one day (18 August 1960).

In my attempt to make sense of the emotions revealed in these letters, it became increasingly clear that the differences in emotional experiences between migrants and loved ones were extremely subtle, if they existed at all. Both perspectives strongly resonated with pleas not to be forgotten, the loneliness and nostalgia for one's distant lover and the envy of other couples who appeared happy together in public. Inevitably, individuals experienced the reality of separation differently because of their particular psychological makeup. But it also seems clear that different writers' responses were strongly shaped by their personal situations as migrants and loved ones, and by the kind of support they received from kin. Significantly, despite the obvious differences in their contexts, the findings of the analysis suggest that there were strong similarities between the emotional experiences of migrants and the loved ones they left behind.

Finally, the study shows that the use of letters as tools of communication was not gender-specific. As Lystra observes in her study of love letters, "both sexes energetically articulated their emotional ties with each other."[58] Indeed, in contrast to the classic image of the woman as the letter writer, especially where the affective expression of love and other emotions was concerned, this study illustrates that men and women were equally articulate in reaching out to their loved ones and conveying emotions on paper. These findings bear out Gerber's warning that "there can be no easy generalizations about gender and the expression of emotions in immigrant epistolarity."[59]

Emotions in letters of migration are heterogeneous, multi-faceted, and complex. This analysis points to the finding that letters of Italian migrants and loved ones "whether the result of a long epistolary exchange or the beginning of it, reveal the energy that forges the links together."[60] The letters exchanged between lovers and kin describe at an intimate level the writers' constant efforts to negotiate separation, whether temporary or permanent, and to build bridges across borders. The emotions in the letters also functioned as forces of agency, soul-sustaining and world-making to the correspondents involved. The emotions expressed in letters of migration were part of an intense "epistolary conversation," a *complicité*[61] shared between correspondents who wrote to each other to keep their connection alive.

Emotions in the letters exchanged between lovers, parents, and children served a vital purpose, corresponding to the experience of two lifelong friends, described by David Gerber in *Authors of Their Lives* as one of their "strongest ties to life."[62] In the context of postwar migration, the letter served as the most important form of communication between migrants and loved ones, and was key to maintaining emotional bonds.

Finally, letters emanated from and circulated in a world of their own, separate from the rationalities and realities experienced by letter writers in their everyday lives. Bruce Redford observes that the practice of letter writing and letters themselves created "a distinctive world at once internally consistent, vital, and self-supporting."[63] As we imagine Sara writing to her husband in the early morning hours or late at night while the children were asleep, we also imagine what she was saying, in effect, to him: that she had entered into another world which allowed her to reach into the depths of her soul and communicate her innermost *pensiero*. For her, as for many correspondents, the paper on which letters were written was a unique space with its own language and its own silences.

A family working together in the fields, Ripabottoni, Italy, 1953

CONCLUSION

THIS BOOK TELLS THE HUMAN STORY of migration perceived through the pulsating current of thoughts, norms, and intimacies inscribed in personal correspondence. The letters of those who emigrated in concert with those of loved ones who remained behind compel us to listen to their stories. They ask us to reflect on the preoccupations, emotions, and viewpoints expressed and experienced by migrants and their loved ones writing from both sides of the ocean.

The correspondence highlighted in this book shows that writers were equally impacted by their own and their loved ones' migration to Canada. For those who stayed behind in Italy, that translated into an empty plate at the dinner table, where they would reminisce about the absent migrant with family and old friends, and, more poignantly, where they would write—often long letters to the migrant in the search of much-needed solace and reassurance. Likewise, these letters remind us of migrants' efforts to make do with new surroundings, new friends, and a new life among new-found relatives. They recorded these initial steps to feeling at home in Canada while writing to their loved ones, expressing their nostalgia for them and their homeland.

Although migration to Canada was motivated by hope and economic opportunity, the process of negotiating travel arrangements, adjusting to new conditions, and coping with separation placed extraordinary demands on people. While the nature of those demands and the means by which migrants attempted to meet them in their own words and their own voices have been described by other scholars, *Families, Lovers, and their Letters* gives an intense emotional voice to both the migrants themselves and to the family members and lovers who remained behind. Through a series of collections that captures two sides of the correspondence, the study shows the kind of personal, and familial worries, changes and overall dynamics that migration entailed for individuals and families writing from both sides of the Atlantic Ocean. The resilience with which these letter writers stayed in touch and remained connected perhaps strikes us today as remarkable, given the availability of instantaneous digital communication technologies that we have become accustomed to recently. However, long before the days of cellphones and satellite videos, people found effective and creative ways to be "present to each other" while absent. Through the written word and the postal system, their news and concerns, coupled with their emotions, imagination and literary agility became increasingly accessible as they strove to reach out to each other as a result of their separation in international migration.

In my analysis I have endeavoured, in the words of Bruno Ramirez, "to reach the past in its raw nature—one that grows from the complexity, confusion, and muddiness of everyday life, where human sentiments in all their varieties interact to produce events that carry a story."[1] At one level, the correspondence is especially revealing about the salience of kinship in the lives of postwar Italians and the multiple ways in which kinship networks were sustained through and because of migration. The flow of people back and forth across the Atlantic in the postwar period was also characterized by communication movements as news, advice, and objects travelled along an invisible, electric current that transferred feelings, perceptions, and norms across space and time. Because the migration project was family-centred in its overall goals, kinship networks provided vital functions of support while attempting to exercise social control. The letters I examined are replete with advice and encouragement, reminders of social and gender roles, and warnings about duties and obligations, including the need to stay in touch, that had to be fulfilled.

Within the broad spectrum of kinship, however, the letters demonstrate the circulation of gender norms. In this case, the letters crystallize the extent to which both the expectations and the experiences of migration were different for women and men. The authors of the correspondence inhabited a deeply gendered universe in postwar Italian society that made distinctions between the public and the private, as well as the productive and reproductive spheres that were considered appropriate for women and men. As the ruptures caused by migration became increasingly evident to the actors involved, gender norms and roles were invariably reified and reinforced as a defence mechanism against change.

In some respects, however, the most disruptive effect of migration was its impact on the emotions of migrants and loved ones who experienced the changes first-hand. In recent years, scholars have illustrated the involvement of women and men facing complex realities of migration and negotiating them through individual, social, and collective strategies, whether as migrants or loved ones who remained behind. To this approach, I have added the analysis of emotions through intimate letters shared between parents and children, and between lovers. The intensity with which the words of despair, love, frustration, and dreams were expressed in the letters allows us to appreciate traits of humanity that are rarely accessible to historical observation. Throughout the correspondence, I found unmistakable evidence in the many expressions of affection and love, of the letter writers' desires to bridge the realities of separation and to stay connected emotionally. By drawing on letters that were never intended for public consumption but were written instead from the hearts and minds of individuals wrestling with major life events, this analysis throws light on the emotional intensity with which migration was felt.

Through these letter collections, we have intercepted voices that offer more than an "unusual look into a broad spectrum of lives... that speak directly to us out of the past."[2] The letters reveal a cultural language of practices and relationships sustained through separation and migration. Read from our perspective, the letters crystallize the narratives of personal and emotional realities and fantasies, desires and dilemmas, concerns and joys, juxtaposed by hopes and fears, woes of despair, and visions of dreams. Postwar modernity and the acceleration of communication technologies coupled with increasing levels of education in Italy and Canada contributed to the proliferation of the letter as a reliable, sustainable source of communication between loved ones living apart in the postal age. Despite the sporadic frustration of letter writers concerning problems with the occasional postal delays or lost deliveries, the letter served as a crucial metaphorical bridge that crossed physical and symbolic "highways" and borders over lands and oceans for loved ones to stay connected. The impact of this kind of document on the personal and the everyday of these actors' lives is unquestionable. As Dante del Moro put it in a letter to his wife, Sara on 12 October 1956, "I received your letters, one day after the other, in the first, your news brought me relief, in the second, you took it away twice, this is to tell you how badly I felt. To you, the person who knows me more than anyone else, I can say that this time the tears flowed incessantly, I don't know what else to say."

The letters written and received by migrants and their loved ones were vital conversations spanning across enormous temporal and spatial distances between individuals and families writing during postwar Canada and Italy. Because of the scale of Italian migration to Canada in the postwar period, it is often tempting to interpret the phenomenon from a macro perspective that focuses on the collective experiences of different cohorts. Without discounting the value of such studies, we must remember that migration was experienced first and foremost by individuals and families, and that it had personal faces and individual voices.

In this book, the themes of separation and reunification through the world-making and intimate spaces invoked in the letters are inextricably linked to the practice of letter writing activated through migration. Letters exchanged in a process of migration created transnational connections that were maintained and sustained both materially and emotionally over time and space through the everyday language of communication—well before our own global times.

The relationship between the life of the letters' material and the symbolic meanings embossed in the letters for the writers, their descendants, and their archivists further underscores the intersections between what is remembered and what was written, what is silenced and what is revealed both in the present and in the past. The juxtaposition of these two sources raises a myriad of questions from a plethora of perspectives as much for the letters' content and hidden meanings, as for the life of the letters themselves and their writers and family archivists. More research is needed in the field, especially in relation to the historical and cultural meanings of migration letters as sites of memory, emotions, and subjectivities. By interweaving these themes, the exploration of oral and written life stories in connection to their authors and their archivists would illustrate more in depth the reconstruction of a diversity of migration experiences in their own terms.

In situations of separation of loved ones, letter writing was a highly valued means of staying in touch, no matter the distance that separated them. It also required letter writers and family members around them to respond quickly to letters of kin and other loved ones. In situations of family reunification, and especially over a longer time span, letter writing was transformed into a less urgent activity for individuals, dwindling almost to non-existent in some households, while still thriving in others. A number of epistolary stories included in *Families, Lovers, and their Letters* reveal that several immediate family members were reunited through their subsequent migrations to Canada. This inevitably resulted in an interruption or a halting in correspondence between these individuals. However, reunification with immediate family members did not arrest the practice of letter writing altogether in these households. As in many families, a number of extended family members had remained in Italy and others settled among the diaspora disseminated to other corners of the world. In this case, the practice of letter writing continued. In situations where reunification did not follow, the early stages of urgently bridging separation through letter writing were replaced by a more resigned pace in correspondence. Still, letter writing persisted into the 1980s and 1990s, even once the technology of the telephone became affordable in both Italian and Canadian households. The collections of Clara Renzi and Maurizio Trevisan and of Luciano Colonello and Marianna Domenica, for instance, include a number of letters written in the last decades of the twentieth century, where it would appear that telecommunications technology was quickly replacing the ancient practice of letter writing.

Available letters from these years suggest that letter writing is in fact a resilient and viable means of communication. Not only is it still commonly in use in the twenty-first century through its continued practice by individuals of Italian origin and other ethnic groups separated through global migration movements, it is ensuring its survivability by means of preservation and access, made possible by the letter writers themselves and their descendants privately archiving the letters in their own homes.

Why some people save some letters—ranging from one to over one hundred—and have safely stored them for years, while others have allowed them to vanish minutes after receiving them is a difficult—perhaps impossible—question to answer. Undoubtedly, much depends on a constellation of emotional and social dynamics and on the personal experiences of the letter writers themselves and their families. The need to safeguard letters can be as much a pragmatic decision as an intensely personal and emotional one, much of it depending on the meanings that the content and context of the letters hold, including issues related to identity and relationships, the symbolic significance of the letters in relation to the language of expression and the silences in between, the link between a letter and a personal life story, and the infusion or absence of memories that the letters conjure up.

For Anita Losanto, daughter of Domenico Losanto and Lucia Valessi, the letters she inherited from her father are treasures from a past that is no longer recoverable—a difficult past, nonetheless, as she recalls her father, towards the end of his life, reluctantly coming to terms with the reality that it was no longer possible for him to contemplate returning to his home in Italy—the home that had been the destination of his earnings for years while he lived in Canada. For Maddalena Franchi, the letters represent a place and time in her life when they kept her company from the sways of loneliness and melancholy. For Gianlorenzo Colonello, whose parents are no longer living, the letters that he rereads from time to time symbolize both his youth and his desire for adventure in Canada and memories of his parents' presence in his life. For Clara Renzi, who finds herself rereading on occasion the letters that she and Maurizio had exchanged over sixty years ago, the letters offer her a place of solace, nostalgia, and reflection enabling her mind to wander to a coveted, yet distant past. For Ester's husband, the letters are symbolic of the woman that he loved and lost recently. For Paolo del Moro, the letters he has preserved offer a looking glass into his childhood and the romantic love shared between his mother and father. The meanings for archiving these documents are multiple and complex even as we attempt to give an explanation for their safe storage.

NOTES

Introduction

1   Oral interview with Gianlorenzo Colonello, 17 August 2009.

2   The expression, "loved ones," is borrowed from Robert F. Harney, "Men without Women: Italian Migrants in Canada, 1885–1930," *The Italian Immigrant Woman in North America*, ed., Betty Boyd Caroli, Robert F. Harney, and Lydio F. Tomasi (Toronto: Multicultural History Society of Ontario, 1978), 79–102. Throughout the book, all excerpts of the letters have been transcribed and translated as per the original texts. All translations from Italian to English of the letter quotations are mine. To preserve the confidentiality of the letter writers and the family archivists in possession of the letters, I have changed all the names to pseudonyms. In some cases, I have also changed other identifying information. In the book, references to "loved ones," "dear ones," and "significant others" are used interchangeably. In a general sense, the terms mean individuals within kin and non-kin networks to which individuals feel affectionately close. In a context of specific relationships, "loved ones" is used to mean intergenerational relationships, such as between parents and children, and other relationships within kin networks, such as relationships between siblings, aunts, uncles, nieces and nephews, grandparents and grandchildren, and cousins. In contrast, the term "lovers" is specifically used to mean relationships between husband and wife, fiancé and fiancée, and courting couples.

3   David A. Gerber, *Authors of Their Lives: The Personal Correspondence of British Immigrants to North America in the Nineteenth Century* (New York: New York University Press, 2006); Bruce S. Elliott, David A. Gerber, and Suzanne M. Sinke, ed., *Letters across Borders: The Epistolary Practices of International Migrants* (New York: Palgrave, 2006); and Yves Frenette, Marcel Martel, and John Willis, ed., *Envoyer et recevoir. Lettres et correspondances dans les diasporas francophones* (Québec: les Presses de l'Université Laval, 2006).

4   A careful reading of the letters reveals that these letters were read and shared among family members when they were addressed to family or about family concerns,

152   *Families, Lovers, and their Letters*

depending on the level of trust between family members. Conversely, in the case of letters exchanged between lovers, it is highly improbable that correspondents shared their correspondence publicly with others—unless they felt they could confide in a third party. On the question of private and public letters, historian Dirk Hoerder writes, "In the old country, letters might be passed from hand to hand among neighbours in a village, shtetl, or urban neighbourhood; they might be read to the neighbours in a local tavern. The audience was not anonymous, it was people the writer knew. 'Public letters' written by men from the immigrant intelligentsia, such as priests or teachers, for newspapers back home resemble information brochures and guidebooks more than personal correspondence." Dirk Hoerder, *Creating Societies: Immigrant Lives in Canada* (Montreal and Kingston: McGill-Queen's University Press, 1999), 19. Moreover, if the writing and reading of letters was shared among family members, it is likely that the expression and content of intimacy was restricted. On this point, see especially Yves Frenette and Gabriele P. Scardellato, "The Immigrant Experience and the Creation of a Transatlantic Epistolary Space," in *More than Words: Readings in Transport, Communication and the History of Postal Communication*, ed. John Willis (Ottawa: Canadian Museum of Civilization, 2007), 197.

5   To my knowledge, Robert F. Harney is the first Canadian historian to acknowledge the importance of studying migration through the first-hand experiences and words of migrants themselves. For reference to the US and European historiography, see especially Marcus Lee Hansen, *The Atlantic Migration, 1607–1860: A History of the Continuing Settlement of the United States* (Cambridge, MA: Harvard University Press, 1940); Charlotte Erickson, *Invisible Immigrants: Adaptation of English and Scottish Immigrants in Nineteenth-century America* (Coral Gables, FL.: University of Miami Press, 1972); and Walter D. Kamphoefner, Wolfgang Helbich and Ulrike Sommer, *News From the Land of Freedom: German Immigrants Write Home* (Ithaca, NY: Cornell University Press, 1991).

6   Sonia Cancian, "Una raccolta di lettere italiane inviate agli emigrati in Canada, 1954–1955" (MA thesis, McGill University, 1999).

7   The terms "transnational households" and "transnational families" are used interchangeably in this book to mean, "families whose core members are located in at least two nation-states." See Rhacel S. Parreñas, *Servants of Globalization: Women, Migration, and Domestic Work* (Stanford: Stanford University Press, 2001).

8   Of the more relevant studies, consider Marcus Lee Hansen, "Migrations: Old and New," in *The Immigrant in American History*, ed. Marcus Lee Hansen (Cambridge, MA: Harvard University Press, 1940), 3-29. For a concise history of the Minnesota School, see Donna R. Gabaccia, "The Minnesota School and Immigration and Refugee Studies," http://www.ihrc.umn.edu/publications/pdf/MinnesotaSchool-1.pdf.

9   Gerber, *Authors of Their Lives*, 40.

10   Ibid., 41.

11   Ibid., 11.

12 Gerber, *Authors of Their Lives*; and David Fitzpatrick, *Oceans of Consolation: Personal Accounts of Irish Migration to Australia* (Ithaca: Cornell University Press, 1994), vii. In this study, Fitzpatrick provides a three-fold "bottom-up" approach that includes complete transcriptions of the letters, detailed commentaries on the texts and a thematic historical analysis of the daily preoccupations of migrants and their kin in both Ireland and Australia. Other works that adopt this innovative approach to letters written in a context of migration include Kerby A. Miller, *Emigrants and Exiles: Ireland and the Irish Exodus to North America* (New York and Oxford: Oxford University Press, 1985); Dirk Hoerder and Horst Rössler, ed. *Distant Magnets: Expectations and Realities in the Immigrant Experience, 1840–1930* (New York and London: Holmes and Meier, 1993); Kamphoefner, Helbich and Sommer, ed. *News from the Land of Freedom;* Dirk Hoerder, *Creating Societies;* and from a literary perspective, Stephen Fender, *Sea Changes: British Emigration and American Literature* (Cambridge: Cambridge University Press, 1992).

13 See also the collaborative contribution by Yves Frenette, Bianca Gendreau, Gabriele P. Scardellato and John Willis, "L'expérience immigrante et la création d'un espace épistolaire: une étude de cas," *Prendre la route. L'expérience migratoire en Europe et en Amérique du Nord du XIVe au XXe siècle,* ed. Andrée Courtemanche and Martin Paquet (Hull: Vents d'Ouest), 172–193; and Willis, ed., *More Than Words.*

14 Bruce S. Elliott, David A. Gerber, Suzanne M. Sinke, "Introduction," *Letters across Borders,* ed. Elliott, Gerber, and Sinke, 4.

15 Beginning in 1960 with Frank Thistlethwaite, "Migration from Europe Overseas in the Nineteenth and Twentieth Centuries" (1960), reprinted in *A Century of European Migrations, 1830–1930,* ed. Rudolph J. Vecoli and Suzanne M. Sinke (Urbana and Chicago: University of Illinois Press, 1991), 22.

16 A number of important works that examine narratives of those who remained behind within a process of migration include Fortunata Piselli, *Parentela ed emigrazione. Mutamenti e continuità in una comunità calabrese* (Turin: Einaudi, 1981); Vito Teti, "Note sui comportamenti delle donne sole degli americani durante la 1a emigrazione in Calabria," *Studi Emigrazione/Etudes Migrations* 24 (1987):13–46; Bruno Ramirez, *On the Move: French-Canadian and Italian Migrants in the North Atlantic Economy, 1860–1914* (Toronto: McClelland and Stewart, 1991); Linda Reeder, *Widows in White: Migration and the Transformation of Rural Italian Women, Sicily, 1880–1920* (Toronto: University of Toronto Press, 2003); Rhacel Salazar Parreñas, *Servants of Globalization;* Bruna Bianchi, "Lavoro ed emigrazione femminile (1880–1915)," *Storia dell'emigrazione italiana,* ed. Piero Bevilacqua, Andreina De Clementi and Emilio Franzina (Rome: Donzelli editore, 2001), 257–274; Franca Iacovetta and Donna R. Gabaccia, ed. *Women, Gender, and Transnational Lives: Italian Workers of the World* (Toronto: University of Toronto Press, 2002); Caroline Brettell, *Men who Migrate, Women who Wait: Population and History in a Portuguese Parish* (Princeton: Princeton University Press, 1986); Sally Cole, *Women of the Praia: Work and Lives in a Portuguese Coastal Community* (Princeton: Princeton University Press, 1991); and for a global perspective, see Donna R. Gabaccia, *Italy's Many Diasporas* (Seattle: University of Washington Press, 2000). Among the handful of works that include letters from the homeland are: David A. Gerber, *Authors of Their Lives;* David Fitzpatrick, *Oceans of*

Consolation; Samuel L. Baily and Franco Ramella, ed. *One Family, Two Worlds: An Italian Family's Correspondence across the Atlantic, 1901-1922* (New Brunswick and London: Rutgers University Press, 1988); and Judith Beattie and Helen Buss, ed. *Undelivered Letters to Hudson's Bay Company Men on the Northwest Coast of America, 1830–57* (Vancouver and Toronto: University of British Columbia, 2003). While Beattie and Buss (2003) is based on the undelivered correspondence sent to the Hudson's Bay workers in North America, it nonetheless provides a window into the mental and social worlds of the individuals and families who remained in their homeland. Consider also, Andrey Pyée, "'Mon Révérend Père, [...] Je m'inquiète pour mon fils.' Relations familiales transnationales et épistolaires," in *Envoyer et recevoir*, ed. Frenette, Martel, and Willis, 201–226.

17   In fact, a good number of studies that examine migration through personal letters draw primarily from immigrants' letters. See especially, Theodore C. Blegen, *Land of their Choice. The Immigrants Write Home* (St. Paul, MN.: University of Minnesota Press, 1955); Alan Conway, ed. *The Welsh in America. Letters from the Immigrants* (St. Paul, MN.: University of Minnesota Press, 1961); Erickson, *Invisible Immigrants*; Arnold Barton, *Letters from the Promised Land. Swedes in America, 1840-1914* (Minneapolis, MN: University of Minnesota Press, 1975); Frederick Hale, ed. *Danes in North America* (Seattle and London: University of Washington Press, 1984); Josephine Wtulich et al., ed. *Writing Home: Immigrants in Brazil and the United States, 1890-1891* (New York: Columbia University Press, 1986); Cecil Houston and William Smyth, *Irish Emigration and Canadian Settlement: Patterns, Links, and Letters* (Toronto: University of Toronto Press, 1990); Kamphoefner, Helbich, and Sommer, ed. *News from the Land of Freedom Home*; Herbert Brinks, ed. *Dutch American Voices: Letters from the United States, 1850-1930* (Ithaca and London: Cornell University Press, 1995); Kathleen Anne De Haan, "'He looks like a Yankee in his new suit.' Immigrant Rhetoric: Dutch Immigrant Letters as Forums for Shifting Immigrant Identities," (PhD diss., Northwestern University, 1998); Patrick O'Farrell, *Letters from Irish Australia, 1825–1929* (1984), Donald H. Akenson, *Half the World from Home: Perspectives on the Irish in New Zealand, 1860-1950* (1990); Kerby Miller, Arnold Schrier, Bruce Boling, and David Doyle, *Irish Immigrants in the Land of Canaan: Letters and Memoirs from Colonial and Revolutionary America, 1675--1815* (2003); and Wendy Cameron, Sheila Haines and Mary M. Maude, ed. *English Immigrant Voices: Labourers' Letters from Upper Canada in the 1830s* (Montreal and Kingston: McGill-Queen's University Press, 2000). For a critical assessment on the uses of the immigrant letter in historical studies, see especially the following articles by David A. Gerber: "The Immigrant Letter between Positivism and Populism: the Uses of Immigrant Personal Correspondence in Twentieth-Century American Scholarship," *Journal of American Ethnic History* 16, 4 (1997): 3–34; "Epistolary Ethics: Personal Correspondence and the Culture of Emigration in the Nineteenth Century," *Journal of American Ethnic History* 19 (Summer 2000): 3–23; "Forming a Transnational Narrative: New Perspectives on European Migrations to the United States," *The History Teacher* 35, 1 (Nov. 2001): 61–78; "What is it we seek to find in first-person documents? Documenting Society and Cultural Practices in Irish Immigrant Writings," *Reviews in American History* 32 (2004): 305-316; and "Acts of Deceiving and Withholding in Immigrant Letters: Personal Identity and Self-

presentation in Personal Correspondence," *Journal of Social History* 39.2 (Winter 2005): 315-330. See also, Matteo Sanfilippo, "Un'occasione mancata? A proposito di un libro di David A. Gerber sulle lettere degli emigranti—A Missed Chance? A Book about the Letters from Migrants by David A. Gerber," *Studi Emigrazione/ Migration Studies*, 170 (2008): 475-488. Aside from the availability of sources, another reason is likely due to the predominant emphasis by historians suggesting that the immigration experience is best embodied on privileging immigrants themselves rather than those who were left behind. The general consensus among migration scholars was that letters of those who remained behind would, as historian George Stephenson observes, "betray the spirit, hopes, and aspirations of the humble folk who tilled the soil, felled the forest, and tended the loom." Gerber, "What is it we seek to find in first-person documents?", 308.

18   Gerber, "What is it we seek to find in first-person documents?",308.

19   Fitzpatrick, *Oceans of Consolation*, vii–viii.

20   As Dirk Hoerder accurately observes, "most letter collections provide one side of a story only: in an age of handwriting, few writers made copies of their own letters but kept those received." Hoerder, *Creating Societies*, 18. See also Yves Frenette and Gabriele P. Scardellato, "The Immigrant Experience and the Creation of a Transatlantic Epistolary Space," in Willis, *More than Words*.

21   Clifford Geertz, "Thick Description: Toward an Interpretive Theory of Culture," *The Interpretation of Cultures*, Clifford Geertz (New York: Basic Books, 1973), 3–30.

22   Personal communication with Bruno Ramirez, August 2006.

23   The term "wire" is used by Bruno Ramirez as a metaphor in reference to an invisible, yet indelible cable of communication through which emotions, energies, private reflections and confidences of correspondents flowed throughout the intense and frequent epistolary communication across borders. Bruno Ramirez, personal communication, August 2006.

24   Recent Italian migration studies to Canada include, Bruno Ramirez, *Les premiers italiens de Montréal: L'origine de la Petite Italie du Québec* (Montreal: Boréal Express, 1984); Bruno Ramirez and Michael Del Balso, *The Italians of Montreal: From Sojourning to Settlement, 1900-1921* (Montreal: Les Éditions du Courant, 1980); Franca Iacovetta, *Such Hardworking People: Italian Immigrants in Postwar Toronto* (Montreal and Kingston: McGill-Queen's University Press, 1992); Franc Sturino, *Forging the Chain: Italian Migration to North America, 1880–1930* (Toronto: Multicultural History Society of Ontario, 1990); John E. Zucchi, *Italians in Toronto: Development of a National Identity, 1875-1935* (Montreal and Kingston: McGill-Queen's University Press, 1988); Matteo Sanfilippo, *Problemi di storiografia dell'emigrazione italiana* (Viterbo, Italy: Sette Città, 2002); and by Robert F. Harney, see especially, *If One Were to Write a History... Selected Writings by Robert F. Harney*, ed. Pierre Anctil and Bruno Ramirez (Toronto: Multicultural History Society of Ontario, 1991), and Harney's "Men without Women."

25   Hoerder, *Creating Societies*, 18.

26   Nicole Constable, *Romance on a Global Stage: Pen Pals, Virtual Ethnography, and 'Mail Order' Marriages* (Berkeley: California University Press, 2003), 14–15.

27 Fabio Caffarena, *Lettere dalla Grande Guerra: Scritture del quotidiano, monumenti della memoria, fonti per la storia. Il caso italiano* (Milano: Edizioni Unicopli, 2005) 17.

28 Ibid., 19.

29 Cécile Dauphin and Danièle Poublan, "S'Écrire au XIXe siècle en France: Histoire d'une acculturation," in Willis, *More than Words*, 160. See also, Liz Stanley,"The Epistolarium: On Theorizing Letters and Correspondences," *Auto/Biography* 12 (2004): 201-235.

30 See Martha Hanna, *Your Death Would be Mine: Paul and Marie Pireaud in the Great War* (Cambridge, MA and London: Harvard University Press, 2006).

31 Caffarena, *Lettere dalla Grande Guerra*, 20. Cited from L. Sepúlveda, *Raccontare, resistere. Conversazioni con Bruno Arpaia* (Parma, Italy: Guanda, 2002), 42.

32 Antonio Gibelli, *L'officina della Guerra: La Grande Guerra e le trasformazioni del mondo mentale* (Torino: Bollati Boringhieri editore, 1998), 55.

33 Ibid., 55.

34 Gerber, *Authors of Their Lives*, 2.

35 Ibid., 2.

36 Ibid., 28.

Chapter One

1 Paul Ginsborg, *A History of Contemporary Italy: Society and Politics 1943-1988* (London: Penguin, 1990); Tony Judt, *Postwar: A History of Europe Since 1945* (London: Penguin 2005); Anna Maria Torriglia, *Broken Time, Fragmented Space: A Cultural Map for Postwar Italy* (Toronto: University of Toronto Press, 2002); Christopher Duggan and Christopher Wagstaff, ed., *Italy in the Cold War: Politics, Culture and Society 1948-58* (Oxford and Washington, DC: Berg, 1995); Patrick McCarthy, ed., *Italy since 1945* (Oxford: Oxford University Press, 2000).

2 Ginsborg, *Contemporary Italy*, 122.

3 Ibid., 122.

4 Stefano Gensini, *Elementi di storia linguistica italiana* (Bergamo: Minerva Italica, 1990), 424.

5 Ginsborg, *Contemporary Italy*, 129-137.

6 Historian Franc Sturino estimates that in the first phase of Italian mass migration to Canada between 1900 and World War I, 119,770 migrants were documented as having entered the country. In the years between 1950 and 1970, 514,000 Italians arrived to Canada. Franc Sturino, "Italians," *Encyclopedia of Canada's People*, ed. Paul Robert Magosci (Toronto: University of Toronto Press, 1999), 789. The number is slightly higher than the figure indicated in the frequently cited Italian statistics (440,000) based on departing numbers for the period from 1946 to 1976, referred to in Luigi Favero and Graziano Tassello, "Cent'anni di emigrazione

italiana (1876–1976)," *Un secolo di emigrazione italiana 1876–1976*, ed. Gianfausto Rosoli (Rome: Centro Studi Emigrazione, 1976), 9–64.

7   Franca Iacovetta, *Such Hardworking People*, 48. See also Franca Iacovetta, "Ordering in Bulk: Canada's Postwar Immigration Policy and the Recruitment of Contract Workers from Italy," *Journal of American Ethnic History* 11, 1 (Fall 1991): 50–81.

8   William Lyon Mackenzie King, "Canada's Postwar Immigration Policy," House of Commons Debates, 1 May 1947, in *Immigration and the Rise of Multiculturalism*, ed. Howard Palmer (Toronto: Copp Clark, 1975), 58.

9   Donald H. Avery, *Reluctant Host: Canada's Response to Immigrant Workers, 1896–1994* (Toronto: McClelland and Stewart, 1995), 167. On the Canadian government's role in shaping immigrants' lives in the postwar years, consider Franca Iacovetta, *Gatekeepers: Reshaping Immigrant Lives in Cold War Canada* (Toronto: Between the Lines, 2006).

10 Kenneth McNaught, *The Pelican History of Canada* (Middlesex and Baltimore: Penguin Books, 1969), 272.

11 Alvin Finkel and Margaret Conrad, *History of the Canadian Peoples: 1867 to the Present*, 2nd ed. (Toronto: Copp Clark, 1998), 385. On Montreal families in the postwar period, see Magda Fahrni, *Household Politics: Montreal Families and Postwar Reconstruction* (Toronto: University of Toronto Press, 2005).

12 A recent historical overview of Italian migration to Canada is offered in Sonia Cancian and Bruno Ramirez, "Post-migration 'Italo-Canada': New Perspectives on its Past, Present, and Future," *Studi Emigrazione/Migration Studies* 170 (2007): 259–272. For a discussion on links between labour activity and kin networks within Italian migration families in Canada and Italy across borders in the postwar period, see Sonia Cancian, "Intersecting labour and social networks across cities and borders," *Studi Emigrazione/Migration Studies* 166 (2007): 313–326.

13 King, "Canada's Postwar Immigration Policy," 60.

14 Ibid., 60.

15 Ibid.

16 Ibid., 61.

17 Robert F. Harney, "'So Great a Heritage as Ours' Immigration and the Survival of the Canadian Polity," in *If One Were to Write a History... Selected Writings by Robert F. Harney*, ed. Anctil and Ramirez, 232.

18 Freda Hawkins, *Canada and Immigration: Public Policy and Public Concern* (Kingston and Montreal: McGill-Queen's University Press, 1988), 90.

19 Alan G. Green, *Immigration and the Postwar Canadian Economy* (Toronto: Macmillan, 1976), 22–24.

20 Bruno Ramirez, personal communication, August 2006.

21 Iacovetta, *Such Hardworking People*, 48.

22 Ibid.

23   Bruno Ramirez, "Canada's Immigration and Policy-making of the 19th and 20th Centuries: From Empire to Globalisation," published as "La immigration y la politica inmigratoria en Canada en los siglos XIX y XX: del imperio a la globalizacion," *Estudios migratorios latinoamericanos* 18 (Abril 2004): 43–74 (unpublished English manuscript, 21).

24   Ramirez, "Canada's Immigration and Policy-making," unpublished manuscript, 21.

25   On the theme of the economic implications for French-Canadian immigrant families in New England, see especially Tamara K. Hareven, *Family Time and Industrial Time* (Cambridge, UK: Cambridge University Press, 1982); Bruno Ramirez, *On the Move: French-Canadian and Italian Migrants in the North Atlantic Economy, 1860–1914* (Toronto: McClelland and Stewart, 1991); and Yukari Takai, *Gendered Passages: French-Canadian Migration to Lowell, Massachusetts, 1900–1920* (New York: Peter Lang, 2008). For a related study involving letters, see Magda Fahrni and Yves Frenette, " 'Don't I long for Montreal': L'identité hybride d'une migrante franco-américaine pendant la première Guerre Mondiale." *Histoire sociale/Social History* 41.81 (May 2008): 75-98. Concerning immigrants from multiple ethnic groups in Canada, see especially Hoerder, *Creating Societies*.

26   In this book, all names of the married women writers reflect pseudonyms acquired at birth, rather than names acquired at marriage.

27   The farm fields of the Molise region were "marked by a harsh topography that bore the brunt of massive deforestation and whose vast land surfaces were constantly vulnerable to rock slides. Under these conditions, soil improvement was a daunting enterprise—when at all possible." Bruno Ramirez, *Les premiers Italiens de Montréal*, 26.

28   Oral interviews and conversations with Marco Colledani, March 2003, and Irene Motta, January 2007.

29   The Church Madonna della Difesa was erected in 1911. It was the first Italian church to be built in large part with the financial support of the Italian community in Montreal. For further details on the founding of the Church Madonna della Difesa in Montreal's Mile End, refer to Ramirez, *Les premiers Italiens* (1984) and Guglielmo Vangelisti, *Gli Italiani in Canada* (Montreal: 1956).

30   Oral interviews and conversations with Maurizio Trevisan and Clara Renzi, June 2003, February 2004, April 2004, and April 2007.

31   *Friulani* means natives of the Friuli region in Italy, and *Trevisano* means a man from the Treviso area in the Veneto region.

32   Mauro Peressini, *Migration, Famille et Communauté: Les Italiens du Frioul à Montréal 1945–1980* (Montreal: Université de Montréal, 1990), 45.

33   Oral interviews and conversations with Gianlorenzo Colonello and Elsa Contini, December 2004, November 2005, December 2006, and January 2007.

34   Clara Renzi is referring here to an immigration regulation that had recently come into effect at the time and that provided conditions upon which a fiancé or fiancée could be sponsored for immigrating to Canada. One of these conditions stipulated that the marriage of the couple take place within a short period of time.

Chapter Two

1 Gayle Rubin, "The Traffic in Women: Notes on the 'Political Economy' of Sex," *Toward an Anthropology of Women*, ed. Rayna R. Reiter (New York and London: Monthly Review Press, 1975), 170.

2 Ibid., 177.

3 The term "personal courier" is borrowed from Gerber, *Authors of Their Lives*, and means "travelling friends and willing passersby who were headed toward the right destination" (146). In my analysis, the expression includes kin and acquaintances of migrants and loved ones in both sending and receiving societies who delivered in person their letters, objects and/or greetings because they were headed toward the same or close to the personal courier's original destination.

4 Hareven, *Family Time and Industrial Time*, 4.

5 Micaela Di Leonardo, *The Varieties of Ethnic Experience: Kinship, Class, and Gender among California Italian-Americans* (Ithaca and London: Cornell University Press, 1984).

6 Colleen Leahy Johnson, *Growing Up and Growing Old in Italian-American Families* (New Brunswick, NJ: Rutgers University Press, 1985). While Johnson's study does not examine Italian families and kinship engaged in the early stages of a migration process, it nonetheless examines family life of first- and second-generation Italian-American families.

7 Piselli, *Parentela ed Emigrazione*.

8 Consider, for instance, Robert F. Harney's essays in the collection *If One Were to Write a History... Selected Writings by Robert F. Harney*, ed. Ramirez and Anctil, 19–36; and Harney, "Men Without Women."

9 Gabaccia identifies "transnationalism" "as a way of life that connects family, work, and consciousness in more than one national territory. Migration made transnationalism a normal dimension of life for many, perhaps even most, working-class families in Italy in the nineteenth and twentieth centuries. Family discipline, economic security, reproduction, inheritance, romance and dreams transcended national boundaries and bridged continents." Gabaccia, *Italy's Many Diasporas*, 11.

10 Roger Rouse, "Mexican Migration and the Social Space of Postmodernism," *Diaspora* 1, 1 (1991): 8–23; Caroline Brettell, *We Have Already Cried Many Tears: The Stories of Three Portuguese Migrant Women* (Cambridge: Schenkman, 1982); Cole, *Women of the Praia*; Sally Cole, "Reconstituting Households, Retelling Culture: Emigration and Portuguese Fisheries Workers," *Transgressing Borders: Critical Perspectives on Gender, Household and Culture*, ed. S. Ilcan and L. Phillips (Westport: Bergin and Garvey, 1998), 75–92; Rhacel S. Parreñas, *Servants of Globalization: Women, Migration, and Domestic Work* (Stanford: Stanford University Press, 2001); Rhacel S. Parreñas, *Children of Global Migration: Transnational Families and Gendered Woes* (Stanford: Stanford University Press, 2005). Consider also: Nina Glick Schiller, Linda Basch and Cristina Szanton Blanc, "From Immigrant to Transmigrant: Theorizing Transnational Migration," *Anthropological Quarterly* 68.1 (January 1995): 48–63; Nina Glick Schiller,

"Transnational Projects: A New Perspective," *Nations Unbound: Transnational Projects, Postcolonial Predicaments, and Deterritorialized Nation-States,*ed. Linda Basch, Nina Glick Schiller, and Cristina Szanton Blanc (Amsterdam: Gordon and Breach Science Publishers, 1994); S. Grasmuck and P. Pessar, *Between Two Islands: Dominican International Migration* (Berkeley: University of California Press, 1991); Ulf Hannerz, *Transnational Connections: Culture, People, Places* (New York: Routledge, 1996).

11   Rouse, "Mexican Migration and the Social Space," 14.

12   Glick Schiller, Basch and Szanton Blanc, "From Immigrant to Transmigrant," 48.

13   Ibid., 50. On the concepts of transnational, translocal, transregional and transcultural, some historians also argue that we cannot consider all types of separation through migration or the reproductions of family ties through long distance as transnational, "for they existed long before national states came to dominate human life or geographies around the world." Christiane Harzig and Dirk Hoerder with Donna Gabaccia, *What is Migration History?* (Cambridge, UK: Polity Press, 2009) 124. See also Dirk Hoerder, "Migration and Cultural Interaction across the Centuries: German History in a European Perspective," *German Politics & Society* 26, 2 (Summer 2008); and Christiane Harzig and Dirk Hoerder, "Internationalizing Working-Class History Since the 1970s: Challenges from Historiography, Archives, and the Web," *Library Trends* 56, 3 (Winter 2008): 635-649.

14   Gerber, *Authors of Their Lives*, 155.

15   Letter from Luciano Colonello to Gianlorenzo Colonello and Mariangela Colonello and Mario Colani.

16   Letter from Dante del Moro to Sara Franceschetti.

17   Letter from Luciano Colonello to Gianlorenzo Colonello and Mariangela Colonello and Mario Colani.

18   Loretta Baldassar, "Missing Kin and Longing to be Together: Emotions and the Construction of Co-Presence in Transnational Relationships," *Journal of Intercultural Studies* 29, 3 (August 2008): 258.

19   Ibid., 257.

20   Ibid., 255.

21   Ibid., 259.

22   Gerber, *Authors of Their Lives*, 157.

23   Hareven, *Family Time and Industrial Time*, 114–115.

24   Tamara K. Hareven, "Les grands thèmes de l'histoire de la famille aux États-Unis," *Revue d'histoire de l'Amérique française* 39, 3 (1985): 193.

25   Baldassar, "Missing Kin," 258.

26   Gabaccia, *Italy's Many Diasporas*, 9.

27   This writer's encouragement coupled with a measure of reservation as he urges Dante to travel first to Canada alone and decide for himself if life in Canada suits him, illustrates Dirk Hoerder's observation that "A contextual approach does

not support the hypothesis that immigrant letters paint a rosy picture of post-migration life. In the case of chain migration, letters provide clues as to whether prospective migrants should venture out or stay put." Hoerder, *Creating Societies*, 18. See also Kamphoefner, Helbich and Sommer, *News From the Land of Freedom*.

28 Gabaccia, *Italy's Many Diasporas*, 11.

29 Piselli, *Parentela ed Emigrazione*, 171.

30 Quintin Hoare and Geoffrey Nowell Smith, ed. *Selections from the Prison Notebooks of Antonio Gramsci* (New York: International Publishers, 1971), 199.

31 Clifford Geertz, "Common Sense as a Cultural System," *The Antioch Review* 50, 1–2 (1992): 221–241, reprinted from *The Antioch Review* 33, 1 (1975).

32 Pierre Bourdieu, *Outline of a Theory of Practice* (London: Cambridge University Press, 1977), 164.

33 Johnson, *Growing Up*, 219.

34 The reference to Belgium here serves as a good example of the immigrants' and their loved ones' reach beyond the Italy-Canada axis.

35 The expression "migration project," is borrowed from Bruno Ramirez, *On the Move* and it refers to a strategy or purpose conceived by the migrant and his or her kin carried through to completion for the benefit of family members involved in the migration experience, whether as migrants or as those who remained behind.

36 Johnson, *Growing Up*, 206.

37 Ibid., 219.

38 I examine this concept and the related excerpt more closely in the next chapter on gender relations and dynamics.

Chapter Three

1 Iacovetta, *Such Hardworking People*, 47–48 and 80.

2 Sarah J. Mahler and Patricia R. Pessar, "Gendered Geographies of Power: Analyzing Gender Across Transnational Spaces," *Identities* 7, 4 (2001): 450.

3 Joan W. Scott, *Gender and the Politics of History*, revised ed. (New York: Columbia University Press, 1999), 86.

4 Candace West and Don H. Zimmerman, "Doing Gender," in *The Social Construction of Gender*, ed. Judith Lorber and Susan A. Farrell (Newbury Park, CA: Sage Publications, 1991), 34.

5 Judith Lorber, *Paradoxes of Gender* (New Haven and London: Yale University Press, 1994), 6.

6 The articles included in this special issue of the *International Migration Review* 40, 1 (Spring 2006) are: Katharine M. Donato, Donna R. Gabaccia, Jennifer Holdaway, Martin Manalansan IV, and Patricia R. Pessar, "A Glass Half Full? Gender in Migration Studies"; Sarah Mahler and Patricia Pessar, "Gender Matters:

Ethnographers Bring Gender from the Periphery toward the Core of Migration Studies"; Suzanne M. Sinke, "Gender and Migration: Historical Perspectives"; Rachel Silvey, "Geographies of Gender and Migration: Spatializing Social Difference"; Nicola Piper, "Gendering the Politics of Migration"; Carola Suarez-Orozco, Desiree Baolian Qin, "Gendered Perspectives in Psychology: Immigrant Origin Youth"; Kitty Calavita, "Gender, Migration, and Law: Crossing Borders and Bridging Disciplines"; Sara R. Curran, Steven Shafer, Katharine M. Donato, Filiz Garip, "Mapping Gender and Migration in Sociological Scholarship: Is it Segregation or Integration?"; and Martin F. Manalansan IV, "Queer Intersections: Sexuality and Gender in Migration Studies."

7   Joan W. Scott, "Experience," *Feminists Theorize the Political*, ed. Joan W. Scott and Judith Butler (New York and London: Routledge, 1992), 24.

8   Donato, Gabaccia, Holdaway, Manalansan IV, and Pessar "A Glass Half Full?" 21.

9   Ibid., 22.

10   See, for example, Gerber, *Authors of Their Lives*, Elliott, Gerber, and Sinke, ed. *Letters across Borders*; and Frenette, Martel and Willis, ed. *Envoyer et recevoir*. In the term "correspondence," I include private letters in the traditional sense as well as communication via the Internet.

11   Constable, *Romance on a Global Stage*, 8.

12   Ibid., 4.

13   Ibid., 225.

14   Iacovetta, *Such Hardworking People*, 96.

15   Diane Elson and Ruth Pearson, "The Subordination of Women and the Internationalisation of Factory Production," in *Of Marriage and the Market: Women's Subordination in International Perspective*, ed. Kate Young, Carol Wolkowitz, and Roslyn McCullagh (London: CSE Books, 1981), 154. See also Olivia Harris, "Households as Natural Units," in *Of Marriage and the Market*, ed. Young, Wolkowitz, and McCullagh, 49–68; Scott, *Gender and the Politcs of History*; Heidi Hartmann, "Capitalism, Patriarchy, and Job Segregation by Sex," *Signs* 1, 3 (Spring 1976): 137–169.

16   In her study on Italian postwar immigrants in Toronto, Iacovetta observes, "While working women accounted for more than one-third of the total Italian adult female population in Canada and Ontario in 1961, for Toronto this figure was 41.5 per cent. And these statistics do not cover the numerous women who earned money informally by taking in children or laundry, or by cleaning homes." Iacovetta, *Such Hardworking People*, 92–94.

17   Maila Stivens, "Women, Kinship and Capitalist Development," in *Of Marriage and the Market: Women's Subordination in International Perspective*, ed. Young, Wolkowitz and McCullagh, 114.

18   Ibid., 115.

19   The epistolary pact is defined by Dauphin, Lebrun-Pezerat and Poublan, as "the more or less explicit pact which engages the sender to use rhetorical tools to bring to fruition the encounter with the other … the letter seals the engagement with the

self in relation to the other." Cécile Dauphin, P. Lebrun-Pezerat, and D. Poublan, *Ces bonnes lettres: Une correspondance familiale au XIX siècle* (Paris: Editions Albin Michel, 1995), 131.

20 As Joan Scott argues, "subjects have agency. They are not unified, autonomous individuals exercising free will, but rather subjects whose agency is created through situations and statuses conferred on them. Being a subject means being 'subject to definite conditions of existence, conditions of endowment of agents and conditions of exercise.' These conditions enable choices, although they are not unlimited." Scott, "Experience," 34.

21 See Hawkins, *Canada and Immigration*.

22 For an anthropological analysis on prospective immigrants' distresses in passing the official interview as part of visa procedures for migration to the US, see Constable, *Romance on a Global Stage*.

23 Emphasis added. Cited from Jane F. Collier and Michelle Z. Rosaldo, "Politics and Gender in Simple Societies," in *Sexual Meanings: The Cultural Construction of Gender and Sexuality*, ed. Sherry B. Ortner, and Harriet Whitehead (Cambridge, UK: Cambridge University Press, 1981).

24 Elson and Pearson, "Subordination of Women," 156–157.

25 Ibid., 154.

26 Ibid., 151. As Elson and Pearson argue, in contrast to social power, "private power is purely individual power, contingent as the specific characteristics of particular individuals, reproducible only by chance."

27 Obviously, other dynamics also came into play. These include rural people travelling to the big city and semi-literate individuals dealing with bureaucracy.

28 On American influences to Italian way of life in immediate postwar, see Paul Ginsborg, *A History of Contemporary Italy: Society and Politics, 1943–1988* (London: Penguin, 1990); Victoria de Grazia, *Irresistible Empire: America's Advance through 20th-Century Europe* (Cambridge, MA and London: Harvard University Press, 2005); Penelope Morris, ed. *Women in Italy, 1945–1960: An Interdisciplinary Study* (New York: Palgrave Macmillan, 2006); Anna Maria Torriglia, *Broken Time, Fragmented Space: A Cultural Map for Postwar Italy* (Toronto: University of Toronto press, 2002); and Silvia Cassamagnaghi, *Immagini dall'America: Mass media e modelli femminili nell'Italia del secondo dopoguerra, 1945–1960* (Milan: FrancoAngeli, 2007).

29 Stanley Brandes, "Like Wounded Stags: Male Sexual Ideology in an Andalusian Town," *Sexual Meanings: the Cultural Construction of Gender and Sexuality*, ed. Sherry B. Ortner and Harriet Whitehead (Cambridge: Cambridge University Press, 1981), 218.

30 As excerpts from the Archivio dell'Istítuto Luce show in their archive of images of postwar Italy, Italian women models and celebrities, such as Maria Fiore, Piera Arico, Eleonora Rossi Drago, and Silvana Mangano, were sporting trousers in the 1950s, and fashion houses were featuring women wearing pants. See especially, la Casa di Moda Myricae in the Archivio dell'Istituto Luce. Refer to http://www.archivioluce.com/archivio/. Studies that examine women's fashions in postwar

Italy include: Stephen Gundle, "Feminine Beauty, National Identity and Political Conflict in Postwar Italy, 1945–1954," *Contemporary European History* 8, 3 (1999): 359–378; Emanuela Scarpellini. *Comprare all'Americana. Le origini della rivoluzione commerciale in Italia, 1945–1971* (Bologna: Il Mulino, 2001); Anna Maria Curcio, ed., *La Dea delle apparenze: Conversazioni sulla moda* (Rome: Franco Angeli, 2000); and Sofia Gnoli, *Un Secolo di Moda Italiana, 1900–2000* (Rome: Meltemi Editore, 2005), in which she discusses the Church's banning of women's trousers in 1941 (p. 97).

31   Judith Lorber, "Dismantling Noah's Ark," *The Social Construction of Gender*, ed. Judith Lorber and Susan A. Farrell (Newbury Park, CA: Sage Publications, 1991), 361.

32   See Gabriele P. Scardellato, "Italian Immigrant Workers in Powell River, BC: A Case Study of Settlement Before World War II," *Labour/Le Travail* 16 (Fall 1985): 145–163.

33   Harney, "Men without Women," 217.

34   Ibid., 214.

35   Ramirez, *On the Move*, 64.

36   Dirk Hoerder, "From Dreams to Possibilities: The Secularization of Hope and the Quest for Independence," in Hoerder and Rössler, *Distant Magnets*, 8.

37   Jessie Bernard, "The Good-Provider Role: Its Rise and Fall," *American Psychologist* 36, 1 (January 1981): 4.

38   Elson and Pearson, "Subordination of Women," 152.

39   In his essay, "Men without Women," Robert Harney makes reference to the interrelationship between hometown gossip and the male migrant's state of mind in the course of his migration experience and separation from his immediate family while working in Canada.

40   Bernard, "Good-Provider Role," 3.

41   These weekly *fotoromanzi* (photo-novels of a romantic nature), as they were called, including *Grand Hotel*, *Intimità* and *Bolero Film*, were a form of *feuilleton* invented in 1946 that became bestsellers overnight, capturing a non-elite female readership internationally. Single and married women working in the factories, *casalinghe* (housewives) toiling in the industrial North and rural South across Italy, Europe, and overseas (including Canada) avidly read the weekly episodes of these romantic *fotoromanzi*. At a mere 12 to 25 lire a copy, these impossible love stories ending happily ever after represented an opportunity for working-class women to dream of romantic love and class mobility during one of their breaks from their daily duties. *Fotoromanzi* like *Grand Hotel*, *Intimità*, and *Bolero Film* are considered the most typical byproducts of mass culture in the postwar period. For references, consider Anna Bravo, *Il Fotoromanzo* (Bologna: Il Mulino, 2003); Barbara Garbin, "Fotoromanzo," in *Encyclopedia of Italian Literary Studies*, ed. Gaetana Marrone, Paolo Puppa, Luca Somigli (New York: Routledge, 2006), 769–770.

42   See Ruth Schwartz Cowan, *More Work for Mother: The Ironies of Household Technology from the Open Hearth to the Microwave* (New York: Basic Books, 1983);

Maxine L. Margolis, *Mothers and Such: Views of American Women and Why They Changed* (Berkeley: University of California Press, 1984).

43 Elson and Pearson, "Subordination of Women," 154.

44 Michelle Z. Rosaldo, "Woman, Culture, and Society: A Theoretical Overview," in *Woman, Culture and Society*, ed. Michelle Zimbalist Rosaldo and Louise Lamphere (Stanford, CA: Stanford University Press, 1974), 42.

45 Iacovetta, *Such Hardworking People*. See also, Franca Iacovetta, "From Contadina to Worker: Southern Italian Immigrant Working Women in Toronto 1947–62," in *Looking into My Sister's Eyes: An Exploration in Women's History*, ed. Jean Burnet (Toronto: Multicultural History Society of Ontario, 1986), 195–222.

46 Arlene B. Gaal, '*Memoirs' of Michel-Natal, 1899–1971* (n.p.: 1971); Arlene B. Gaal, '*Times to Remember...' Michel-Natal, 1899–1980* (n.p.: 1980); and Tom Langford and Wayne Norton, ed., *A World Apart: The Crowsnest Communities of Alberta and British Columbia* (Kamloops: Plateau Press, 2002).

47 See Meg Luxton, *More than a Labour of Love: Three Generations of Women's Work in the Home* (Toronto: Women's Educational Press, 1980); specifically concerning the mining towns of Elk Valley in British Columbia and Alberta, see Langford and Norton, ed., *A World Apart*.

48 *Caffé Italia, Montréal*, dir. Paul Tana (Montreal: ACPAV, 1984).

49 Parreñas, *Children of Global Migration*, 84–87.

50 In Italian transnational households, other female roles are observed in a process of reconfiguration, including, for instance, the role that changed from cousin to sister. Daniela Perini writes to her daughter, urging her to stay close to her female cousin in Montreal: "I hope that you are close to each other, and that you see each other often, given that Giovanna is like a sister to you" (28 October 1961).

51 Harriet Perry offers a definition of what "good" means in relation to a young woman's roles in Italian family households in postwar Toronto. She suggests: "A 'good' girl is one reputed to be chaste, obedient to her father, and knowledgeable about the running of a household. It is a great bonus if the girl is considered intelligent and if at school she has gained certain practical skills that will be helpful to her in getting a job. Secretarial, dressmaking, and hairdressing skills are the most common, not least because they can to some extent be done in the home after marriage and motherhood, and also because part-time jobs are possible in these occupations." Harriet Perry, "The Metonymic Definition of the Female and the Concept of Honour Among Italian Immigrant Families in Toronto," in *The Italian Immigrant Woman in North America*, ed. Caroli, Harney, and Tomasi, 225.

52 "*Mia cara... I hope you will be happy here and thankful...*," cfr. letter from Dante del Moro to Sara Franceschetti, 24 July 1956.

53 See Parreñas, *Children of Global Migration*, esp. 92–140.

Chapter Four

1   According to William Reddy, one reason for the scholarly lacunae in the study of emotions is linked to the understanding that, "For a long time, our common sense supported a certain division of labor among the disciplines that assigned emotions to the sphere of psychology." William M. Reddy, *The Navigation of Feeling: A Framework for the History of Emotions* (New York: Cambridge University Press, 2001), 316.

2   Gerber, *Authors of Their Lives*, 108.

3   Gerber, *Authors of Their Lives*, 107–108.

4   Willis, "De votre chère," 83.

5   William Reddy observes that the study of emotions has produced a number of works cutting across various disciplines in the humanities and social sciences, including psychology, anthropology, history and literary studies. See especially the contributions of Michelle Z. Rosaldo, Catherine Lutz, and Lila Abu-Lughod. See also Lucien Febvre, "La sensibilité et l'histoire: Comment reconstituer la vie affective d'autrefois," *Les Annales d'histoire sociale* 3 (January–June 1941): 5–20; Barbara H. Rosenwien, "Worrying about Emotions in History," *American Historical Review* 107, 3 (June 2002): 823–824; Peter N. Stearns with Carol Z. Stearns, "Emotionology: Clarifying the History of Emotions and Emotional Standards," *American Historical Revew* 90, 4 (1985): 813–835.

6   Rosaldo, "Toward an Anthropology," 149. On the social construction of emotions, especially maternal love, see Nancy Scheper-Hughes, *Death without Weeping: The Violence of Everyday Life in Brazil* (Berkeley and Los Angeles: University of California Press, 1992), 341. See also William Jankowiak, ed., *Romantic Passion: A Universal Experience?* (New York: Columbia University Press, 1995); Michelle Z. Rosaldo. *Knowledge and Passion: Ilongot Notions of Self and Social life* (New York: Cambridge University Press, 1980); Michelle Z. Rosaldo, "Toward an Anthropology of Self and Feeling," *Culture Theory: Essays on Mind, Self and Emotion*, ed. Richard A. Shweder and Robert A. LeVine (Cambridge, UK: Cambridge University Press, 1984); Catherine A. Lutz and Lila Abu-lughod, eds., *Language and the Politics of Emotion* (New York: Cambridge University Press, 1990); Catherine Lutz and Geoffrey M. White, "The Anthropology of Emotions," *Annual Review of Anthropology* 15 (1986): 405–436; and Laura M. Ahearn, *Invitations to Love: Literacy, Love Letters, and Social Change in Nepal* (Ann Arbor: University of Michigan Press, 2001).

7   Catherine A. Lutz and Lila Abu-Lughod, "Introduction," in *Language and the Politics of Emotion*, ed. Lutz and Abu-Lughod, 1. On the importance of analyzing emotions, see also Catherine A. Lutz, "Emotion, Thought, and Estrangement: Emotion as a Cultural Category," *Cultural Anthropology* 1, 3 (Aug. 1986). See also Lutz and White, "The Anthropology of Emotions,"; and Lila Abu-Lughod, *Veiled Sentiments: Honor and Poetry in a Bedouin Society* (Berkeley and Los Angeles: University of California Press, 1986).

8   Karen Lystra, *Searching the Heart: Women, Men, and Romantic Love in Nineteenth-Century America* (New York and Oxford: Oxford University Press, 1989). Anya Jabour, "'The Language of Love': The Letters of Elizabeth and William Wirt, 1802–

1834," in *A Shared Experience: Men, Women, and the History of Gender*, ed. Laura McCall and Donald Yacovone (New York and London: New York University Press, 1998), 119–140; Martha Hanna, "A Republic of Letters: The Epistolary Tradition in France during World War I," *American Historical Review* 108, 5 (Dec. 2003): 1338–1361; Hanna, *Your Death Would Be Mine*; Robert K. Nelson, "'The Forgetfulness of Sex': Devotion and Desire in the Courtship Letters of Angelina Grimke and Theodore Dwight Weld," *Journal of Social History* 37, 3 (2004): 663–679; William E. French, "'Te Amo Muncho': The Love Letters of Pedro and Enriqueta," in *The Human Tradition in Mexico*, ed. Jeffrey M. Pilcher (Wilmington, DE: Scholarly Resources, 2003), 123–135; Mireille Bossis and Charles Porter, ed., *L'Epistolarité à Travers les Siècles: Geste de communication et/ou d'écriture* (Stuttgart: Franz Steiner Verlag, 1990); Mireille Bossis, ed., *La lettre à la croisée de l'individuel et du social* (Paris: Editions Kimé, 1994); Marie-Claire Grassi, "Des lettres qui parlent d'amour," *Romantisme* 68, 2 (1990): 23-32; Roger Chartier, ed., *La Correspondance: Les usages de la lettre au XIXe siècle* (Paris: Fayard, 1991); Mary A. Favret, *Romantic Correspondence: Women, Politics and the Fiction of Letters* (Cambridge, UK: Cambridge University Press, 1993); Bruce Redford, *The Converse of the Pen: Acts of Intimacy in the Eighteenth-Century Familiar Letter* (Chicago and London: University of Chicago Press, 1986); Susan Albertine, "Heart's Expression: the Middle-Class Language of Love in Late Nineteenth-Century Correspondence," *American Literary History* 4, 1 (Spring 1992): 141-164; Martyn Lyons, "Love Letters and Writing Practices: On Ecritures Intimes in the Nineteenth Century," *Journal of Family History* 24 (1999): 232-239; William Merrill Decker, *Epistolary Practices: Letter writing in America before Telecommunications* (Chapel Hill and London: University of North Carolina Press, 1998); and the special issue, "Men/Women of Letters," *Yale French Studies* 71 (1986). On the intersections of letter writing and social practice, consider Niko Besnier, *Literacy, Emotion, and Authority: Reading and Writing on a Polynesian Atoll* (New York: Cambridge University Press, 1995); David Barton and Nigel Hall, ed., *Letter Writing as a Social Practice* (Amsterdam: John Benjamins, 2000); and Stanley, "The Epistolarium".

9   Gerber, *Authors of Their Lives*, 286.

10 In *Invitations to Love*, Ahearn examines the emotions of romantic love in courtship and marriage between young couples in relation to social development in Nepali villages. Marriage, courtship, love, and correspondence via the Internet is explored in Nicole Constable, *Romance on a Global Stage*. See also Constable's *Cross-Border Marriages: Gender and Mobility in Transnational Asia* (Philadelphia: University of Pennsylvania Press, 2005); Lystra, *Searching the Heart*; Jennifer S. Hirsch, *A Courtship after Marriage: Sexuality and Love in Mexican Transnational Families* (Berkeley and Los Angeles: University of California Press, 2003); Jennifer S. Hirsch and Holly Wardlow, *Modern Loves: The Anthropology of Romantic Courtship and Companionate Marriage* (Ann Arbor: University of Michigan Press, 2006); Suzanne Sinke, "Marriage through the Mail: North American Correspondence Marriage from Early Print to the Web," in *Letters across Borders*, ed. Elliott, Gerber, and Sinke.

11 Janet Gurkin Altman, *Epistolarity: Approaches to a Form* (Columbus: Ohio University Press, 1982), 131.

12 Ibid., 131. Temporal dynamics in correspondence have been examined by other literary theorists as well, including, Cécile Dauphin, "Les manuels épistolaires au XIXe siècle," in Chartier, *La correspondance*, 209-272.

13 Altman, *Epistolarity*, 129–130.

14 Parreñas, *Servants of Globalization*. See also Parreñas, *Children of Global Migration*.

15 Loretta Baldassar, Cora V. Baldock, and Raelene Wilding. *Families Caring across Borders: Migration, Aging and Transnational Caregiving* (London: Palgrave MacMillan, 2007).

16 Gerber, *Authors of Their Lives*, 46. Part of the reason for caution is the letter writers' knowledge of writing conventions, as Roger Chartier explains in the case of French middle-class individuals. Yet the art of epistolary writing did not involve precise conventions, but was based in the ease and naturalness of the writing itself. Roger Chartier, "Préface," *Ces bonnes lettres*.

17 See also Brettell, *Men Who Migrate: Women Who Wait*.

18 Grassi, "Des lettres qui parlent d'amour," 27.

19 The name "Nina" here is affectionately used to mean "little girl" in general. This expression is commonly used in the northeastern regions of Italy.

20 Grassi, "Des lettres qui parlent d'amour," 26.

21 Martha Hanna, "A Republic of Letters," 1348.

22 Lystra, *Searching the Heart*, 25.

23 On the relationship between photography, photo albums, family, and memory, see: Marianne Hirsch, *Family Frames: Photography, Narrative and Postmemory* (Cambridge: Harvard University Press, 1997); Marianne Hirsch, ed. *The Familial Gaze* (Hanover, NH: University Press of New England, 1999); Julia Hirsch, *Family Photographs: Content, Meaning and Effect* (Oxford: Oxford University Press, 1981) and Martha Langford, *Suspended Conversations: The Afterlife of Memory in Photographic Albums* (Montreal-Kingston: McGill-Queen's University Press, 2001).

24 Roland Barthes, *A Lover's Discourse: Fragments*, trans. Richard Howard (New York: Hill and Wang, 1978), 157.

25 Mireille Bossis, "Table Ronde: la lettre d'amour," *L'Epistolarité à Travers les Siècles*, 39. As Bernard Bray suggests, "the love letter—even if, as we know, is about love—doesn't merely speak of love, but accompanies it, surpasses it, claims it, comments on it, regrets it. An impure genre, the love letter combines in the analysis and in the observation of feelings, also narratives, descriptions, autobiographical fragments, ornamentation that constitute as many personality projections. By addressing the other, the individual endeavours to establish a communication that helps to pull her/him, ie. the other out of her/his subjective solitude. The love sentiment is the motivation for which the letter is written, but the content of the letter is of interest to us especially for reasons outside the sentiment itself, quickly identified... we know more about a life, a temperament, a culture, a style." Bernard Bray, "Treize Propos sur la Lettre d'Amour," *L'Epistolarité à Travers les Siècles*, 40-41.

26 Lystra, *Searching the Heart*, 17.

27 William Jankowiak, "Introduction," in *Romantic Passion: A Universal Experience?* ed. William Jankowiak (New York: Columbia University Press, 1995), 4.

28 Leonard Plotnicov, "Love, Lust and Found in Nigeria," in *Romantic Passion*, ed. Jankowiak, 129.

29 The archived correspondence dates from the first letter Giordano Rossini wrote to Ester di Leonardi once she left for Canada, that is from 10 March 1957 and continues until 18 August 1960 with an interruption between the years.

30 Much as emotions are socially constructed, the notion of "romantic love" is also, I believe, dependent on its social and historical context. My understanding of the social and historical construction of romantic love is drawn from Laura Ahearn's suggestion that "there is no universal, ahistorical experience of romantic love that all humans share." Ahearn, *Invitations to Love*, 48. Also, my concern here is not to investigate whether the discourse of romantic love in the letters is true, or not. As Nicole Constable suggests, "It would be impossible to 'prove' whether love is present in these relationships… There is no question, however, that a discourse about romantic love is often present among couples involved in correspondence relationships." Constable, *Romance on a Global Stage*, 128.

31 Jan Clanton Collins and Thomas Gregor, "Boundaries of Love," in *Romantic Passion*, ed. Jankowiak, 73.

32 Grassi, "Des lettres qui parlent d'amour," 23.

33 Ahearn, *Invitations to Love*, 48–49.

34 Ibid.

35 Lystra, *Searching the Heart*, 51–52.

36 Ibid., 55.

37 Ahearn, *Invitations to Love*, 152.

38 Barthes, *Lover's Discourse*, 112.

39 Lystra, *Searching the Heart*, 47.

40 This letter refers to the long-standing television quiz show, *Lascia o Raddoppia* hosted by the Italian-American journalist, Mike Bongiorno. Viewed as "the Italian equivalent of 'The 64,000 Dollar Question'" (Ginsborg, *A History of Contemporary Italy*, 240), the quiz show quickly became extremely popular as television made its way into Italian homes. On the popularity of the television show, see Ginsborg, *A History of Contemporary Italy*; Silvio Lanaro, *Storia dell'Italia repubblicana: L'economia, la politica, la cultura, la società dal dopoguerra agli anni '90* (Venezia: Marsilio Editori, 1992); Cassamagnaghi, *Immagini dall'America*; and John Foot, "Television and the City: the Impact of Television in Milan, 1954–1960," *Contemporary European History* 8, 3 (1999): 379–394.

41 Emotional dependency is viewed as a characteristic of romantic love. See Helen Harris, "Rethinking Polynesian Heterosexual Relationships: A Case Study on Mangaia, Cook Islands," in *Romantic Passion*, ed. Jankowiak, 95–127.

42 Lystra, *Searching the Heart*, 52.

43 A letter in the Del Moro collection refers to Lisbon as an embarkation point for the *S.S. Saturnia*, which sailed from the Strait of Messina to Naples to Palermo, Gibraltar, and then to Lisbon, from which point it sailed to its final destination, Halifax, arriving on 6 March 1956. Ocean liners, like the *S.S. Saturnia* and *S.S. Argentina*, en route to Canada from Italy were often scheduled to stop in Lisbon, Portugal, in addition to other points along the way to pick up passengers and cargo.

44 Altman, *Epistolarity*, 148.

45 On the dialogic element in letters of migration, David Gerber suggests, "in personal letters the voice of the other is always present, for the letter-writer composes for a particular, known individual in a process that is an implicit conversation with, or a psychological probing of, the addressee. Conversation or correspondence, much of the creative activity in living, consists of anticipating responses to one's utterances and, in consequence, crafting one's responses in certain ways suited to the other, while attempting not to sacrifice one's own individuality." Gerber, *Authors of Their Lives*, 72.

46 Hoerder, *Creating Societies*, 18.

47 Ibid., 18.

48 The appearance of poetry or poetic devices in love letters is not an anomaly. Bray suggests, "this is where we observe how written love is different from spoken love, or love as it is experienced. The lover becomes a poet and poetry opens an infinity of image expressions that call for their writing." Bray, "Treize Propos," 41.

49 Italo Calvino, *Six Memos for the Next Millennium* (Cambridge, MA: Harvard University Press, 1988), 91.

50 Bray, "Treize Propos," 42–43.

51 The expression, "*non ti scordar di me*" likely originates in the Italian song of the bel canto that was popular in the 1950s entitled "Non ti scordar di me," composed by Ernesto De Curtis in the mid-1930s.

52 Fitzpatrick, *Oceans of Consolation*, 494.

53 Grassi, "Des lettres qui parlent d'amour," 23–24.

54 My understanding of Dauphin's "le temps épistolaire" is that it encompasses the temporal dynamics involved in the waiting, reading, writing practices of a letter. She suggests, "epistolary writing externalizes, crystallizes and emphasizes the break from oral communication by providing spatial and temporal dimensions that subject it to eventual manipulations. However, written communication also creates its own ritual within a coded temporal framework. First, the exchange is punctuated by the waiting for a response... This obligation, (part of a code of politeness) denotes, in fact, a relationship to the specific time of the correspondence. In contrast to oral communication, the exchange can at any time be interrupted. It is always postponed, as a result of the time it takes to deliver the letter and the reply... The relationship with time finds expression also in the progression of the yearly cycle—with its recurring and hectic moments... and

with its dull moments which the letter must fill." Cécile Dauphin, "Les manuels épistolaires au XIXe siècle," 235–236.

55 Gerber, *Authors of Their Lives*, 149–154.

56 Lystra, *Searching the Heart*, 4.

57 According to Bernard Bray, the letters of Victor Hugo and Juliette Drouet, and Musset and George Sand are a case in point. Bray, "Treize Propos," 45.

58 Lystra, *Searching the Heart*, 20.

59 Gerber, *Authors of Their Lives*, 121.

60 Altman, *Epistolarity*, 61.

61 Willis, "De votre chère," 83.

62 Gerber, *Authors of Their Lives*, 210.

63 Redford, *Converse of the Pen*, 9.

Conclusion

1 Bruno Ramirez, "Clio in Words and in Motion: Practices of Narrating the Past," *Journal of American History* 86, 3 (Dec. 1999), 987.

2 Beattie and Buss, ed. *Undelivered Letters*, 7.

BIBLIOGRAPHY

Primary Sources

Letter Collections and Family Archivists

Letter series, Gianlorenzo Colonello (1951–1986).

Letter series, Paolo del Moro (1956–1960).

Letter series, Maddalena Franchi (1961–1988).

Letter series, Anita Losanto (1958–1972).

Letter series, Maurizio Trevisan and Clara Renzi (1946–1982).

Letter series, Ester di Leonardi and Marco Colledani (1957–1960).

Oral Interviews and Informal Conversations with Research Participants

Gianlorenzo Colonello and Elsa Contini, December 2004, November 2005, December 2006, January 2007, and August 2009 (Canada).

Marco Colledani, March 2003 (Canada).

Paolo del Moro, August 2004, May 2006, August 2007 (Canada).

Maddalena Franchi, June 2003, August 2003 and November 2003 (Canada).

Davide Franchi and Assunta Sordi, June 2005 (Italy).

Anita Losanto, July 2003, August 2003, June 2007 and August 2007 (Canada).

Irene Motta, January 2007 (Canada).

Anna Cavallero, November 2005 (Canada).

Maurizio Trevisan and Clara Renzi, June 2003, February 2004, April 2004 (Canada), June 2005 (with Giuliana Trevisan and Mario Trevisan, Italy) and April 2007 (Canada).

Secondary Sources

Abu-Lughod, Lila. *Veiled Sentiments: Honor and Poetry in a Bedouin Society.* Berkeley and Los Angeles: University of California Press, 1986.

Ahearn, Laura M. *Invitations to Love: Literacy, Love Letters, and Social Change in Nepal.* Ann Arbor: University of Michigan Press, 2001.

Akenson, Donald H. "Reading the Texts of Rural Immigrants: Letters from the Irish in Australia, New Zealand, and North America." *Canadian Papers in Rural History* 7 (1990): 387–406.

_____. *Half the World from Home: Perspectives on the Irish in New Zealand, 1860–1950.* Wellington, New Zealand: Victoria University Press, 1990.

Albertine, Susan. "Heart's Expression: the Middle-Class Language of Love in Late Nineteenth-Century Correspondence." *American Literary History* 4, 1 (Spring 1992): 141–164.

Altman, Janet Gurkin. *Epistolarity: Approaches to a Form.* Columbus: Ohio University Press, 1982.

Avery, Donald H. *Reluctant Host: Canada's Response to Immigrant Workers, 1896–1994.* Toronto: McClelland and Stewart, 1995.

Baily, Samuel. *Immigrants in the Lands of Promise: Italians in Buenos Aires and New York City, 1870 to 1914.* Ithaca: Cornell University Press, 1999.

Baily, Samuel, and Franco Ramella. *One Family, Two Worlds. An Italian Family's Correspondence across the Atlantic, 1901–1922.* New Brunswick and London: Rutgers University Press, 1988.

Baldassar, Loretta. "Missing Kin and Longing to be Together: Emotions and the Construction of Co-presence in Transnational Relationships." *Journal of Intercultural Studies* 29, 3 (August 2008): 247–266.

Baldassar, Loretta, Cora V. Baldock, and Raelene Wilding. *Families Caring across Borders: Migration, Aging and Transnational Caregiving.* London: Palgrave Macmillan, 2007.

Barthes, Roland. *A Lover's Discourse: Fragments,* trans. Richard Howard. New York: Hill and Wang, 1978.

Barton, Arnold. *Letters from the Promised Land: Swedes in America, 1840–1914.* Minneapolis: University of Minnesota Press, 1975.

Barton, David and Nigel Hall, ed. *Letter Writing as a Social Practice.* Amsterdam: John Benjamins, 2000.

Basch, Linda, Nina Glick Schiller, and Cristina Szanton Blanc. *Nations Unbound: Transnational Projects, Postcolonial Predicaments, and Deterritorialized Nation-States.* Amsterdam: Gordon and Breach Science Publishers, 1994.

Beattie, Judith, and Helen Buss, ed. *Undelivered Letters to Hudson's Bay Company Men on the Northwest Coast of America, 1830–57.* Vancouver and Toronto: University of British Columbia, 2003.

Bernard, Jessie. "The Good-Provider Role: Its Rise and Fall." *American Psychologist* 36, 1 (January 1981): 1–12.

Besnier, Niko. *Literacy, Emotion, and Authority: Reading and Writing on a Polynesian Atoll*. New York: Cambridge University Press, 1995.

Bianchi, Bruna. "Lavoro ed emigrazione femminile (1880–1915)." In *Storia dell'emigrazione italiana*, ed. Piero Bevilacqua, Andreina De Clementi, and Emilio Franzina. Rome: Donzelli editore, 2001.

Blegen, Theodore C. *Land of their Choice: The Immigrants Write Home*. St. Paul, MN: University of Minnesota Press, 1955.

Bossis, Mireille, ed. *La lettre à la croisée de l'individuel et du social*. Paris: Editions Kimé, 1994.

_____. "Table Ronde: la lettre d'amour." In *L'epistolarité à Travers les Siècles. Geste de communication et/ou d'écriture*. Ed. Mireille Bossis. Centre Culturel International de Cerisy la Salle France. Stuttgart: Franz Steiner Verlag, 1990.

Bossis, Mireille, and Charles A. Porter, ed. *L'Epistolarité à Travers les Siècles: Geste de communication et/ou d'écriture*. Stuttgart: Franz Steiner Verlag, 1990.

Bourdieu, Pierre. *Outline of a Theory of Practice*. London: Cambridge University Press, 1977.

Brandes, Stanley. "Like Wounded Stags: Male Sexual Ideology in an Andalusian town." In *Sexual Meanings: The Cultural Construction of Gender and Sexuality*, ed. Sherry B. Ortner and Harriet Whitehead. Cambridge: Cambridge University Press, 1981.

Bravo, Anna. *Il Fotoromanzo*. Bologna: Il Mulino, 2003.

Bray, Bernard. "Treize Propos sur la Lettre d'Amour." In *L'Epistolarité à Travers les Siècles: Geste de communication et/ou d'écriture*, ed. Mireille Bossis, and Charles Porter. Stuttgart: Franz Steiner Verlag, 1990.

Brettell, Caroline. *We Have Already Cried Many Tears: Portuguese Women and Migration*. Cambridge, MA: Schenkman Pub. Co., 1982.

_____. *Men who Migrate, Women who Wait: Population and History in a Portuguese Parish*. Princeton: Princeton University Press, 1986.

Brinks, Herbert, ed. *Dutch American Voices: Letters from the United States, 1850–1930*. Ithaca and London: Cornell University Press, 1995.

Brown, Helen. "Negotiating Space, Time, and Identity: The Hutton-Pellett Letters and a British Child's Wartime Evacuation to Canada." In *Letters Across Borders: The Epistolary Practices of International Migrants*, ed. Bruce S. Elliott, David A. Gerber, and Suzanne M. Sinke. New York: Palgrave Macmillan, 2006.

Bruneton-Governatori, Ariane, and Bernard Moreux. "Un modèle épistolaire populaire. Les lettres d'émigrés béarnais." In *Par Ecrit. Ethnologie des écritures quotidiennes*, ed. Daniel Fabre. Paris: Editions de la Maison des sciences de l'homme, 1997.

_____. "L'avènement d'une source privée: lettres et correspondances d'émigrés pyrénéens." In *Envoyer et recevoir: Lettres et correspondances dans les diasporas francophones*, ed. Yves Frenette, Marcel Martel, and John Willis. Québec: Presses de l'Université Laval, 2006.

Caffarena, Fabio. *Lettere dalla Grande Guerra: Scritture del quotidiano, monumenti della memoria, fonti per la storia. Il caso italiano.* Milano: Edizioni Unicopli, 2005.

Caffé Italia, Montréal. Dir. Paul Tana. Montreal: ACPAV, 1984.

Calavita, Kitty. "Gender, Migration, and Law: Crossing Borders and Bridging Disciplines." *International Migration Review* 40, 1 (Spring 2006): 104–132.

Calvino, Italo. *Six Memos for the Next Millennium.* Cambridge, MA: Harvard University Press, 1988.

Cameron, Wendy, Sheila Haines, and Mary M. Maude, ed. *English Immigrant Voices: Labourers' Letters from Upper Canada in the 1830s.* Montreal and Kingston: McGill-Queen's University Press, 2000.

Cancian, Sonia. "Una raccolta di lettere italiane inviate agli emigrati in Canada, 1954–1955." MA thesis, McGill University, 1999.

_____. "Intersecting labour and social networks across cities and borders." *Studi Emigrazione/Migration Studies* 166 (2007): 313–326.

Cancian, Sonia, and Bruno Ramirez. "Post-migration 'Italo-Canada': new perspectives on its past, present, and future." *Studi Emigrazione/Migration Studies* 170 (2007): 259–272.

Cassamagnaghi, Silvia. *Immagini dall'America: Mass media e modelli femminili nell'Italia del secondo dopoguerra, 1945–1960.* Milano: FrancoAngeli, 2007.

Chartier, Roger, ed. *La Correspondance: Les usages de la lettre au XIXe siècle.* Paris: Fayard, 1991.

Chartier, Roger. "Préface." *Ces bonnes lettres: Une correspondance familiale au XIXe siècle,* ed. C. Dauphin, P. Lebrun-Pezerat, and D. Poublan. Paris: Editions Albin Michel, 1995.

Cole, Sally. *Women of the Praia: Work and Lives in a Portuguese Coastal Community.* Princeton: Princeton University Press, 1991.

_____. "Reconstituting Households, Retelling Culture: Emigration and Portuguese Fisheries Workers." In *Transgressing Borders: Critical Perspectives on Gender, Household and Culture,* ed. S. Ilcan and L. Phillips. Westport: Bergin and Garvey, 1998.

Collins, Jan Clanton, and Thomas Gregor. "Boundaries of Love." In *Romantic Passion: A Universal Experience?* ed. William Jankowiak. New York: Columbia University Press, 1995.

Constable, Nicole. *Romance on a Global Stage: Pen Pals, Virtual Ethnography, and "Mail Order" Marriages.* Berkeley and Los Angeles: University of California Press, 2003.

_____. *Cross-Border Marriages: Gender and Mobility in Transnational Asia.* Philadelphia: University of Pennsylvania Press, 2005.

Conway, Alan, ed. *The Welsh in America. Letters from the Immigrants.* St. Paul, MN: University of Minnesota Press, 1961.

Courtemanche, Andrée, and Martin Paquet, ed. *Prendre la route. L'expérience migratoire en Europe et en Amérique du Nord du XIVe au XXe siècle.* Hull, QC: Editions Vents d'Ouest, 2001.

Cowan, Ruth Schwartz. *More Work for Mother: The Ironies of Household Technology from the Open Hearth to the Microwave.* New York: Basic Books, 1983.

Curcio, Anna Maria, ed. *La Dea delle apparenze: Conversazioni sulla moda.* Rome and Milan: Franco Angeli, 2000.

Curran, Sara R., Steven Shafer, Katharine M. Donato, and Filiz Garip. "Mapping Gender and Migration in Sociological Scholarship: Is it Segregation or Integration?" *International Migration Review* 40, 1 (Spring 2006): 199–223.

Dauphin, Cécile. "Les manuels épistolaires au XIXe siècle." *La Correspondance. Les usages de la lettre au XIXe siècle,* ed. Roger Chartier. Paris: Fayard, 1991.

Dauphin, Cécile, P. Lebrun-Pezerat, and D. Poublan. *Ces bonnes lettres: Une correspondance familiale au XIXe siècle.* Paris: Editions Albin Michel, 1995.

Dauphin-Memeteau, Cécile, and Danièle Poublan. "S'Écrire au XIXe siècle en France : Histoire d'une acculturation." In *More than Words :Readings in Transport, Communication and the History of Postal Communication,* ed. John Willis. Gatineau, QC: Canadian Museum of Civilzation, 2007.

Decker, William Merrill. *Epistolary Practices: Letter Writing in America before Telecommunications.* Chapel Hill and London: University of North Carolina Press, 1998.

De Grazia, Victoria. *Irresistible Empire: America's Advance through 20th-Century Europe.* Cambridge, MA: Harvard University Press, 2005.

De Haan, Kathleen Anne. "'He looks like a Yankee in his new suit.' Immigrant Rhetoric: Dutch Immigrant Letters as Forums for Shifting Immigrant Identities." PhD diss., Northwestern University, 1998.

Di Leonardo, Micaela. *The Varieties of Ethnic Experience: Kinship, Class, and Gender among California Italian-Americans.* Ithaca and London: Cornell University Press, 1984.

Donato, Katherine M., Donna R. Gabaccia, Jennifer Holdaway, Martin Manalansan IV, and Patricia Pessar. "A Glass Half Full? Gender in Migration Studies." *International Migration Review* 40, 1 (Spring 2006): 3–26.

Duggan, Christopher, and Christopher Wagstaff, ed. *Italy in the Cold War: Politics, Culture & Society 1948–58.* Oxford and Washington, DC: Berg, 1995.

Elliott, Bruce S., David A. Gerber, and Suzanne M. Sinke, ed. *Letters across Borders: The Epistolary Practices of International Migrants.* New York: Palgrave Macmillan, 2006.

Elson, Diane, and Ruth Pearson. "The Subordination of Women and the Internationalisation of Factory Production." In *Of Marriage and the Market: Women's Subordination in International Perspective,* ed. Kate Young, Carol Wolkowitz, and Roslyn McCullagh. London: CSE Books, 1981.

Erickson, Charlotte. *Invisible Immigrants: The Adaptation of English and Scottish Immigrants in 19th Century America.* Coral Gables, FL: Miami University Press, 1972.

Fahrni, Magda. *Household Politics: Montreal Families and Postwar Reconstruction.* Toronto: University of Toronto Press, 2005.

Fahrni, Magda and Yves Frenette. " 'Don't I long for Montreal': L'identité hybride d'une migrante franco-américaine pendant la première Guerre Mondiale." *Histoire sociale/Social History* 41.81 (May 2008): 75-98.

Favero, Luigi, and Graziano Tassello. "Cent'anni di emigrazione italiana (1876-1976)." In *Un secolo di emigrazione italiana 1876-1976*, ed. Gianfausto Rosoli. Rome: Centro Studi Emigrazione, 1976.

Favret, Mary A. *Romantic Correspondence: Women, Politics and the Fiction of Letters.* Cambridge, UK: Cambridge University Press, 1993.

Febvre, Lucien. "La sensibilité et l'histoire: Comment reconstituer la vie affective d'autrefois." *Les Annales d'histoire sociale* 3 (January–June 1941): 5-20.

Feldman-Bianco, B. "Multiple Layers of Time and Space: The Construction of Class, Race, Ethnicity and Nationalism among Portuguese Immigrants." In *Towards a Transnational Perspective on Migration: Race, Class, Ethnicity and Nationalism Reconsidered*, ed. Nina Glick Schiller, Linda Basch, and Cristina Szanton Blanc. New York: New York Academy of Sciences, 1992. 145-171.

Fender, Stephen. *Sea Changes: British Emigration and American Literature.* Cambridge: Cambridge University Press, 1992.

Finkel, Alvin, and Margaret Conrad. *History of the Canadian Peoples: 1867 to the Present.* 2nd edition. Toronto: Copp Clark, 1998.

Fitzpatrick, David. *Oceans of Consolation: Personal Accounts of Irish Migration to Australia.* Ithaca and London: Cornell University Press, 1994.

Foot, John. "Television and the City: the Impact of Television in Milan, 1954-1960." *Contemporary European History* 8, 3 (1999): 379-394.

Foner, Nancy. "What's New About Transnationalism? New York Immigrants Today and at the Turn of the Century." *Diaspora* 6, 3 (Winter): 355-376.

Franzina, E. *Merica! Merica! Emigrazione e colonizzazione nelle lettere dei contadini veneti e friulani in America Latina, 1876-1902.* Milano: Feltrinelli, 1979.

French, William E. "'*Te Amo Muncho*': The Love Letters of Pedro and Enriqueta." In *The Human Tradition in Mexico*, ed. Jeffrey M. Pilcher. Wilmington, DE: Scholarly Resources, 2003.

Frenette, Yves, Marcel Martel, and John Willis, ed. *Envoyer et recevoir. Lettres et correspondances dans les diasporas francophones.* Quebec: Presses L'Université Laval, 2006.

Frenette, Yves, Bianca Gendreau, Gabriele Scardellato, and John Willis. "L'expérience immigrante et la création d'un espace épistolaire: une étude de cas." In *Prendre la route. L'expérience migratoire en Europe et en Amérique du Nord du XIVe au XXe siècle*, ed. Andrée Courtemanche and Martin Paquet. Hull, QC: Vents d'Ouest, 2001.

Frenette, Yves, and Gabriele Scardellato. "The Immigrant Experience and the Creation of a Transatlantic Epistolary Space." In *More Than Words: Readings in Transport, Communication and the History of Postal Communication*, ed. John Willis. Gatineau, QC: Canadian Museum of Civilzation, 2007.

Gaal, Arlene B. '*Memoirs' of Michel-Natal, 1899–1971*. N.p.: 1971.

———. '*Times to Remember…' Michel-Natal, 1899–1980*. N.p.: 1980.

Gabaccia, Donna R. *From Sicily to Elizabeth Street: Housing and Social Change Among Italian Immigrants, 1880–1930*. Albany: State University of New York Press, 1984.

———. "Is Everywhere Nowhere? Nomads, Nations, and the Immigrant Paradigm of United States History." *Journal of American History* 86, 3 (1999): 1115–1134.

———. *Italy's Many Diasporas*. Seattle: University of Washington Press, 2000.

———. "The Minnesota School of Immigration and Refugee Studies." http://www.ihrc.umn.edu/publications/pdf/MinnesotaSchool-1.pdf (accessed 15 August 2009).

Gabaccia, Donna R., and Fraser M. Ottanelli, ed. *Italian Workers of the World: Labor Migration and the Formation of Multiethnic States*. Urbana and Chicago: University of Illinois Press, 2001.

Gabaccia, Donna R., and Franca Iacovetta, ed. *Women, Gender, and Transnational Lives: Italian Workers of the World*. Toronto: University of Toronto Press, 2002.

Garbin, Barbara. "Fotoromanzo." In *Encyclopedia of Italian Literary Studies*, ed. Gaetana Marrone, Paolo Puppa, and Luca Somigli. New York: Routledge, 2006.

Geertz, Clifford. "Thick Description: Toward an Interpretive Theory of Culture." In *The Interpretation of Cultures*, ed. Clifford Geertz. New York: Basic Books, 1973.

———. "Common Sense as a Cultural System." *Antioch Review* 50, 1–2 (1992): 221–241. Reprinted from *Antioch Review* 33, 1 (1975).

Gensini, Stefano. *Elementi di storia linguistica italiana*. Bergamo: Minerva Italica, 1990.

Gerber, David A. "The Immigrant Letter between Positivism and Populism: the Uses of Immigrant Personal Correspondence in Twentieth-Century American Scholarship." *Journal of American Ethnic History* 16, 4 (Summer 1997): 3–34.

———. "Epistolary Ethics: Personal Correspondence and the Culture of Emigration in the Nineteenth Century." *Journal of American Ethnic History* 19 (Summer 2000): 3–23.

———. "Forming a Transnational Narrative: New Perspectives on European Migrations to the United States." *The History Teacher* 35, 1 (2001): 61–78.

———. "What is it we seek to find in first-person documents? Documenting society and cultural practices in Irish Immigrant Writings." *Reviews in American History* 32 (2004): 305–316.

———. "Acts of Deceiving and Withholding in Immigrant Letters: Personal Identity and Self-presentation in Personal Correspondence." *Journal of Social History* 39, 2 (2005): 315–330.

———. *Authors of Their Lives: The Personal Correspondence of British Immigrants to North America in the Nineteenth Century*. New York: New York University Press, 2006.

Gibelli, Antonio. "'Fatemi unpo sapere...' Scrittura e fotografia nella corrispondenza degli emigranti liguri." In *La via delle Americhe. L'emigrazione ligure tra evento e racconto. Catalogo della mostra*, ed. Antonio Gibelli. Genova: Sagep, 1989.

_____. *L'officina della Guerra: La Grande Guerra e le trasformazioni del mondo mentale.* Torino: Bollati Boringhieri editore, 1998.

Gibelli, Antonio, and Fabio Caffarena. "Le lettere degli emigranti." In *Storia dell'emigrazione italiana. Vol. 1 Partenze*, ed. Piero Bevilacqua, E. Franzina, and Maddalena Tirabassi. Rome: Donzelli, 2001.

Ginsborg, Paul. *A History of Contemporary Italy: Society and Politics, 1943–1988.* London: Penguin, 1990.

Glick Schiller, Nina, Linda Basch, and Cristina Blanc-Szanton. "Transnationalism: A New Analytic Framework for Understanding Migration." In *Towards a Transnational Perspective on Migration: Race, Class, Ethnicity and Nationalism Reconsidered*, ed. Nina Glick Schiller, Linda Basch, and Cristina Blanc-Szanton. New York: New York Academy of Sciences, 1992.

_____. "Towards a Definition of Transnationalism: Introductory Remarks and Research Questions." In *Towards a Transnational Perspective on Migration: Race, Class, Ethnicity, and Nationalism Reconsidered*, ed. Nina Glick Schiller, Linda Basch, and Cristina Szanton Blanc. New York: New York Academy of Sciences, 1992.

_____. "From Immigrant to Transmigrant: Theorizing Transnational Migration." *Anthropological Quarterly* 68, 1 (January 1995): 48–63.

Gnoli, Sofia. *Un Secolo di Moda Italiana, 1900–2000.* Rome: Meltemi Editore, 2005.

Grasmuck, S. and P. Pessar. *Between Two Islands: Dominican International Migration.* Berkeley: University of California Press, 1991.

Grassi, Marie-Claire. "Des lettres qui parlent d'amour." *Romantisme* 68, 2 (1990): 23–32.

Green, Alan G. *Immigration and the Postwar Canadian Economy.* Toronto: Macmillan, 1976.

Gundle, Stephen. "The legacy of the Prison Notebooks: Gramsci, the PCI and Italian Culture in the Cold War Period." In *Italy in the Cold War: Politics, Culture & Society 1948–58*, ed. Christopher Duggan and Christopher Wagstaff. Oxford and Washington, DC: Berg, 1995.

_____. "Feminine Beauty, National Identity and Political Conflict in Postwar Italy, 1945–1954." *Contemporary European History* 8, 3 (1999): 359–378.

Hale, Frederick, ed. *Danes in North America.* Seattle and London: University of Washington Press, 1984.

Hanna, Martha. "A Republic of Letters: The Epistolary Tradition in France during World War I." *American Historical Review* 108, 5 (2003): 1338–1361.

_____. *Your Death Would Be Mine: Paul and Marie Pireaud in the Great War.* Cambridge, MA: Harvard University Press, 2006.

Hannerz, Ulf. *Transnational Connections: Culture, People, Places.* New York: Routledge, 1996.

Hansen, Marcus Lee. *The Atlantic Migration, 1607–1860: A History of the Continuing Settlement of the United States.* Cambridge, MA: Harvard University Press, 1940.

_____. "Migrations: Old and New." In *The Immigrant in American History*, ed. Marcus Lee Hansen. Cambridge, MA: Harvard University Press, 1940.

Hareven, Tamara K. *Family Time and Industrial Time: The Relationship Between the Family and Work in a New England Industrial Community.* Cambridge: Cambridge University Press, 1982.

_____. "Les grands thèmes de l'histoire de la famille aux États-Unis." *Revue d'histoire de l'Amérique française* 39, 3 (1985): 185–209.

Harney, Robert F. Harney. "Men without Women: Italian Migrants in Canada, 1885–1930." In *The Italian Immigrant Woman in North America*, ed. Betty Boyd Caroli, Robert F. Harney, and Lydio F. Tomasi. Toronto: Multicultural History Society of Ontario, 1978.

_____. "'So Great a Heritage as Ours' Immigration and the Survival of the Canadian Polity." In *If One Were to Write a History... Selected Writings by Robert F. Harney*, ed. Pierre Anctil and Bruno Ramirez. Toronto: Multicultural History Society of Ontario, 1991.

Harris, Helen. "Rethinking Polynesian Heterosexual Relationships: A Case Study on Mangaia, Cook Islands." In *Romantic Passion: A Universal Experience?* ed. William Jankowiak. New York: Columbia University Press, 1995.

Harris, Olivia. "Households as Natural Units." In *Of Marriage and the Market: Women's Subordination in International Perspective*, ed. Kate Young, Carol Wolkowitz, and Roslyn McCullagh. London: CSE Books, 1981.

Hartmann, Heidi. "Capitalism, Patriarchy, and Job Segregation by Sex." *Signs* 1, 3 (Spring 1976): 137–169.

_____. "The Family as the Locus of Gender, Class, and Political Struggle: The Example of Housework." *Signs* 6, 3 (1981): 366–394.

Harzig, Christiane, and Dirk Hoerder with Donna Gabaccia, *What is Migration History?* Cambridge, UK: Polity Press, 2009.

Harzig, Christiane, and Dirk Hoerder, "Internationalizing Working-Class History Since the 1970s: Challenges from Historiography, Archives, and the Web," *Library Trends* 56, 3 (Winter 2008): 635–649.

Hawkins, Freda. *Canada and Immigration: Public Policy and Public Concern.* 2nd ed. Kingston and Montreal: McGill-Queen's University Press, 1988.

Hirsch, Jennifer S. *A Courtship after Marriage: Sexuality and Love in Mexican Transnational Families.* Berkeley and Los Angeles: University of California Press, 2003.

Hirsch, Jennifer S., and Holly Wardlow. *Modern Loves: The Anthropology of Romantic Courtship and Companionate Marriage.* Ann Arbor: University of Michigan Press, 2006.

Hirsch, Julia. *Family Photographs: Content, Meaning and Effect.* Oxford: Oxford University Press, 1981.

Hirsch, Marianne. *Family Frames: Photography, Narrative, and Postmemory.* Cambridge, MA: Harvard University Press, 1997.

Hirsch, Marianne, ed. *The Familial Gaze.* Hanover, NH: Dartmouth College, 1999.

Hoare, Quintin, and Geoffrey N. Smith, ed. *Selections from the Prison Notebooks of Antonio Gramsci.* New York: International Publishers, 1971.

Hoerder, Dirk. "Migration and Cultural Interaction across the Centuries: German History in a European Perspective." *German Politics & Society* 26, 2 (Summer 2008).

Hoerder, Dirk. *Creating Societies. Immigrant Lives in Canada.* Montreal and Kingston: McGill-Queen's University Press, 1999.

Hoerder, Dirk, and Horst Rössler, ed. *Distant Magnets: Expectations and Realities in the Immigrant Experience, 1840–1930.* New York and London: Holmes and Meier, 1993.

Houston, Cecil, and William Smyth. *Irish Emigration and Canadian Settlement: Patterns, Links, and Letters.* Toronto: University of Toronto Press, 1990.

Iacovetta, Franca. *Gatekeepers: Reshaping Immigrant Lives in Cold War Canada.* Toronto: Between the Lines, 2006.

_____. *Such Hardworking People: Italian Immigrants in Postwar Toronto.* Montreal and Kingston: McGill-Queen's University Press, 1992.

_____. "From Contadina to Worker: Southern Italian Immigrant Working Women in Toronto 1947–62." In *Looking into My Sister's Eyes: An Exploration in Women's History,* ed. Jean Burnet. Toronto: Multicultural History Society of Ontario, 1986.

_____. "Ordering in Bulk: Canada's Postwar Immigration Policy and the Recruitment of Contract Workers from Italy." *Journal of American Ethnic History* 11, 1 (1991): 50–81.

Jabour, Anya. "'The Language of Love': The Letters of Elizabeth and William Wirt, 1802–1834." In *A Shared Experience: Men, Women, and the History of Gender,* ed. Laura McCall and Donald Yacovone. New York and London: New York University Press, 1998.

Jankowiak, William, ed. *Romantic Passion: A Universal Experience?* New York: Columbia University Press, 1995.

Johnson, Colleen Leahy. *Growing Up and Growing Old in Italian-American Families.* New Brunswick, NJ: Rutgers University Press, 1985.

Judt, Tony. *Postwar: A History of Europe Since 1945.* London: Penguin 2005.

Kamphoefner, Walter, D., Wolfgang Helbich, and Ulrike Sommer, ed. *News from the Land of Freedom: German Immigrants Write Home.* Ithaca and London: Cornell University Press, 1991.

Kearney, Michael. "The Local and the Global: The Anthropology of Globalization and Transnationalism." *Annual Review of Anthropology* 24 (1995): 547–565.

King, William Lyon Mackenzie. "Canada's Postwar Immigration Policy." House of Commons Debates, 1 May 1947. In *Immigration and the Rise of Multiculturalism,* ed. Howard Palmer. Toronto: Copp Clark, 1975.

Lamphere, Louise. *From Working Mothers to Working Daughters: Immigrant Working Women in a New England Industrial Community*. Ithaca: Cornell University Press, 1987.

Lanaro, Silvio. *Storia dell'Italia repubblicana: L'economia, la politica, la cultura, la società dal dopoguerra agli anni '90*. Venezia : Marsilio Editori, 1992.

Langford, Martha. *Suspended Conversations: The Afterlife of Memory in Photographic Albums*. Montreal-Kingston: McGill-Queen's University Press, 2001.

Langford, Tom and Wayne Norton, ed. *A World Apart: The Crowsnest Communities of Alberta and British Columbia*. Kamloops: Plateau Press, 2002.

Lorber, Judith. *Paradoxes of Gender*. New Haven and London: Yale University Press, 1994.

_____. "Dismantling Noah's Ark." In *The Social Construction of Gender*, ed. Judith Lorber and Susan A. Farrell. Newbury Park, CA: Sage Publications, 1991.

Lutz, Catherine A. "Emotion, Thought, and Estrangement: Emotion as a Cultural Category." *Cultural Anthropology* 1, 3 (1986): 287–309.

Lutz, Catherine A., and Lila Abu-Lughod, ed. *Language and the Politics of Emotion*. New York: Cambridge University Press, 1990.

Lutz, Catherine A., and Lila Abu-Lughod. "Introduction: Emotion, Discourse, and the Politics of Everyday Life." In *Language and the Politics of Emotion*, ed. Catherine A. Lutz, and Lila Abu-Lughod. New York: Cambridge University Press, 1990.

Lutz, Catherine, and Geoffrey M. White. "The Anthropology of Emotions." *Annual Review of Anthropology* 15 (1986): 405–436.

Luxton, Meg. *More than a Labour of Love: Three Generations of Women's Work in the Home*. Toronto: Women's Educational Press, 1980.

Lyons, Martyn. "Love Letters and Writing Practices: On Ecritures Intimes in the Nineteenth Century." *Journal of Family History* 24 (1999): 232–239.

Lystra, Karen. *Searching the Heart: Women, Men, and Romantic Love in Nineteenth-Century America*. New York and Oxford: Oxford University Press, 1989.

Mahler, Sarah. "Transnational Relationships: The Struggle to Communicate Across Borders." *Identities* 7, 4 (2001): 583–619.

Mahler, Sarah, and Patricia Pessar. "Gender Matters: Ethnographers Bring Gender from the Periphery toward the Core of Migration Studies." *International Migration Review* 40, 1 (Spring 2006): 27–63.

_____. "Gendered Geographies of Power: Analyzing Gender Across Transnational Spaces." *Identities* 7, 4 (2001): 441–459.

Manalansan IV, Martin F. "Queer Intersections: Sexuality and Gender in Migration Studies." *International Migration Review* 40, 1 (Spring 2006): 224–249.

Margolis, Maxine L. *Mothers and Such: Views of American Women and Why They Changed*. Berkeley: University of California Press, 1984.

Markelis, Daiva. "'Every Person Like a Letter': The Importance of Correspondence in Lithuanian Immigrant Life." *Letters across Borders: The Epistolary Practices of*

International Migrants, ed. Bruce S. Elliott, David A. Gerber, and Suzanne M. Sinke. New York: Palgrave Macmillan, 2006.

Martel, Marcel. "'Gardons contact': l'expérience epistolaire de Jean-Henri et de Maxime-Ovila Freniere en Nouvelle-Angleterre, 1912–1929." In *Envoyer et recevoir: Lettres et correspondances dans les diasporas francophones*, ed. Yves Frenette, Marcel Martel, and John Willis. Québec: Presses de l'Université Laval, 2006.

May, Elaine Tyler. *Homeward Bound: American Families in the Cold War Era*. New York: Basic Books, 1988.

McCarthy, Patrick, ed. *Italy since 1945*. Oxford: Oxford University Press, 2000.

McNaught, Kenneth. *The Pelican History of Canada*. Middlesex and Baltimore: Penguin Books, 1969.

Miller, Kerby A. *Emigrants and Exiles: Ireland and the Irish Exodus to North America*. Oxford: Oxford University Press, 1985.

Miller, Kerby A., Arnold Schrier, Bruce D. Boling, and David N. Doyle. *Irish Immigrants in the Land of Canaan: Letters and Memoirs from Colonial and Revolutionary America, 1675–1815*. Oxford and New York: Oxford University Press, 2003.

Morris, Penelope, ed. *Women in Italy, 1945–1960: An Interdisciplinary Study*. New York: Palgrave Macmillan, 2006.

Nelson, Robert K. "'The Forgetfulness of Sex': Devotion and Desire in the Courtship Letters of Angelina Grimke and Theodore Dwight Weld." *Journal of Social History* 37, 3 (2004): 663–679.

O'Farrell, Patrick, with Brian Trainor. *Letters from Irish Australia, 1825–1929*. Sydney: New South Wales University Press and Belfast: Ulster Historical Foundation, 1984.

Parreñas, Rhacel Salazar. *Servants of Globalization: Women, Migration and Domestic Work*. Stanford: Stanford University Press, 2001.

———. *Children of Global Migration: Transnational Families and Gendered Woes*. Stanford: Stanford University Press, 2005.

Peressini, Mauro. *Migration, Famille et Communauté: Les Italiens du Frioul à Montréal 1945–1980*. Montreal: Presses L'Université de Montréal, 1990.

Perry, Harriet. "The Metonymic Definition of the Female and the Concept of Honour Among Italian Immigrant Families in Toronto." In *The Italian Immigrant Woman in North America*, ed. Betty Boyd Caroli, Robert F. Harney, and Lydio F. Tomasi. Toronto: Multicultural History Society of Ontario, 1978.

Piper, Nicola. "Gendering the Politics of Migration." *International Migration Review* 40, 1 (2006): 133–164.

Piselli, Fortunata. *Parentela ed Emigrazione. Mutamenti e continuità in una comunità calabrese*. Torino: Einaudi, 1981.

Plotnicov, Leonard. "Love, Lust and Found in Nigeria." In *Romantic Passion: A Universal Experience?* ed. William Jankowiak. New York: Columbia University Press, 1995.

Pyée, Audrey. "'Mon Révérend Père, [...] Je m'inquiète pour mon fils.' Relations familiales transnationales et épistolaires." In *Envoyer et recevoir. Lettres et correspondances dans les diasporas francophones*, ed. Yves Frenette, Marcel Martel, and John Willis. Quebec City: Presses de L'Université Laval, 2006.

Ramirez, Bruno. *Les premiers Italiens de Montréal: L'origine de la Petite Italie du Québec.* Montreal: Boréal Express, 1984.

_____. *On the Move: French-Canadian and Italian Migrants in the North Atlantic Economy, 1860–1914.* Toronto: McClelland and Stewart, 1991.

_____. "Clio in Words and in Motion: Practices of Narrating the Past." *Journal of American History* 86, 3 (1999): 987–1014.

_____. *Crossing the 49th Parallel: Migration from Canada to the United States, 1900–1930.* Ithaca and London: Cornell University Press, 2001.

_____. "Canada's Immigration and Policy-making of the 19th and 20th Centuries: From Empire to Globalisation." Published as "La immigration y la politica inmigratoria en Canada en los siglos XIX y XX: del imperio a la globalizacion," *Estudios migratorios latinoamericanos* 18 (2004): 43–74. Unpublished English manuscript.

Ramirez, Bruno and Michael Del Balso. *The Italians of Montreal: From Sojourning to Settlement, 1900-1921.* Montreal: Les Éditions du Courant, 1980.

Ramirez, Bruno and Pierre Anctil, ed. *If One Were to Write a History... Selected Writings by Robert F. Harney.* Toronto: Multicultural History Society of Ontario, 1991.

Reddy, William M. "Against Constructionism: The Historical Ethnography of Emotions." *Current Anthropology* 30, 3 (1997): 327–351.

_____. *The Navigation of Feeling: A Framework for the History of Emotions.* New York: Cambridge University Press, 2001.

Redford, Bruce. *The Converse of the Pen: Acts of Intimacy in the Eighteenth-Century Familiar Letter.* Chicago and London: University of Chicago Press, 1986.

Reeder, Linda. *Widows in White: Migration and the Transformation of Rural Italian Women, Sicily, 1880-1920.* Toronto: University of Toronto Press, 2003.

Rosaldo, Michelle Z. "Toward an Anthropology of Self and Feeling." In *Culture Theory: Essays on Mind, Self and Emotion*, ed. Richard A. Shweder and Robert A. LeVine. Cambridge, UK: Cambridge University Press, 1984.

_____. "Woman, Culture, and Society: A Theoretical Overview." In *Woman, Culture and Society*, ed. Michelle Zimbalist Rosaldo and Louise Lamphere. Stanford, CA: Stanford University Press, 1974.

_____. *Knowledge and Passion: Ilongot Notions of Self and Social Life.* New York: Cambridge University Press, 1980.

Rosenwein, Barbara H. "Worrying about Emotions in History." *American Historical Review* 107, 3 (2002): 821–845.

Rouse, Roger. "Mexican Migration and the Social Space of Postmodernism." *Diaspora* 1, 1 (1991): 8–23.

_____. "Thinking Through Transnationalism: Notes on the Cultural Politics of Class Relations in the Contemporary United States." *Public Culture* 7, 2 (1996): 353–402.

Rubin, Gayle. "The Traffic in Women: Notes on the 'Political Economy' of Sex." In *Toward an Anthropology of Women*, ed. Rayna R. Reiter. New York and London: Monthly Review Press, 1975.

Sanfilippo, Matteo. *Problemi di storiografia dell'emigrazione italiana.* Viterbo, Italy: Sette Città, 2002.

_____. "Un'occasione mancata? A proposito di un libro di David A. Gerber sulle lettere degli emigranti—A Missed Chance? A Book About the Letters from Migrants by David A. Gerber." *Studi Emigrazione/Migration Studies* 170 (2008): 475–488.

Scardellato, Gabriele P. "Italian Immigrant Workers in Powell River, B.C.: A Case Study of Settlement Before World War II." *Labour/Le Travail* 16 (1985): 145–163.

Scarpellini, Emanuela. *Comprare all'Americana. Le origini della rivoluzione commerciale in Italia, 1945–1971.* Bologna: Il Mulino, 2001.

Scheper-Hughes, Nancy. *Death Without Weeping: The Violence of Everyday Life in Brazil.* Berkeley and Los Angeles: University of California Press, 1992.

Scott, Joan W. *Gender and the Politics of History.* Revised ed. New York: Columbia University Press, 1999.

Scott, Joan W. "'Experience.'" In *Feminists Theorize the Political*, ed. Joan W. Scott and Judith Butler. New York and London: Routledge, 1992.

Silvey, Rachel. "Geographies of Gender and Migration: Spatializing Social Difference." *International Migration Review* 40, 1 (2006): 64–81.

Sinke, Suzanne M. "Gender and Migration: Historical Perspectives." *International Migration Review* 40, 1 (Spring 2006): 82–103.

Stanley, Liz. "The Epistolarium: On Theorizing Letters and Correspondences." *Auto/Biography* 12 (2004): 201-235.

Stearns, Peter N., and Carol Z. Stearns. "Emotionology: Clarifying the History of Emotions and Emotional Standards." *American Historical Review* 90, 4 (1985): 813–835.

Stephenson, George. "When America was the Land of Canaan." *Minnesota History* 10, 3 (Sept. 1929).

Stivens, Maila. "Women, Kinship and Capitalist Development." In *Of Marriage and the Market: Women's Subordination in International Perspective*, ed. Kate Young, Carol Wolkowitz, and Roslyn McCullagh. London: CSE Books, 1981.

Sturino, Franc. *Forging the Chain: Italian Migration to North America, 1880–1930.* Toronto: Multicultural History Society of Ontario, 1990.

_____. "Italians." In *Encyclopedia of Canada's People*, ed. Paul Robert Magosci. Toronto: University of Toronto Press, 1999.

Suarez-Orozco, Carola, and Desiree Baolian Qin. "Gendered Perspectives in Psychology: Immigrant Origin Youth." *International Migration Review* 40, 1 (2006): 165–198.

Takai, Yukari. *Gendered Passages: French-Canadian Migration to Lowell, Massachusetts, 1900–1920.* New York: Peter Lang, 2008.

Teti, Vito. "Note sui comportamenti delle donne sole degli americani durante la 1a emigrazione in Calabria." *Studi Emigrazione/Etudes Migrations* 24 (1987): 13–46.

Thistlethwaite, Frank. "Migration from Europe Overseas in the Nineteenth and Twentieth Centuries." In *A Century of European Migrations, 1830–1930*, ed. Rudolph J. Vecoli and Suzanne M. Sinke. Urbana and Chicago: University of Illinois Press, 1991.

Torriglia, Anna Maria. *Broken Time, Fragmented Space: A Cultural Map for Postwar Italy.* Toronto: University of Toronto press, 2002.

Vangelisti, Guglielmo. *Gli Italiani in Canada.* Montreal: n.p., 1956.

West, Candace and Don H. Zimmerman. "Doing Gender." In *The Social Construction of Gender*, ed. Judith Lorber and Susan A. Farrell. Newbury Park, CA: Sage Publications, 1991.

Willis, John. "'De votre chère soeur qui ne vous oublie jamais': A Postal Perspective on French-Canadian Migration in North America." In *Envoyer et recevoir: Lettres et correspondances dans les diasporas francophones*, ed. Yves Frenette, Marcel Martel, and John Willis. Quebec City: Presses de l'Université Laval, 2006.

Wtulich, Josephine, et al., ed. *Writing Home: Immigrants in Brazil and the United States, 1890–1891.* New York: Columbia University Press, 1986.

Zavella, Patricia. *Women's Work and Chicano Families.* Ithaca: Cornell University Press, 1987.

Zucchi, John. E. *Italians in Toronto: Development of a National Identity 1875–1935.* Montreal and Kingston: McGill-Queen's University Press, 1988.

INDEX

Index   189

G

Gabaccia, Donna, 42, 43, 55, 159n9
garment industry, 74–77, 79
Geertz, Clifford, 62
gender roles: daughters acting as mothers,
99–100; and division of labour, 62,
66, 95, 96; emotional cost of, 92–93,
142; husband as breadwinner,
87–89, 90–91; husband as protector,
89; and kinship, 42, 77–78; and
migration, 71–74, 146–47; and
social power, 83–84; studies
on, 73–74; wife as babymaker,
98–99; wife as domestic, 93–97,
101, 165n51; wife as extension of
husband, 91, 100–102; and women
in waged work, 75–76, 77, 95–96;
and women's fashion, 84–86; and
women's freedom, 78–81
Gensini, Stefano, 23
Gerber, David: and *Authors of Their
Lives,* 7, 9; and migrants' letters,
12, 106, 142, 143, 170n45; and
time consciousness, 136; and
transnationalism, 43–44
Gibelli, Antonio, 11
Ginsborg, Paul, 84
Glick Schiller, Nina, 43
gossip, 91–92
Gramsci, Antonio, 62
Grassi, Marie-Claire, 109, 112, 136
gratitude, 115
Gregor, Thomas, 119

H

Hanna, Martha, 11, 115–16
Hansen, Marcus, 6–7
happiness: children for parents, 114; from
family, 28, 47, 53, 55–56, 57, 127;
between lovers/couples, 67, 78, 79,
92, 97–98, 105, 121, 128–30, 132–
34, 136, 138–39; over births, 44–45,
98–99; over settling in, 44, 57, 87,
122; parents for daughter, 64–65,
101, 110, 111, 122; parents for son,
3, 37, 63. *See also* joy
Hareven, Tamara, 42, 53
Harney, Robert, 25, 43, 87, 108
helplessness, 45, 112–13
Hoerder, Dirk, 90, 132, 152n4, 155n20, 161
houses, 28, 31, 57, 63, 123

I

Iacovetta, Franca, 24, 26, 71, 95, 162n16
illness/ailments, 21, 37, 45–46, 63, 112–13
imagination, 113–14, 132–35, 140
immigrant letters: as historical documents,

105–6, 107, 168n16; new historical
approaches to, 4–5, 6–9; and sense
of time, 107; sharing of, 106, 151n4;
timelessness of, 149–50
immigration, 24, 25–27, 38, 156n6. *See also*
sponsorship program; visa process
individuality, 57

J

Jankowjak, William, 118
jealousy: between Del Moro and
Franceschetti, 81–82, 85; by G.
Rossini, 67–68, 78, 80, 128
Johnson, Colleen L., 42, 64
joy, 116, 122, 129–30. *See also* happiness

K

King, Mackenzie, 24, 25
kinship: caring for those feeling abandoned,
54–55, 117; and employment, 55–
56; extended support for migrants,
55–56; and gender roles, 42, 77–78;
and interference in personal affairs,
34, 60–61; and life events, 44, 45;
maintaining in Canada, 56–57;
as provider of support, 29, 30, 31,
33; as source of parental control,
56, 61–66; as source of security,
53–54; and stress with in-laws,
32; studies on, 42–43; support
for romances, 60–61; support on
arrival in Canada, 59–60; and travel
support, 58–59, 160n27. *See also*
transnational kinship networks

L

labour. *See* employment
land reform, 23
landowners, 90
language blocks, 44
leisure activities, 33, 40, 93, 130–31, 164n41
letter writing: as akin to personal presence,
116–17, 132–33, 138; and breaking
down barriers of time and space,
107, 136–37, 138, 143; comfort
from, 11, 130–32; connection to war
and migration, 10–11; conventions
of, 8; and dynamics of love, 119–21;
frustration with, 137–38; as link to
home, 12, 44, 149; and reflections
on separation, 138–42; resiliency of,
149–50
Letters across Borders, 7–8
life events: celebrating, 44–45, 46–47;
markers for, 45, 48–52, 99. *See also*
births; death; marriage; weddings
literacy, 23, 53

loneliness: of D. del Moro, 92–93, 120; of
    family in Italy, 54–55; of G. Rossini,
    67, 78–79, 121, 125; kinship as cure
    for, 56; of migrant housewives, 94–
    95, 98, 101; of S. Franceschetti, 28
longing: among siblings, 33; father-children,
    111, 114; between lovers, 124–30,
    137; mother-daughter, 30, 31, 110–
    11, 115; mother-son, 109–10
Lorber, Judith, 72–73, 84, 86
Losanto, Anita, 15, 32, 51, 150
Losanto, Carmela: care of in-laws at home,
    54–55; illness, 45–46; letters from,
    21; and life events, 44, 45, 46–47; life
    in Ripabottoni, 31–33, 57; and lost
    letters, 47; and religious festivities,
    50; use of personal couriers, 53
Losanto, Domenico, 21, 31, 150
lost letters, 47
love: anxiety over, 80, 125, 130; as comfort,
    130–32; definition of, 118–19; and
    dynamic of time, 107, 136–38; and
    fear of abandonment, 125, 141–42;
    and feelings of desperation, 124–30;
    and feelings of empowerment,
    122–23; and feelings of joy, 122,
    129–30; forms of control on, 66–69;
    and inadequacy of letters, 137–38;
    and possessiveness, 67–68, 85; and
    reflections on separation, 138–42;
    and sadness, 124–28, 129, 139, 140;
    and use of dreams, 135–36; use of
    imagination to bring closer, 132–35,
    140; and worry: 67-68, 79, 140. *See
    also* Del Moro, Dante; Franceschetti,
    Sara; Renzi, Clara; Rossini,
    Giordano; Trevisan, Maurizio
love letters: definition of, 118, 168n25;
    dynamics of, 119–20, 121–22,
    169n30
lovesickness, 33–34, 67–68, 120, 124–30
Lutz, Catherine, 106
Lystra, Karen: effect of letter writing, 116;
    effect of love letters, 107, 118, 138;
    gender differences in writing love
    letters, 142; on highs and lows of
    love, 126, 130; and romantic love,
    122

M

Madonna della Difesa (church), 35, 37,
    158n29
Mahler, Sarah, 72
Manfredi, Giovanni, 90
Marche, Italy, 30
marriage: in Ascoli Piceno, 20, 30; as
    important kinship event, 45; in
    Montreal, 34–35, 37, 38, 139

Martino, Guiseppe, 30
melancholy, 49, 129, 140. *See also* sadness
Mestre, Italy, 35
Michel, BC, 35, 36, 40
migration from Italy: after WWII, 23;
    to Canada, 24, 26–27, 38, 71,
    156n6; and employment, 38; and
    gender roles, 71–74, 146–47; in
    Ripabottoni, 31–32; to US, 24
migration project, 63, 146, 161n35
Milan, Italy, 32
mining, 36, 37, 41
Molise, Italy, 32, 158n27
money problems: advice on, 41; in
    Colonello family, 36; in Del Moro-
    Franceschetti marriage, 29, 88; as
    part of parental control, 63–64; in
    Renzi-Trevisan partnership, 76;
    in Rossi-Di Leonardi partnership,
    122–23. *See also* remittances
Montreal, QC: and D. Perini, 30; and E. Di
    Leonardi, 34; employment in, 34,
    37, 100; G. Colonello's move to, 65;
    marriage in, 34–35, 37, 38, 139; and
    Ripabottoni, 31
Morris, Penelope, 84
myths of America, 90–91, 94–95

N

nostalgia, 56, 94, 98, 101, 117, 127, 150

O

objects/gifts: as bridging mechanisms,
    113–14, 115–17, 149; as life event
    markers, 45, 48–52, 99; for practical
    reasons, 50–51, 88; as sites of
    memory, 48, 49, 99, 116–17, 149
One Family, Two Worlds (Baily and
    Ramella), 9

P

patriarchy, 61, 72, 102, 162n15
Parreñas, Rhacel, 74, 99, 107, 108
Pearson, Ruth, 76, 84, 91, 95
Perini, Daniela: advice for daughter, 56,
    64–65, 66, 98–99, 101, 165n50;
    background, 30–31; birth of
    grandchild, 44–45; joy of, 116;
    kinship care of, 54; sadness over
    separation from daughter, 110–11,
    112, 117; sends gifts, 49; sends news
    to daughter, 117
Perry, Harriet, 165n51
personal courier, 46, 48, 51–53, 117, 159n3
Pessar, Patricia, 72
photographs, 113–14, 116–17, 130
Piselli, Fortunata, 43, 61–62